Better Homes and Gardens®

Dinnertime EXPRESS

BETTER HOMES AND GARDENS® BOOKS
Des Moines, Iowa

If you would like to purchase any of our books, check wherever quality books are sold.

Visit our website at bhgbooks.com.

All of us at Better Homes and Gardens® Books are dedicated to providing you with the information and ideas you need to create delicious foods. We welcome your comments and suggestions. Write to us at: Better Homes and Gardens Books, Cookbook Editorial Department, 1716 Locust St., Des Moines, IA 50309-3023.

Our seal assures you that every recipe in *Dinnertime Express* has been tested in the Better Homes and Gardens® Test Kitchen. This means that each recipe is practical and reliable, and meets our high standards of taste appeal. We guarantee your satisfaction with this book for as long as you own it.

Pictured on front cover:
Bow Ties with Sausage & Sweet Peppers
(see recipe, page 11)

Better Homes and Gardens® Books
An imprint of Meredith® Books

Dinnertime Express
Editor: Chuck Smothermon
Contributing Editor: Spectrum Communication Services, Inc.
Associate Art Director: Mick Schnepf
Contributing Designer: Shelton Design Studios
Copy Chief: Catherine Hamrick
Copy and Production Editor: Terri Fredrickson
Managers, Book Production: Pam Kvitne, Marjorie J. Schenkelberg
Contributing Proofreaders: Gretchen Kauffman, Susan J. Kling, Elizabeth Duff-Popplewell
Electronic Production Coordinator: Paula Forest
Editorial and Design Assistants: Judy Bailey, Mary Lee Gavin, Karen Schirm
Test Kitchen Director: Lynn Blanchard

Meredith® Books
Editor in Chief: James D. Blume
Design Director: Matt Strelecki
Managing Editor: Gregory H. Kayko

Director, Retail Sales and Marketing: Terry Unsworth
Director, Sales, Special Markets: Rita McMullen
Director, Sales, Premiums: Michael A. Peterson
Director, Sales, Retail: Tom Wierzbicki
Director, Sales, Home & Garden Centers: Ray Wolf
Director, Book Marketing: Brad Elmitt
Director, Operations: George A. Susral
Director, Production: Douglas M. Johnston

Vice President, General Manager: Jamie L. Martin

Better Homes and Gardens® Magazine
Editor in Chief: Jean LemMon
Executive Food Editor: Nancy Byal

Meredith Publishing Group
President, Publishing Group: Christopher M. Little
Vice President, Finance & Administration: Max Runciman

Meredith Corporation
Chairman and Chief Executive Officer: William T. Kerr

Chairman of the Executive Committee: E. T. Meredith III

F ast, fresh, and healthful...Different but doable...Food with personality...Tall order for a weeknight dinner? Sure, but that's what busy cooks tell Better Homes and Gardens® Books they crave. And that's what you'll get with every easy-to-make recipe in **Dinnertime Express.** Every recipe has appealing, innovative flavors created from easy-to-find meats, poultry, and fish, garden-fresh produce, and creative seasonings. The prep time for every recipe is minimal and so is the mess, leaving you with luscious dishes and plenty of time to savor every bite—even on your busiest days.

TABLE OF CONTENTS

dependable pasta	4
perfect poultry	34
meats in minutes	90
fast and fabulous fish	148
vegetarian dinners	188
appetizers, sides, and desserts	252
index	282

Pasta Rosa-Verde
See recipe, page 31

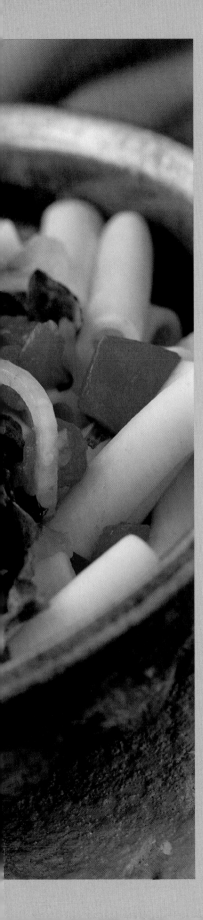

dependable pasta

Chicken & Pasta Primavera 6
Wide Noodles with Chicken & Lima Beans 7
Soba Noodles with Spring Vegetables 8
White Bean & Sausage Rigatoni 9
Shells Stuffed with Turkey & Lentils 10
Bow Ties with Sausage & Sweet Peppers 11
Spaetzle with Caramelized Onions 12
Shanghai Pork Lo Mein 13
Linguine with Steak & Spicy Garlic Sauce 14
Fresh Tomato Fusilli 15
Roasted Red Pepper Sauce over Tortellini 16
Tomatoes & Ravioli with Escarole 17
Pasta with Smoked Salmon & Lemon Cream 18
Strawberries, Salmon, & Fettuccine 19
Capellini with Shrimp in Pesto Sauce 20
Party Pancit 21

Linguine with Fennel & Shrimp in Orange Sauce 22
Trattoria-Style Spinach Fettuccine 23
Tomato Ravioli with Grilled Portobellos & Spinach . . . 24
Wild Mushroom Ravioli with Sage Butter 25
Teriyaki Penne 26
Penne with Broccoli & Dried Tomatoes 27
Pasta with Chèvre 28
Cavatelli with Arugula & Dried Cranberries 29
Rotini & Sweet Pepper Primavera 30
Pasta Rosa-Verde 31
Mostaccioli with Green Beans & Tomatoes 32
Garlic Asparagus & Pasta with Lemon Cream 33

chicken & pasta primavera

This almost effortless saucepan pasta gets a flavor boost from year-round market staples. A sour cream and mustard combo infused with fresh herbs wraps the meal in a creamy, tangy sauce.

INGREDIENTS

1 9-ounce package refrigerated spinach or plain fettuccine

2 medium carrots, thinly sliced

1 medium zucchini, halved lengthwise and thinly sliced

¾ cup frozen whole kernel corn

12 ounces deli-roasted chicken, cut into ½-inch strips (about 2½ cups)

1½ cups chicken broth

4 teaspoons cornstarch

1 tablespoon snipped fresh tarragon or basil

2 teaspoons finely shredded lemon peel

½ cup dairy sour cream

2 tablespoons Dijon-style mustard

Start to finish: 25 minutes

DIRECTIONS

1. Cook pasta according to package directions, adding carrots, zucchini, and corn to the water with pasta. Drain pasta and vegetables. Return all to saucepan; add chicken. (If the chicken has been refrigerated, place it in a colander. Pour the pasta, vegetables, and cooking liquid over chicken; drain.)

2. Meanwhile, in a medium saucepan combine chicken broth, cornstarch, tarragon, and lemon peel. Cook and stir over medium heat until thickened and bubbly. Cook and stir for 2 minutes more. Remove from heat.

3. Stir in sour cream and mustard. Pour over pasta mixture; toss gently to coat. Serve immediately. Makes 6 servings.

NUTRITION FACTS PER SERVING:

321 calories
9 g total fat
4 g saturated fat
97 mg cholesterol
425 mg sodium
32 g carbohydrate
1 g fiber
27 g protein

INGREDIENTS

- 8 ounces dried pappardelle or mafalda pasta, fettuccine, or wide egg noodles
- 1 10-ounce package frozen baby lima beans
- 1 14½-ounce can Italian-style stewed tomatoes
- 6 ounces skinless, boneless chicken breast halves
- 1 small onion, cut into wedges
- ¼ teaspoon coarsely ground pepper
- 1 tablespoon olive oil
- ¼ cup chicken broth
- ¼ cup whipping cream
-    Finely shredded Parmesan cheese (optional)
-    Snipped fresh chives (optional)

wide noodles with chicken & lima beans

Any width pasta will do here, but the wider the noodle, the more you get per mouthful of this luscious, creamy sauce. The ruffled edges of the pappardelle or mafalda pasta create even more places for the sauce to cling.

Start to finish: 30 minutes

DIRECTIONS

1. Cook pasta according to package directions, adding lima beans to the water with pasta. Drain pasta and beans; return to saucepan.

2. Meanwhile, place undrained tomatoes in a food processor bowl or blender container. Cover and process or blend until pureed; set aside.

3. Cut chicken into bite-size pieces. For sauce, in a large skillet cook chicken, onion, and pepper in hot oil over medium-high heat for 2 to 3 minutes or until chicken is no longer pink. Reduce heat; stir in tomatoes and chicken broth. Simmer about 5 minutes or until liquid is reduced by half. Stir in cream; simmer for 2 to 3 minutes more or until sauce is desired consistency.

4. Pour sauce over pasta mixture; toss gently to coat. Transfer pasta mixture to a warm serving dish. If desired, sprinkle with Parmesan cheese and chives. Makes 4 servings.

Substitute lasagna noodles

for the suggested pasta, if you like. Cook them according to package directions. Drain and cut crosswise into 1-inch pieces. (If you use frozen lasagna noodles, cook the beans separately because they will cook longer than the noodles.)

NUTRITION FACTS PER SERVING:

503 calories
12 g total fat
4 g saturated fat
43 mg cholesterol
438 mg sodium
75 g carbohydrate
7 g fiber
25 g protein

soba noodles with spring vegetables

This Japanese-style noodle soup satisfies any time of year. For added appeal, try using reduced-sodium chicken broth and stirring in 2 teaspoons of white or yellow miso—a soybean paste used in Asian cooking to boost flavor—with the chicken.

INGREDIENTS

- 1 14½-ounce can vegetable or chicken broth
- 1 tablespoon finely chopped fresh ginger
- 1 tablespoon reduced-sodium soy sauce
- 4 ounces dried soba (buckwheat) noodles or whole wheat spaghetti, broken
- 1 medium carrot, thinly sliced
- 1 cup cubed cooked chicken or turkey
- 1 cup shredded bok choy
- ½ cup halved pea pods
- ⅓ cup sliced radishes or chopped daikon
- ½ teaspoon toasted sesame oil
   Green onion strips

Start to finish: 25 minutes

DIRECTIONS

1. In a medium saucepan combine broth, ginger, and soy sauce. Bring to boiling; reduce heat. Simmer, covered, for 5 minutes.

2. Stir in the noodles and carrot. (If using whole wheat spaghetti, stir in spaghetti and cook for 6 minutes before adding carrot.) Bring to boiling; reduce heat. Simmer, uncovered, about 4 minutes or until noodles and carrot are tender. Stir in chicken, bok choy, pea pods, radishes, and sesame oil. Heat through. Sprinkle each serving with green onion strips. Makes 3 servings.

NUTRITION FACTS PER SERVING:

276 calories
8 g total fat
2 g saturated fat
39 mg cholesterol
1,092 mg sodium
37 g carbohydrate
3 g fiber
22 g protein

INGREDIENTS

- 8 ounces dried rigatoni pasta
- 1 15-ounce can white kidney (cannellini), Great Northern, or navy beans, rinsed and drained
- 1 14½-ounce can Italian-style stewed tomatoes
- 6 ounces cooked smoked turkey sausage, sliced ½ inch thick
- ⅓ cup snipped fresh basil
- ¼ cup shaved or finely shredded Asiago cheese (1 ounce)

white bean & sausage rigatoni

Reminiscent of a wonderful baked Italian casserole that comes bubbling from the oven, this dish is done on the stovetop instead, so it's ready to put on the table in less than half the time. Snipped fresh basil adds a hint of licorice flavor.

Start to finish: 20 minutes

DIRECTIONS

1. Cook pasta according to package directions, except do not add salt to the cooking water; drain. Return the pasta to saucepan.

2. Meanwhile, in a large saucepan combine beans, undrained tomatoes, and sausage; heat through. Add bean mixture and basil to pasta; toss gently to combine. Sprinkle each serving with cheese. Makes 4 servings.

NUTRITION FACTS PER SERVING:

401 calories
6 g total fat
1 g saturated fat
32 mg cholesterol
964 mg sodium
67 g carbohydrate
5 g fiber
25 g protein

shells stuffed with turkey & lentils

If you love the flavors of lasagna, but not its richness, try this stuffed pasta created with health-conscious diet in mind. Ground turkey, low-fat lentils, and a lighter, herb-seasoned sauce make the difference.

INGREDIENTS

- 15 dried jumbo pasta shells or 10 manicotti shells
- 8 ounces uncooked ground turkey
- 1 small onion, finely chopped
- 3 large plum tomatoes, seeded and finely chopped
- 1 tablespoon dried Italian seasoning, crushed
- ½ teaspoon ground nutmeg
- ¼ teaspoon pepper
- 1 cup canned lentils, rinsed and drained, or cooked lentils
- 1 15-ounce container refrigerated light alfredo sauce
- ½ cup fat-free ricotta cheese or cream-style cottage cheese
- ½ cup shredded reduced-fat mozzarella cheese
- ¼ cup snipped fresh parsley
- ¼ cup grated Parmesan cheese

To make ahead,

fill the pasta shells and arrange in baking dish. Pour remaining sauce over top. Seal, label, and freeze. (Freeze the cheese topping separately.) Before cooking, thaw overnight in the refrigerator. Bake, covered, in a 350° oven for 55 minutes. Uncover; sprinkle with the cheese topping. Bake about 10 minutes more or until cheese is golden and pasta is heated through.

Prep time: 30 minutes
Baking time: 25 minutes

DIRECTIONS

1. Cook pasta according to package directions; drain. Meanwhile, for filling, in a large saucepan cook turkey and onion until turkey is no longer pink. Add tomatoes, Italian seasoning, nutmeg, and pepper; reduce heat. Simmer for 5 minutes, stirring often. Stir in lentils. Remove from heat.

2. Stir in ½ cup of the alfredo sauce, the ricotta cheese, half of the mozzarella cheese, and the parsley. Spoon about 2 tablespoons filling into each pasta shell or about ⅓ cup into each manicotti shell.

3. Arrange filled pasta shells in a lightly greased 2-quart rectangular baking dish. Bake, covered, in a 375° oven for 15 minutes. Sprinkle with remaining mozzarella cheese and the Parmesan cheese. Bake about 10 minutes more or until cheese is golden brown.

4. Meanwhile, heat the remaining alfredo sauce; spoon sauce onto plates. Place 3 pasta shells or 2 manicotti shells on each plate. Makes 5 servings.

NUTRITION FACTS PER SERVING:

474 calories
19 g total fat
9 g saturated fat
64 mg cholesterol
986 mg sodium
50 g carbohydrate
3 g fiber
28 g protein

INGREDIENTS

- 8 ounces dried large bow-tie pasta
- 12 ounces uncooked spicy Italian sausage links
- 2 medium red sweet peppers, cut into ¾-inch pieces
- ½ cup vegetable broth or beef broth
- ¼ teaspoon coarsely ground black pepper
- ¼ cup snipped fresh Italian flat-leaf parsley

bow ties with sausage & sweet peppers

You will be amazed that so few ingredients generate so much flavor. For a lower-fat version, use uncooked spicy Italian turkey sausage links.

Start to finish: 25 minutes

DIRECTIONS

1. Cook pasta according to package directions; drain. Return pasta to saucepan.

2. Meanwhile, cut the sausage into 1-inch pieces. In a large skillet cook sausage and sweet peppers over medium-high heat until sausage is brown. Drain well.

3. Stir the broth and black pepper into skillet. Bring to boiling; reduce heat. Simmer, uncovered, for 5 minutes. Remove from heat. Pour over pasta; add parsley. Toss gently to coat. Transfer to a warm serving dish. Makes 4 servings.

NUTRITION FACTS PER SERVING:

397 calories
18 g total fat
6 g saturated fat
94 mg cholesterol
713 mg sodium
38 g carbohydrate
3 g fiber
24 g protein

11

spaetzle with caramelized onions

In every Swiss kitchen you'll find a spaetzle maker, a type of sieve cooks use to shape these tiny dumplings. Dried spaetzle, available at most markets, saves all the old-country flavor—and you many steps.

INGREDIENTS

2 large onions, cut into thin wedges (2 cups)
2 tablespoons margarine or butter
¾ cup yellow, orange, and/or red sweet pepper cut into bite-size strips
4 teaspoons brown sugar
1 tablespoon cider vinegar
⅓ cup chicken broth

⅓ cup half-and-half or light cream
1 tablespoon snipped fresh dill
⅛ teaspoon black pepper
4 ounces dried spaetzle or kluski-style egg noodles
2 cups halved Brussels sprouts
1 cup cooked lean boneless pork or ham, cut into bite-size strips

Start to finish: 30 minutes

DIRECTIONS

1. In a covered large skillet cook onions in hot margarine over medium-low heat for 13 to 15 minutes or until onions are tender.

2. Uncover; add the sweet pepper strips, brown sugar, and vinegar. Cook and stir over medium-high heat for 4 to 5 minutes or until onions are golden. Stir in chicken broth, half-and-half, dill, and black pepper. Boil gently until mixture is thickened.

3. Meanwhile, cook the spaetzle according to package directions, adding Brussels sprouts to the water with spaetzle. Drain and return to saucepan. Add caramelized onion mixture and pork to saucepan. Cook and stir over low heat until spaetzle are well-coated and mixture is heated through. Transfer to a warm serving dish. Makes 4 servings.

NUTRITION FACTS PER SERVING:

374 calories
15 g total fat
5 g saturated fat
91 mg cholesterol
279 mg sodium
42 g carbohydrate
5 g fiber
20 g protein

shanghai pork lo mein

Forget takeout. Stir-fry this Chinese specialty in 20 minutes—far less time than it takes to place a restaurant order and pick it up. Serve it with hot jasmine or oolong tea and fortune cookies from the grocery store and you won't miss a thing!

INGREDIENTS

- 6 ounces dried somen or fine egg noodles or angel hair pasta
- 2 teaspoons cooking oil
- 8 ounces pork tenderloin, halved lengthwise and sliced ¼ inch thick
- 2 cups sliced bok choy
- ¾ cup reduced-sodium chicken broth
- ¼ cup orange juice
- 3 tablespoons reduced-sodium soy sauce or regular soy sauce
- 2 teaspoons toasted sesame oil
- ¼ to ½ teaspoon crushed red pepper
- 1 11-ounce can mandarin orange sections, drained, or 2 large oranges, peeled and sectioned

Start to finish: 20 minutes

DIRECTIONS

1. Cook noodles according to package directions; drain. Meanwhile, pour oil into a wok or large skillet. Preheat over medium-high heat. Stir-fry pork in hot oil for 3 minutes, adding more oil if necessary. Add bok choy; stir-fry about 2 minutes more or until pork is slightly pink in center and bok choy is crisp-tender.

2. Add the broth, orange juice, soy sauce, sesame oil, and red pepper. Bring to boiling. Stir in the cooked noodles. Cook for 1 minute, stirring occasionally. Gently stir in orange sections. Makes 4 servings.

NUTRITION FACTS PER SERVING:

323 calories
7 g total fat
1 g saturated fat
40 mg cholesterol
1,337 mg sodium
45 g carbohydrate
1 g fiber
20 g protein

linguine with steak & spicy garlic sauce

The lively sauce for this pasta with pepper steak has only a few ingredients, including lots of garlic, so you know it has to be good—and quick. Buy only plump heads of garlic and store them in a dark, cool, dry spot.

INGREDIENTS

- 1 9-ounce package refrigerated tomato or red pepper linguine or fettuccine
- 1 small yellow summer squash or zucchini, halved lengthwise and sliced
- 1 medium green sweet pepper, cut into bite-size strips
- ½ teaspoon coarsely ground black pepper
- 8 ounces beef top loin steak, cut ¾ inch thick
- 1 tablespoon olive oil or cooking oil
- ½ cup chicken broth
- ¼ cup dry white wine
- 6 cloves garlic, minced

Except in salads, pasta is best

enjoyed hot from the pot. Always serve pasta in warmed, heat-conserving dishes. Use one of these easy methods to warm the serving dishes: rinse them under hot water and dry, splash them with the pasta cooking water and dry, or let them sit briefly in the oven at a low temperature.

Start to finish: 25 minutes

DIRECTIONS

1. Cook pasta according to package directions, adding summer squash and sweet pepper the last 2 minutes of cooking; drain. Return pasta and vegetables to saucepan.

2. Meanwhile, rub black pepper onto both sides of steak. In a large skillet cook steak in hot oil over medium heat until desired doneness, turning once. (Allow 10 to 12 minutes for medium.) Remove steak from skillet.

3. For sauce, stir chicken broth, wine, and garlic into skillet. Bring to boiling; reduce heat. Simmer, uncovered, for 2 minutes. Remove skillet from heat.

4. Cut steak into thin bite-size strips. Pour sauce over pasta mixture; add steak slices. Toss gently to coat. Transfer to a warm serving platter. Makes 4 servings.

NUTRITION FACTS PER SERVING:

247 calories
13 g total fat
4 g saturated fat
49 mg cholesterol
238 mg sodium
13 g carbohydrate
1 g fiber
18 g protein

fresh tomato fusilli

What to serve on balmy evenings, when life slows and moves outdoors? Light and easy pasta is an obvious choice, with the season's ambrosial tomatoes, which need little else to show them off.

INGREDIENTS

- 8 ounces dried fusilli pasta
- 4 cups sliced fresh mushrooms
- ¼ cup chopped onion
- 1 clove garlic, minced
- 1 tablespoon olive oil or cooking oil
- ¾ cup chicken broth
- 1 teaspoon all-purpose flour
- 2 cups red and/or yellow cherry tomatoes, halved
- ¼ cup finely chopped prosciutto (Italian ham) or cooked ham
- 2 tablespoons snipped fresh basil
- 1 tablespoon snipped fresh oregano
- ¼ cup shredded Parmesan cheese

Start to finish: 25 minutes

DIRECTIONS

1. Cook pasta according to package directions; drain. Return pasta to saucepan.

2. Meanwhile, for sauce, in a large skillet cook the mushrooms, onion, and garlic in hot oil over medium heat about 5 minutes or until tender. Stir chicken broth into flour; add to mushroom mixture. Cook and stir until slightly thickened and bubbly. Cook and stir for 1 minute more. Stir in tomatoes, prosciutto, basil, and oregano. Pour over pasta; toss gently to coat.

3. Transfer to a warm serving dish. Sprinkle with Parmesan cheese. Makes 4 servings.

NUTRITION FACTS PER SERVING:

363 calories
9 g total fat
1 g saturated fat
5 mg cholesterol
364 mg sodium
56 g carbohydrate
3 g fiber
16 g protein

roasted red pepper sauce over tortellini

For leisurely dining, start in the fast lane. Take advantage of ready-to-use roasted peppers and tortellini to speed up meal preparation. Then, slow down and enjoy the delectable result. The sauce is equally tasty spooned over chicken or fish.

INGREDIENTS

- 1 9-ounce package refrigerated meat- or cheese-filled tortellini
- 1 12-ounce jar roasted red sweet peppers, drained
- ½ cup chopped onion
- 3 cloves garlic, minced
- 1 tablespoon margarine or butter
- 2 teaspoons snipped fresh thyme or ½ teaspoon dried thyme, crushed
- 2 teaspoons snipped fresh oregano or ¼ teaspoon dried oregano, crushed
- 1 teaspoon sugar
     Fresh thyme sprigs (optional)

Start to finish: 20 minutes

DIRECTIONS

1. Cook pasta according to package directions; drain. Return pasta to saucepan.

2. Meanwhile, place the roasted sweet peppers in a food processor bowl. Cover and process until smooth. Set aside.

3. For sauce, in a medium saucepan cook the onion and garlic in hot margarine until tender. Add pureed peppers, snipped fresh or dried thyme, oregano, and sugar. Cook and stir until heated through. Pour sauce over pasta; toss gently to coat. Transfer to a warm serving dish. If desired, garnish with thyme sprigs. Makes 3 servings.

NUTRITION FACTS PER SERVING:

343 calories
15 g total fat
4 g saturated fat
75 mg cholesterol
298 mg sodium
40 g carbohydrate
2 g fiber
14 g protein

tomatoes & ravioli with escarole

INGREDIENTS

- ½ cup chopped onion
- 2 cloves garlic, minced
- 1 tablespoon olive oil or cooking oil
- 3 cups sliced fresh mushrooms
- 2 cups chopped plum tomatoes
- ¾ cup chicken broth
- 4 cups coarsely chopped escarole
- 1 tablespoon snipped fresh basil
- 1 teaspoon snipped fresh rosemary
- 1 9-ounce package refrigerated meat-filled ravioli
- ¼ cup pine nuts, toasted (see tip, page 63)

Serve meat-filled ravioli cloaked in a chunky tomato sauce and suit hectic schedules and hearty appetites to a T. Adding leafy escarole, a winter staple, satisfies palates that crave something fresh and green.

Start to finish: 30 minutes

DIRECTIONS

1. For sauce, in a large skillet cook onion and garlic in hot oil for 2 minutes. Add mushrooms, tomatoes, and chicken broth. Bring to boiling; reduce heat. Simmer, uncovered, about 7 minutes or until mushrooms are tender and sauce is slightly reduced (you should have about 3 cups sauce). Add escarole, basil, and rosemary, stirring just until the escarole is wilted.

2. Meanwhile, cook the pasta according to package directions; drain. Return pasta to saucepan. Pour sauce over pasta; toss gently to coat. Transfer to a warm serving dish. Sprinkle with pine nuts. Makes 4 servings.

Escarole, with its pungent flavor

and sturdy green leaves, adds texture, color, and punch to hearty one-pot meals or wilted salads. This relative of endive is slightly chewy and very tasty. Spinach is an acceptable substitute when escarole is scarce (although it's milder in flavor and less crisp).

NUTRITION FACTS PER SERVING:

339 calories
14 g total fat
3 g saturated fat
34 mg cholesterol
454 mg sodium
43 g carbohydrate
4 g fiber
16 g protein

17

pasta with smoked salmon & lemon cream

You can prepare this dish in 20 minutes, hardly longer than it takes to cook the pasta. The elegant result tastes as if preparation had taken hours.

INGREDIENTS

8 ounces dried medium pasta shells, cavatelli, or orecchiette pasta

1 5-ounce container semisoft cheese with garlic and herbs

⅓ cup milk

1 teaspoon finely shredded lemon peel

1 tablespoon lemon juice

2 medium zucchini and/or yellow summer squash, halved lengthwise and thinly sliced (2 cups)

6 ounces thinly sliced, smoked salmon (lox-style), cut into ½-inch strips

2 tablespoons snipped fresh chives

Can you tell real lox from a fishy imposter?

If it's draped over a cream-cheese-slathered bagel, that's one clue. If you buy it at a Jewish deli, that's another. But most of all, to pass the lox test, those rosy, translucent, paper-thin salmon slices must be brine-cured, with a bold, salty flavor. Nova Scotia smoked salmon (or Nova) is more delicate in flavor—and more expensive.

Start to finish: 20 minutes

DIRECTIONS

1. Cook pasta according to package directions; drain. Return pasta to saucepan.

2. Meanwhile, for sauce, in a medium saucepan heat the cheese and milk over low heat until cheese melts, whisking until smooth. Stir in lemon peel and lemon juice. Stir in zucchini and salmon; heat through. Pour sauce over pasta; toss gently to coat.

3. Transfer to a warm serving platter. Sprinkle with chives. Makes 4 servings.

NUTRITION FACTS PER SERVING:

420 calories
15 g total fat
9 g saturated fat
44 mg cholesterol
347 mg sodium
48 g carbohydrate
1 g fiber
19 g protein

INGREDIENTS

- ⅓ cup raspberry vinegar
- 3 tablespoons olive oil
- 2 teaspoons sugar
- 1 clove garlic, minced
- ¼ teaspoon coarsely ground pepper
- 1 8- to 10-ounce skinless, boneless salmon fillet or other fish fillet
- 1 9-ounce package refrigerated spinach or plain fettuccine
- 1 cup sliced strawberries
- ¼ cup sliced green onions

strawberries, salmon, & fettuccine

Strawberries aren't just for dessert. Partner their delicate sweetness with juicy broiled salmon brushed with raspberry vinaigrette. The reward is a delightful main course for a spring dinner.

Start to finish: 25 minutes

DIRECTIONS

1. In a small bowl whisk together raspberry vinegar, olive oil, sugar, garlic, and pepper. Reserve 1 tablespoon of the oil mixture; set aside.

2. Rinse fish; pat dry. Place fish on the greased, unheated rack of a broiler pan, tucking under any thin edges. Brush fish with reserved oil mixture. Broil 4 inches from the heat until fish flakes easily when tested with a fork (allow 4 to 6 minutes per ½-inch thickness of fish).

3. Meanwhile, cook the pasta according to package directions; drain. Return pasta to saucepan. Pour remaining oil mixture over pasta; toss gently to coat.

4. Flake cooked salmon. Add salmon and strawberries to pasta; toss gently to combine. Transfer to a warm serving platter. Sprinkle with sliced green onions. Makes 4 servings.

NUTRITION FACTS PER SERVING:

357 calories
15 g total fat
3 g saturated fat
70 mg cholesterol
87 mg sodium
40 g carbohydrate
1 g fiber
17 g protein

19

capellini with shrimp in pesto sauce

INGREDIENTS

12 ounces fresh or frozen peeled and deveined shrimp
8 ounces dried tomato-flavored angel hair pasta (capellini), fettuccine, or linguine
    Nonstick cooking spray
2 medium yellow summer squash and/or zucchini, cut into ½-inch chunks (about 2 cups)
⅓ cup pesto
1 medium plum tomato, chopped

It's said that sailors from the Italian port city of Genoa popularized pesto—the aromatic sauce of fresh basil, garlic, olive oil, Parmesan cheese, and pine nuts. Pesto has the earthy, green freshness they undoubtedly yearned for on their long journeys.

Shrimp are sold by the pound.

The price per pound usually is determined by the size of the shrimp—the bigger the shrimp, the higher the price and the fewer per pound. Fresh shrimp should be moist and firm, have translucent flesh, and smell fresh. Signs of poor quality are an ammonia smell and blackened edges or spots on the shells.

Start to finish: 20 minutes

DIRECTIONS

1. Thaw shrimp, if frozen. Rinse shrimp; pat dry. Cook pasta according to package directions. Drain and keep warm.

2. Meanwhile, coat an unheated large nonstick skillet with cooking spray (or, brush with a little oil drained from pesto). Heat skillet over medium-high heat. Add shrimp; cook and stir for 2 minutes. Add squash; cook and stir about 2 minutes more or until shrimp turn pink and squash is crisp-tender. Remove from heat. Add pesto; toss gently to coat.

3. Serve shrimp mixture over pasta; sprinkle with tomato. Makes 4 servings.

NUTRITION FACTS PER SERVING:

428 calories
16 g total fat
0 g saturated fat
134 mg cholesterol
316 mg sodium
47 g carbohydrate
3 g fiber
25 g protein

INGREDIENTS

- 1 tablespoon cooking oil
- ½ cup chopped onion
- 2 teaspoons grated fresh ginger
- 2 cloves garlic, minced
- 1 14½-ounce can reduced-sodium chicken broth
- 1 cup water
- 2 tablespoons reduced-sodium soy sauce
- 1½ cups sliced fresh shiitake or cremini mushrooms
- 12 ounces asparagus spears, trimmed and cut into 1-inch pieces
- 1 cup thinly bias-sliced carrots
- 8 ounces pancit canton noodles or dried spaghetti, broken
- 12 ounces peeled and deveined shrimp, cut lengthwise in half (leave tails intact, if desired)
- Savoy cabbage leaves (optional)

party pancit

Expand your social calendar to busy weeknights with this easy stir-fry that's sure to be the life of any dinner party. Pancit canton is a dried egg noodle—and the name of the Filipino version of Chinese chow mein.

Start to finish: 30 minutes

DIRECTIONS

1. Pour oil into a 12-inch skillet. Preheat over medium-high heat. Stir-fry onion, ginger, and garlic in hot oil for 1 minute. Carefully add chicken broth, water, and soy sauce to skillet. Bring to boiling. Stir in mushrooms, asparagus, carrots, and noodles. Return to boiling; reduce heat to medium. Cook for 4 minutes.

2. Add shrimp to skillet. Cook for 3 to 4 minutes more or until shrimp turn pink, noodles are tender, and most of the liquid is absorbed. If desired, garnish with cabbage leaves. Serve immediately. Makes 4 servings.

NUTRITION FACTS PER SERVING:

353 calories
7 g total fat
1 g saturated fat
180 mg cholesterol
740 mg sodium
47 g carbohydrate
4 g fiber
25 g protein

linguine with fennel & shrimp in orange sauce

Licorice-flavor fennel and the best oranges begin to appear in markets as summer's bounty fades. Serve this easy seafood sauce throughout the cool months to show off its seasonal flavors.

INGREDIENTS

- 8 ounces dried spinach, tomato-basil, or plain linguine or fettuccine
- 8 ounces peeled and deveined shrimp
- 1 medium fennel bulb, trimmed and sliced (about 1½ cups)
- 1 tablespoon olive oil or cooking oil
- 1 cup chicken broth
- 1 tablespoon cornstarch
- 1 teaspoon finely shredded orange peel
- ¼ cup orange juice
- 2 oranges, peeled, halved lengthwise, and sliced
- 1 green onion, thinly sliced
  Snipped fennel leaves

When shopping for fennel, look for firm, smooth bulbs without cracks or brown spots. The stalks should be crisp, the leaves green and fresh. Store fennel in a plastic bag in the refrigerator for up to 4 days.

Start to finish: 25 minutes

DIRECTIONS

1. Cook pasta according to package directions until nearly tender; add shrimp. Return to boiling; reduce heat. Simmer for 1 to 3 minutes more or until shrimp turn pink and pasta is tender but still firm; drain. Return the pasta and shrimp to saucepan.

2. Meanwhile, for sauce, in a medium saucepan cook the fennel in hot oil over medium heat for 3 to 5 minutes or until crisp-tender. In a small bowl stir together chicken broth and cornstarch; add orange peel and orange juice. Add broth mixture to saucepan. Cook and stir until thickened and bubbly. Cook and stir for 2 minutes more. Gently stir in orange slices.

3. Pour sauce over pasta mixture; toss gently to coat. Transfer to a warm serving dish. Sprinkle with green onion and snipped fennel leaves. Makes 4 servings.

NUTRITION FACTS PER SERVING:

342 calories
5 g total fat
1 g saturated fat
87 mg cholesterol
321 mg sodium
54 g carbohydrate
12 g fiber
20 g protein

trattoria-style spinach fettuccine

This fettuccine special is just the kind of soulful pasta dish that neighborhood trattorias take pride in serving. It tosses an intensely flavored double-tomato sauce with tangy feta cheese for a dinner that deserves a red-checked tablecloth and candles.

INGREDIENTS

- 1 9-ounce package refrigerated spinach fettuccine
- 2 tablespoons chopped shallot or green onion
- 1 tablespoon olive oil
- 4 yellow and/or red tomatoes, chopped (2 cups)
- 1 medium carrot, finely chopped
- ¼ cup oil-packed dried tomatoes, drained and snipped
- ½ cup crumbled garlic and herb or peppercorn feta cheese (2 ounces)

Start to finish: 20 minutes

DIRECTIONS

1. Using kitchen scissors, cut fettuccine strands in half. Cook the pasta according to package directions; drain. Return pasta to saucepan.

2. Meanwhile, in a large skillet cook shallot in hot oil over medium heat for 30 seconds. Stir in fresh tomatoes, carrot, and dried tomatoes. Cook, covered, for 5 minutes, stirring once. Spoon tomato mixture over cooked pasta; toss gently to combine. Sprinkle each serving with cheese. Makes 4 servings.

NUTRITION FACTS PER SERVING:

311 calories
11 g total fat
4 g saturated fat
73 mg cholesterol
250 mg sodium
44 g carbohydrate
2 g fiber
13 g protein

tomato ravioli with grilled portobellos & spinach

Rosy-hued purchased sun-dried tomato ravioli are dotted with a green duo of spinach and sweet basil. Slices of smoky, garlic-infused grilled portobello mushrooms are substantial enough you won't notice the absence of meat.

INGREDIENTS

- 2 tablespoons olive oil
- 2 garlic cloves, minced
- 4 to 5 fresh large portobello mushrooms (about 1 pound total), stems removed
- 1 9-ounce package refrigerated cheese-filled sun-dried-tomato-flavored ravioli
- 4 cups torn spinach
- ¼ cup grated Parmesan cheese
- 1 tablespoon snipped fresh basil
- ¼ teaspoon freshly ground pepper Grated Parmesan cheese (optional)

Meaty portobello mushrooms are the mature form of the cremino mushroom, a brown variation of the white button mushroom. Portobellos are great for the grill—simply brush them with olive oil and garlic. The grilled result can be eaten like a steak, sliced and tossed with pasta, rolled in a tortilla with grilled red peppers, or slipped between slices of grilled focaccia or bread.

Prep time: 15 minutes
Grilling time: 10 minutes

DIRECTIONS

1. Combine 1 tablespoon of the oil and the garlic. Lightly brush rounded side of mushrooms with garlic-oil mixture; sprinkle lightly with salt and pepper. Grill the mushrooms on the rack of an uncovered grill directly over medium heat for 10 to 12 minutes or until slightly softened, turning once halfway through cooking. Slice into bite-size pieces.

2. Meanwhile, cook the pasta in lightly salted water according to package directions, adding spinach to the water with pasta the last 1 minute of cooking; drain.

3. Place pasta and spinach in a large bowl. Add the mushrooms, remaining oil, the ¼ cup Parmesan cheese, the basil, and the ¼ teaspoon pepper; toss gently to combine. If desired, serve with additional Parmesan cheese. Makes 4 servings.

NUTRITION FACTS PER SERVING:

336 calories
18 g total fat
7 g saturated fat
61 mg cholesterol
500 mg sodium
31 g carbohydrate
3 g fiber
16 g protein

wild mushroom ravioli with sage butter

INGREDIENTS

- 1 ounce dried porcini mushrooms
- 8 ounces fresh mushrooms, finely chopped (1⅔ cups)
- 2 tablespoons olive oil or cooking oil
- 2 tablespoons snipped fresh Italian flat-leaf parsley
- 2 cloves garlic, minced
- ¼ teaspoon salt
- ⅛ teaspoon pepper
- ¾ cup ricotta cheese
- 1 egg yolk
- 48 wonton wrappers (about 12 ounces)
- 1 slightly beaten egg white
- 2 tablespoons butter, melted
- 2 teaspoons snipped fresh sage
- ¼ cup shaved Parmesan cheese
  Fresh sage sprigs (optional)

Here's a great tip for making quick work of homemade ravioli: Use wonton wrappers. Northern Italian cuisine rules this recipe, from the woodsiness of the porcini mushroom filling to the sage-butter and Parmesan toppings.

Start to finish: 35 minutes

DIRECTIONS

1. Soak dried mushrooms in enough boiling water to cover about 15 minutes or until soft. Drain; squeeze and finely chop mushrooms.

2. Meanwhile, in a large skillet cook fresh mushrooms in hot olive oil over medium-high heat about 5 minutes or until liquid evaporates. Stir in porcini mushrooms, parsley, and garlic; cook for 1 minute more. Sprinkle with salt and pepper. In a medium bowl combine mushroom mixture, ricotta, and egg yolk. If desired, cover and refrigerate until needed.

3. For each ravioli, spoon 1 tablespoon mushroom mixture onto a wonton wrapper. Brush egg white around edges and top with another wrapper; press together to seal.

4. In 2 large saucepans bring large amounts of water to boiling. Add half of the ravioli to each pan; cook for 3 to 5 minutes or until tender. Meanwhile, combine melted butter and the snipped sage. With a large slotted spoon, transfer cooked ravioli to soup plates. Drizzle with butter mixture and sprinkle with Parmesan cheese. If desired, garnish with sage sprigs. Makes 4 servings.

NUTRITION FACTS PER SERVING:

537 calories
21 g total fat
9 g saturated fat
100 mg cholesterol
935 mg sodium
67 g carbohydrate
2 g fiber
21 g protein

teriyaki penne

Tossed with pasta tubes, this easy Asian stir-fry delivers a tasty bonus with every bite. The zippy ginger-spiked sauce coats the pasta inside and out for a double dose of flavor.

INGREDIENTS

8	ounces dried tomato-basil penne or plain penne pasta
½	teaspoon grated fresh ginger
1	clove garlic, minced
1	tablespoon toasted sesame oil or cooking oil
3	cups packaged shredded broccoli (broccoli slaw mix)
2	cups sliced fresh mushrooms
¼	cup teriyaki sauce
¼	cup thinly sliced green onions

Start to finish: 25 minutes

DIRECTIONS

1. Cook pasta according to package directions; drain. Return pasta to saucepan.

2. Meanwhile, in a large skillet cook ginger and garlic in hot oil for 15 seconds. Stir in the shredded broccoli, mushrooms, and teriyaki sauce. Cook and stir about 5 minutes or until broccoli is crisp-tender.

3. To serve, add broccoli mixture to hot pasta; toss gently to combine. Sprinkle with green onions. Makes 4 servings.

NUTRITION FACTS PER SERVING:

286 calories
5 g total fat
1 g saturated fat
0 mg cholesterol
749 mg sodium
50 g carbohydrate
5 g fiber
11 g protein

INGREDIENTS

8 ounces dried tomato-basil penne
or plain cut ziti pasta
(about 2¼ cups)

4 cups broccoli flowerets

½ cup oil-packed dried tomatoes

1 cup sliced fresh shiitake
mushrooms

3 cloves garlic, minced

¼ teaspoon crushed red pepper

½ cup snipped fresh basil
Shredded Parmesan cheese
(optional)

penne with broccoli & dried tomatoes

Is this Italian? Or is it Chinese? With flavors borrowed from both cuisines, this hearty vegetable main course will please almost everyone.

Start to finish: 25 minutes

DIRECTIONS

1. Cook pasta according to package directions, adding broccoli to the water with pasta the last 2 minutes of cooking; drain. Return pasta and broccoli to saucepan.

2. Meanwhile, drain the tomatoes, reserving 2 tablespoons oil. Cut tomatoes into strips.

3. In a medium saucepan cook the mushrooms, garlic, and crushed red pepper in the reserved oil for 3 to 4 minutes or until the mushrooms are tender. Stir in basil. Add the mushroom mixture and tomato strips to pasta; toss gently to combine. Transfer to a warm serving dish. If desired, sprinkle with cheese. Makes 4 servings.

NUTRITION FACTS PER SERVING:

348 calories
10 g total fat
1 g saturated fat
0 mg cholesterol
70 mg sodium
55 g carbohydrate
5 g fiber
12 g protein

pasta with chèvre

Recover from rush hour over a bright, easy-going Mediterranean mélange. Here, pasta shells pair with tangy goat cheese, meaty black olives, juicy tomatoes, yellow sweet peppers, and aromatic fresh basil.

INGREDIENTS

- 8 ounces dried cavatelli pasta or large pasta shells (about 3 cups)
- 2 medium tomatoes, chopped
- 1 yellow sweet pepper, cut into bite-size pieces
- 4 ounces crumbled semisoft mild goat cheese (chèvre) or crumbled feta cheese
- 1/3 cup pitted, chopped kalamata olives or ripe olives
- 2 tablespoons snipped fresh basil
- 2 tablespoons olive oil

If your olives

come only from a can or speared from the depths of a martini, you're missing a world of good eating. Olives grow on six continents and are cured and dressed in countless ways. Specialty food stores and even some supermarkets now offer them in an exciting variety—fat, slender, round, tapered, black, brown, green, purple, smooth, wrinkled, salt-cured, brine-cured, oil-cured—in bulk and prepackaged. Ask for suggestions and for samples, if possible. It's the best way to choose.

Start to finish: 25 minutes

DIRECTIONS

1. Cook pasta according to package directions; drain. Return pasta to saucepan.

2. Add tomatoes, sweet pepper, cheese, olives, basil, and olive oil to pasta; toss gently to combine. Transfer to a warm serving dish. Season to taste with coarsely ground black pepper. Makes 4 servings.

NUTRITION FACTS PER SERVING:

402 calories
18 g total fat
5 g saturated fat
25 mg cholesterol
216 mg sodium
49 g carbohydrate
1 g fiber
14 g protein

INGREDIENTS

- 8 ounces dried cavatelli or rotini pasta (about 3 cups)
- ½ cup vegetable broth
- 2 cloves garlic, minced
- 1 tablespoon olive oil
- 4 cups torn arugula and/or spinach
- ½ cup dried cranberries or raisins
- ½ cup sliced almonds or coarsely chopped pistachio nuts, toasted (see tip, page 63)
- ¼ cup finely shredded Parmesan cheese

cavatelli with arugula & dried cranberries

Unlike some other feasts that feature cranberries, this elegant pasta supper will leave you satisfied, but not stuffed. Peppery Italian arugula and pungent garlic punch up the sweetness of the dried fruit.

Start to finish: 20 minutes

DIRECTIONS

1. Cook pasta according to package directions; drain. Return pasta to saucepan. Add broth to pasta; toss gently to coat. Cover and keep warm.

2. Meanwhile, in a large skillet cook garlic in hot oil over medium heat for 1 minute. Add arugula; cook and stir 1 to 2 minutes or just until the arugula is wilted.

3. To serve, add arugula mixture, cranberries, and nuts to warm pasta mixture; toss gently to combine. Sprinkle each serving with Parmesan cheese. Season to taste with salt or sea salt (as pictured, left). Makes 4 servings.

NUTRITION FACTS PER SERVING:

395 calories
13 g total fat
1 g saturated fat
5 mg cholesterol
331 mg sodium
59 g carbohydrate
2 g fiber
14 g protein

29

rotini & sweet pepper primavera

Primavera means spring in Italian. This creamy pasta punctuated with tender asparagus, crisp sweet peppers, and tiny baby squash is the essence of that welcome season.

INGREDIENTS

- 8 ounces dried rotini or gemelli pasta (about 2½ cups)
- 14 ounces asparagus spears, trimmed and cut into 1-inch pieces
- 1 large red or yellow sweet pepper, cut into 1-inch pieces
- 1 cup halved baby pattypan squash or sliced yellow summer squash
- 1 10-ounce container refrigerated light alfredo sauce
- 2 tablespoons snipped fresh tarragon or thyme
- ¼ teaspoon crushed red pepper

Start to finish: 20 minutes

DIRECTIONS

1. Cook pasta according to package directions, adding asparagus, sweet pepper, and squash to the water with pasta the last 3 minutes of cooking; drain. Return pasta and vegetables to saucepan.

2. Meanwhile, in a small saucepan combine alfredo sauce and tarragon. Cook and stir over medium heat about 5 minutes or until mixture is heated through. Pour over pasta and vegetables; toss gently to coat. Sprinkle each serving with crushed red pepper. Makes 4 servings.

NUTRITION FACTS PER SERVING:

421 calories
12 g total fat
6 g saturated fat
31 mg cholesterol
622 mg sodium
66 g carbohydrate
2 g fiber
15 g protein

pasta rosa-verde

This red, white, and green dish will make any flag-waving Italian feel patriotic, not to mention famished! Tomatoes are quick-cooked with peppery arugula and topped with tangy Gorgonzola cheese.

INGREDIENTS

- 8 ounces dried cut ziti or mostaccioli (penne) pasta
- 1 medium onion, thinly sliced
- 2 cloves garlic, minced
- 1 tablespoon olive oil
- 4 to 6 medium tomatoes, seeded and coarsely chopped (3 cups)
- 1 teaspoon salt
- ½ teaspoon freshly ground black pepper
- ¼ teaspoon crushed red pepper (optional)
- 3 cups arugula, watercress, and/or spinach, coarsely chopped
- ¼ cup pine nuts or slivered almonds, toasted (see tip, page 63)
- 2 tablespoons crumbled Gorgonzola or other blue cheese

Start to finish: 30 minutes

DIRECTIONS

1. Cook pasta according to package directions. Drain and keep warm. Meanwhile, in a large skillet cook onion and garlic in hot olive oil over medium heat until onion is tender. Stir in tomatoes, salt, black pepper, and, if desired, red pepper. Cook and stir over medium-high heat about 2 minutes or until tomatoes are warm and release some of their juices. Stir in arugula and heat just until the arugula is wilted.

2. To serve, divide pasta among individual serving bowls. Top with the tomato mixture. Sprinkle with toasted pine nuts and cheese. Makes 4 servings.

NUTRITION FACTS PER SERVING:

352 calories
11 g total fat
2 g saturated fat
3 mg cholesterol
610 mg sodium
54 g carbohydrate
2 g fiber
12 g protein

31

mostaccioli with green beans & tomatoes

Most string beans are stringless these days, making this wholesome vegetable sauce for pasta good and easy. A little white wine rounds out the sauce, and the flavor's just as full if you choose to substitute vegetable or chicken broth.

INGREDIENTS

- 6 ounces dried mostaccioli (penne) pasta (about 2 cups)
- 4 ounces green beans and/or wax beans, cut into 1-inch pieces
- 1/3 cup chopped onion
- 1 clove garlic, minced
- 2 teaspoons olive oil
- 3 ripe medium plum tomatoes, seeded and chopped (about 1 cup)
- 1/4 cup dry white wine, vegetable broth, or chicken broth
- 2 tablespoons finely shredded Parmesan cheese
- 1 tablespoon snipped fresh Italian flat-leaf parsley

The best sauce tomatoes are called

plum or roma tomatoes. They are oval, meaty rather than juicy, and cook down to a thick, full-flavored sauce. To remove their few seeds, halve each crosswise, then give each half a gentle squeeze over a sink or bowl and the seeds will fall right out. Or, scoop out the seeds with a small spoon. Buy them canned when fresh are unavailable.

Start to finish: 30 minutes

DIRECTIONS

1. In a large saucepan cook pasta and beans in a large amount of boiling, lightly salted water about 14 minutes or until the pasta and beans are tender; drain. Return pasta and beans to saucepan.

2. Meanwhile, in a medium saucepan cook onion and garlic in hot olive oil over medium heat for 2 to 3 minutes or until onion is tender. Reduce heat to low; add tomatoes and wine. Cook and stir for 2 minutes more.

3. Add tomato mixture to pasta mixture; toss gently to combine. Transfer to a serving dish. Sprinkle with Parmesan cheese and parsley. Season to taste with freshly ground pepper. Makes 3 servings.

NUTRITION FACTS PER SERVING:

313 calories
6 g total fat
1 g saturated fat
3 mg cholesterol
65 mg sodium
52 g carbohydrate
3 g fiber
11 g protein

INGREDIENTS

- 8 ounces dried mafalda or rotini pasta
- 2 cups asparagus spears cut into 2-inch pieces
- 8 baby sunburst squash and/or pattypan squash, halved (4 ounces)

- 2 cloves garlic, minced
- 1 tablespoon margarine or butter
- ½ cup whipping cream
- 2 teaspoons finely shredded lemon peel

garlic asparagus & pasta with lemon cream

Delicate asparagus requires tender, loving care to show off its simple perfection. Providing just the coddling it needs are succulent baby squash, curly pasta ribbons, and a low-fuss, lemon-infused cream sauce.

Start to finish: 25 minutes

DIRECTIONS

1. Cook pasta according to package directions; drain. Return pasta to saucepan.

2. Meanwhile, in a large skillet cook asparagus, squash, and garlic in hot margarine for 2 to 3 minutes or until vegetables are crisp-tender, stirring frequently. Remove with a slotted spoon and add to pasta.

3. Combine whipping cream and lemon peel in skillet. Bring to boiling. Boil for 2 to 3 minutes or until mixture is reduced to ⅓ cup. To serve, pour the cream mixture over pasta mixture; toss gently to coat. Makes 4 servings.

If you can't find baby sunburst

or pattypan squash, substitute 1 medium zucchini or yellow summer squash, cut into 8 pieces.

NUTRITION FACTS PER SERVING:

370 calories
15 g total fat
8 g saturated fat
41 mg cholesterol
49 mg sodium
49 g carbohydrate
4 g fiber
10 g protein

Grilled Vietnamese Chicken Breasts
See recipe, page 41

perfect poultry

Chicken & Prosciutto Roll-Ups 36
Spicy Chicken & Star Fruit 37
Sautéed Chicken Breasts with Tomatillo Salsa 38
Sautéed Chicken with Brandied Fruit & Almonds . . . 39
Chicken with Mango Chutney 40
Grilled Vietnamese Chicken Breasts 41
Keys-Style Citrus Chicken 42
Raspberry Chicken with Plantains 43
Chicken with Roquefort Sauce 44
Pesto Chicken Breasts with Summer Squash 45
Herb-Rubbed Grilled Chicken 46
Chicken & Banana Curry 47
Sesame-Ginger Barbecued Chicken 48
Braised Chicken Thighs with Peppers & Olives 49
Chicken Souvlaki 50
Smoky Chicken Wraps 51
Thai Chicken Wraps 52
Chicken, Long Beans, & Tomato Stir-Fry 53
Hawaiian-Style Barbecue Pizza 54
Fabulous Focaccia Sandwiches 55
Stuffed Turkey Tenderloins 56
Turkey Burgers with Fresh Curry Catsup 57
Pineapple-Rum Turkey Kabobs 58
Barbecued Turkey Tenderloins 59
Southwest Chicken Salad 60
Chicken, Pear, & Blue Cheese Salad 61
Sesame Chicken Kabob Salad 62
Chicken & Pears with Pecan Goat Cheese 63
Cool-as-a-Cucumber Chicken Salad 64
Chutney-Chicken Salad 65
Poached Chicken & Pasta with Pesto Dressing 66
Teriyaki Chicken Noodle Salad 67
Citrusy Chicken Salad 68
Curried Chicken Salad 69
Scarlet Salad 70
Southwestern Chicken & Black Bean Salad 71
Strawberry Vinaigrette with Turkey 72
Turkey & Pasta Salad 73
Border Grilled Turkey Salad 74
Turkey-Peach Salad 75
Broiled Turkey Salad with Pineapple Wedges 76
Warm Sweet Potato, Apple, & Sausage Salad 77
BLT Salad with Crostini 78
Chipotle Chile Pepper Soup 79
Mushroom Medley Soup 80
Chicken Stew with Tortellini 81
Spring Vegetable Stew 82
Asian Chicken Noodle Soup 83
Mexican Chicken Posole 84
Soup with Mixed Pastas 85
Chunky Chicken Chili 86
Chicken Chili with Rice 87
Dilled Spinach Soup 88
Turkey & Wild Rice Chowder 89

chicken & prosciutto roll-ups

This pretty dish takes the Italian technique braciola—thin slices of meat wrapped around savories such as Italian ham, cheese, artichokes, spinach, and herbs—and applies it to chicken. Serve the attractive spirals with spinach fettuccine.

INGREDIENTS

- ¼ cup dry white wine
- 2 teaspoons snipped fresh thyme or ½ teaspoon dried thyme, crushed
- 4 medium skinless, boneless chicken breast halves (about 1 pound total)
- 4 thin slices prosciutto (Italian ham), trimmed of fat
- 2 ounces fontina cheese, thinly sliced
- ½ of a 7-ounce jar roasted red sweet peppers, cut into thin strips (about ½ cup)
- Fresh thyme sprigs (optional)

Prep time: 25 minutes
Grilling time: 15 minutes

DIRECTIONS

1. For sauce, in a small bowl combine the wine and the 2 teaspoons fresh or ½ teaspoon dried thyme. Set aside.

2. Place a chicken piece between 2 pieces of plastic wrap. Using the flat side of a meat mallet, pound chicken lightly into a rectangle about ⅛ inch thick. Remove plastic wrap. Repeat with remaining chicken pieces.

3. Place a slice of the prosciutto and one-fourth of the cheese on each chicken piece. Arrange one-fourth of the roasted peppers on cheese near bottom edge of chicken. Starting from bottom edge, roll up into a spiral; secure with wooden toothpicks. (At this point, chicken may be individually wrapped in plastic wrap and refrigerated up to 4 hours.)

4. Grill chicken on the lightly greased rack of an uncovered grill directly over medium heat for 15 to 17 minutes or until chicken is tender and no longer pink, turning to cook evenly and brushing twice with sauce up to the last 5 minutes of grilling. If desired, garnish with thyme sprigs. Makes 4 servings.

NUTRITION FACTS PER SERVING:

214 calories
9 g total fat
4 g saturated fat
76 mg cholesterol
294 mg sodium
2 g carbohydrate
0 g fiber
27 g protein

INGREDIENTS

- 2 tablespoons balsamic vinegar or red wine vinegar
- 1 tablespoon olive oil
- ½ teaspoon dried rosemary, crushed
- ¼ teaspoon ground cumin
- ⅛ teaspoon ground coriander
- ⅛ teaspoon black pepper
  Dash ground red pepper
- 2 star fruit (carambola), sliced

- 8 green onions, cut into 2-inch pieces, and/or 4 small purple boiling onions, cut into wedges
- 4 medium skinless, boneless chicken breast halves (about 1 pound total)
- 2 cups hot cooked rice
- 1 teaspoon finely shredded orange peel (optional)
- 2 tablespoons peach or apricot preserves, melted (optional)

spicy chicken & star fruit

It's a match made in heaven. The celestial star fruit, also called carambola, is a fitting addition to this chicken dish that's a little bit Italian (balsamic vinegar, olive oil, and rosemary) and a little bit Indian (cumin, coriander, and hot red pepper).

Prep time: 15 minutes
Grilling time: 12 minutes

DIRECTIONS

1. In a small bowl combine vinegar, olive oil, rosemary, cumin, coriander, black pepper, and red pepper. On eight 6-inch skewers alternately thread star fruit and green onions. Set aside.

2. Grill chicken on the lightly greased rack of an uncovered grill directly over medium heat for 12 to 15 minutes or until chicken is tender and no longer pink, turning and brushing once with the vinegar mixture halfway through cooking.

Place kabobs on grill rack next to chicken the last 5 minutes of grilling, turning and brushing once with vinegar mixture halfway through cooking.

3. To serve, if desired, toss the hot cooked rice with orange peel. Serve chicken and kabobs over rice. If desired, drizzle with preserves. Makes 4 servings.

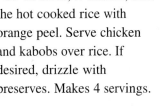

NUTRITION FACTS PER SERVING:

286 calories
7 g total fat
1 g saturated fat
59 mg cholesterol
57 mg sodium
30 g carbohydrate
1 g fiber
24 g protein

sautéed chicken breasts with tomatillo salsa

Although tomatillos look like tiny green tomatoes, their acidic flavor hints of lemon and apple. They're commonly used in Southwest-inspired cooking. Tomatillo salsa puts zest in these chili-cornmeal-breaded chicken breasts.

INGREDIENTS

- 2 tablespoons yellow cornmeal
- 2 tablespoons all-purpose flour
- 4 teaspoons chili powder
- ½ teaspoon salt
- ¼ teaspoon black pepper
- 4 medium skinless, boneless chicken breast halves (about 1 pound total)
- 2 tablespoons cooking oil
- 1 13-ounce can tomatillos
- 3 tablespoons snipped fresh cilantro
- 3 tablespoons finely chopped onion
- 2 tablespoons lime juice
- 1 fresh jalapeño pepper, seeded and finely chopped (see tip, page 158)

Start to finish: 25 minutes

DIRECTIONS

1. In a plastic bag combine cornmeal, flour, 1 tablespoon of the chili powder, the salt, and black pepper. Add the chicken, 2 pieces at a time, and shake to coat.

2. In a large skillet heat cooking oil over medium heat. Add chicken and cook for 8 to 10 minutes or until chicken is tender and no longer pink, turning once halfway through cooking.

3. Meanwhile, for tomatillo salsa, rinse, drain, and coarsely chop tomatillos (you should have about 1 cup). In a small bowl combine tomatillos, cilantro, onion, lime juice, jalapeño pepper, and the remaining 1 teaspoon chili powder. Serve chicken with salsa. Makes 4 servings.

NUTRITION FACTS PER SERVING:

240 calories
10 g total fat
2 g saturated fat
59 mg cholesterol
755 mg sodium
13 g carbohydrate
1 g fiber
23 g protein

INGREDIENTS

- 4 medium skinless, boneless chicken breast halves (about 1 pound total)
- ¼ cup all-purpose flour
- ¼ teaspoon salt
- ⅛ teaspoon ground red pepper
- 1 tablespoon olive oil
- 1 tablespoon butter or margarine
- 3 medium nectarines, pitted and cut into thin wedges
- 3 tablespoons brandy
- 2 tablespoons water
- 1 tablespoon lemon juice
- 2 tablespoons sliced almonds, toasted (see tip, page 63)
  Fresh oregano sprigs (optional)

sautéed chicken with brandied fruit & almonds

Ground red pepper heats, just enough, these scaloppine-style chicken breasts dressed with a sweet, aromatic nectarine sauce. Add a tossed spinach salad on the side.

Start to finish: 30 minutes

DIRECTIONS

1. Place each chicken piece between 2 pieces of plastic wrap. Using the flat side of a meat mallet, pound chicken lightly to ¼-inch thickness. Remove plastic wrap. Combine flour, salt, and red pepper. Coat chicken pieces with flour mixture.

2. In a large skillet heat olive oil and butter over medium heat. Add chicken and cook for 6 to 8 minutes or until chicken is tender and no longer pink, turning once halfway through cooking. Remove skillet from heat. Transfer chicken to a serving platter; cover and keep warm. Add nectarines, brandy, water, and lemon juice to the skillet. Return to heat; cook

for 1 minute, stirring gently.

3. Serve the fruit mixture over chicken. Sprinkle with almonds. If desired, garnish with oregano sprigs. Makes 4 servings.

If you don't have nectarines on hand, substitute fresh plums, peaches, or pears.

NUTRITION FACTS PER SERVING:

303 calories
12 g total fat
3 g saturated fat
67 mg cholesterol
217 mg sodium
19 g carbohydrate
2 g fiber
24 g protein

chicken with mango chutney

A variety of chutneys are available on the market, but homemade is best—and who would have guessed something that seems so exotic could be so easy to make? This chutney features mangoes and is ready in less than 10 minutes.

INGREDIENTS

- 1 ripe mango, seeded, peeled, and sliced
- ¼ cup dried currants or raisins
- ¼ cup thinly sliced green onions
- 2 to 3 tablespoons cider vinegar
- 2 tablespoons brown sugar
- ½ teaspoon mustard seed, crushed
- ⅛ teaspoon salt
- 1 pound skinless, boneless chicken thighs
- 1 teaspoon five-spice powder

One of the happy innovations in the supermarket today is jars of chilled sliced mango and papaya, available year-round. Conveniently peeled and always at the peak of ripeness, they are custom-made for quick meals. Substitute about 1 cup chilled mango or papaya for each fruit.

Start to finish: 25 minutes

DIRECTIONS

1. In a medium saucepan combine half of the mango slices, the currants, green onions, vinegar, brown sugar, mustard seed, and salt. Bring to boiling; reduce heat. Simmer, covered, for 5 minutes. Remove the saucepan from heat.

2. Meanwhile, chop the remaining mango slices; set aside. Rub both sides of the chicken with five-spice powder. Grill chicken on the lightly greased rack of an uncovered grill directly over medium heat for 10 to 12 minutes or until the chicken is tender and no longer pink, turning once halfway through cooking.

3. To serve, stir the chopped mango into cooked mango mixture. Serve with chicken. Makes 4 servings.

NUTRITION FACTS PER SERVING:

205 calories
6 g total fat
2 g saturated fat
54 mg cholesterol
125 mg sodium
22 g carbohydrate
2 g fiber
17 g protein

grilled vietnamese chicken breasts

This is no ho-hum chicken sandwich. Spicy-sweet peanut sauce and crisp broccoli slaw lend an Asian accent to this out-of-the-ordinary grilled chicken.

INGREDIENTS

- 2 teaspoons toasted sesame oil
- ½ teaspoon crushed red pepper
- 4 medium skinless, boneless chicken breast halves (about 1 pound total)
- 2 tablespoons sugar
- 2 tablespoons peanut butter
- 2 tablespoons soy sauce
- 2 tablespoons water
- 1 tablespoon cooking oil
- 1 clove garlic, minced
- 4 French-style rolls, split
- ½ cup packaged shredded broccoli (broccoli slaw mix)
- ¼ cup radish sprouts
- ¼ cup chopped peanuts (optional)

Prep time: 15 minutes
Grilling time: 12 minutes

DIRECTIONS

1. Combine sesame oil and crushed red pepper; brush over chicken.

2. Grill chicken on the lightly greased rack of an uncovered grill directly over medium heat for 12 to 15 minutes or until the chicken is tender and no longer pink, turning once halfway through cooking.

3. Meanwhile, for sauce, in a small saucepan* stir together the sugar, peanut butter, soy sauce, water, oil, and garlic. Place saucepan on the grill rack next to chicken and heat until sugar is dissolved, stirring frequently. Toast split rolls on the grill rack next to chicken the last 1 minute of grilling.

4. To serve, place broccoli and cooked chicken breasts on bottom halves of rolls; spoon on sauce and top with radish sprouts, peanuts (if desired), and roll tops. Makes 4 servings.

*Note: The heat from the grill will blacken the outside of the saucepan, so use an old one or a small cast-iron skillet.

NUTRITION FACTS PER SERVING:

360 calories
14 g total fat
3 g saturated fat
59 mg cholesterol
852 mg sodium
29 g carbohydrate
1 g fiber
28 g protein

keys-style citrus chicken

The tropical island-inspired cooking of the Florida Keys draws on the best of both of its worlds. Here, it combines fresh Florida citrus with the Caribbean penchant for fiery peppers. Soak up the delicious juice with hot cooked rice.

INGREDIENTS

- 4 medium skinless, boneless chicken breast halves (about 1 pound total)
- 2 or 3 cloves garlic, thinly sliced
- 1 tablespoon butter or margarine
- 1 orange
- 1 teaspoon finely shredded lime peel
- 2 tablespoons lime juice
- ¼ teaspoon ground ginger
- ⅛ teaspoon crushed red pepper

Enjoy the great tastes of garlic.

Garlic can be roasted, braised, baked, or as it is in this recipe, sautéed. Cooking of any kind caramelizes the sugars in garlic, mellowing its pungent smell and taming its assertive flavor. Because it is sautéed with the chicken in Keys-Style Citrus Chicken, the garlic cooks long enough to turn light brown. This adds a toasty flavor that pairs well with the tangy lime juice.

Start to finish: 20 minutes

DIRECTIONS

1. In a large skillet cook chicken and garlic in hot butter over medium heat for 8 to 10 minutes or until chicken is tender and no longer pink, turning chicken once and stirring garlic occasionally.

2. Meanwhile, in a small bowl combine lime peel, lime juice, ginger, and red pepper; set aside. Peel orange. Reserving juice, cut orange in half lengthwise; then cut crosswise into slices. Add any reserved orange juice and the lime juice mixture to skillet. Place orange slices on top of chicken. Cook, covered, for 1 to 2 minutes or until heated through. To serve, spoon any reserved drippings over chicken. Makes 4 servings.

NUTRITION FACTS PER SERVING:

167 calories
6 g total fat
3 g saturated fat
67 mg cholesterol
84 mg sodium
5 g carbohydrate
1 g fiber
22 g protein

INGREDIENTS

- 1 cup fresh raspberries or one 10-ounce package frozen unsweetened raspberries
- 2 tablespoons granulated sugar
- 1 teaspoon margarine or butter
- 2 ripe plantains or firm bananas, sliced
- 2 tablespoons brown sugar
- 2 tablespoons white wine vinegar
- 2 green onions, thinly sliced
- 1 small fresh jalapeño pepper, seeded and finely chopped (see tip, page 158)
- 4 medium skinless, boneless chicken breast halves (about 1 pound total)
- Ti leaves (optional)

raspberry chicken with plantains

Plantains are a starchier, less-sweet cousin of the beloved banana. Unlike bananas, though, they must be cooked before eaten. Here they're sautéed in butter, a little brown sugar, and vinegar to make a delicious side to smoky-sweet raspberry chicken.

Start to finish: 30 minutes

DIRECTIONS

1. For sauce, in a small saucepan combine raspberries and granulated sugar. Heat over low heat about 3 minutes or until the berries are softened. Press berries through a fine-mesh sieve; discard seeds.

2. In a large nonstick skillet heat margarine over medium heat. Add plantains (if using) and cook and stir about 2 minutes or until plantains are lightly browned and slightly softened. Stir in bananas (if using), brown sugar, and vinegar; heat through. Remove from heat; stir in green onions and jalapeño pepper.

3. Sprinkle chicken with salt and pepper. Grill chicken on the lightly greased rack of an uncovered grill directly over medium heat for 12 to 15 minutes or until chicken is tender and no longer pink, turning once halfway through cooking. If desired, place a chicken breast on a ti leaf; spoon sauce over chicken. Serve with plantains. Makes 4 servings.

NUTRITION FACTS PER SERVING:

300 calories
5 g total fat
1 g saturated fat
59 mg cholesterol
103 mg sodium
45 g carbohydrate
4 g fiber
23 g protein

43

chicken with roquefort sauce

Roquefort—the king of French blues—is a sheep's milk cheese that, by law, must be aged at least two months in the limestone caves of Roquefort in the South of France. Serve this dish with some French bread, a crisp green salad, and a dry white wine.

INGREDIENTS

- ½ cup plain fat-free yogurt
- ¼ cup chopped red onion
- 2 tablespoons crumbled Roquefort or other blue cheese
- 1 tablespoon snipped fresh chives
- ⅛ teaspoon white pepper

- 2 ripe small pears, halved lengthwise, cored, and stemmed
- Lemon juice
- 4 medium skinless, boneless chicken breast halves (about 1 pound total)

Prep time: 12 minutes
Grilling time: 12 minutes

DIRECTIONS

1. For sauce, in a small bowl combine yogurt, onion, Roquefort cheese, chives, and white pepper. Cover and refrigerate until ready to serve. Brush the cut sides of pears with lemon juice. Set aside.

2. Sprinkle chicken with salt and black pepper. Grill chicken on the lightly greased rack of an uncovered grill directly over medium heat for 5 minutes. Turn chicken. Add pears to grill, cut sides down. Grill chicken and pears for 7 to 10 minutes or until chicken is tender and no longer pink. Serve chicken and pears with sauce. Makes 4 servings.

NUTRITION FACTS PER SERVING:

199 calories
5 g total fat
2 g saturated fat
63 mg cholesterol
168 mg sodium
14 g carbohydrate
2 g fiber
25 g protein

INGREDIENTS

- 2 tablespoons pesto
- 4 small skinless, boneless chicken breast halves (about 12 ounces total)
- 2 cups chopped zucchini and/or yellow summer squash
- 2 tablespoons finely shredded Asiago or Parmesan cheese

pesto chicken breasts with summer squash

This study in green is all about great taste and true simplicity. Crisp-tender diamonds of zucchini accompany juicy, pan-seared chicken breasts flavored with basil-specked pesto and smoky Asiago cheese. Count 'em, there are only four ingredients!

2. Turn the chicken; add squash. Cook for 4 to 6 minutes more or until chicken is tender and no longer pink and squash is crisp-tender, stirring squash gently once or twice. Transfer chicken and squash to 4 dinner plates. Spread pesto over chicken; sprinkle with cheese. Makes 4 servings.

Start to finish: 13 minutes

DIRECTIONS

1. Skim 1 tablespoon oil off pesto (or substitute 1 tablespoon olive oil). In a large nonstick skillet cook chicken in hot oil over medium heat for 4 minutes.

NUTRITION FACTS PER SERVING:

169 calories
8 g total fat
1 g saturated fat
48 mg cholesterol
158 mg sodium
4 g carbohydrate
1 g fiber
19 g protein

Pesto is the essence of Italy all

whirled together into one heady sauce of fresh basil, olive oil, garlic, sharply flavored cheese, and pine nuts. Pesto is most commonly tossed with hot pasta or gnocchi (dumplings), but its uses are nearly limitless. Try spreading pesto on pizza crust before adding other ingredients. Top off a baked potato with pesto instead of sour cream. Spread pesto lightly over a whole chicken or under its skin before roasting. Or, blend pesto with butter and serve it with grilled fish or warm bread.

45

herb-rubbed grilled chicken

Here's an aromatic way to flavor grilled chicken that doesn't depend on having fresh herbs. Try this rub on steak or pork chops, too.

INGREDIENTS

½ teaspoon salt

½ teaspoon dried thyme, crushed

½ teaspoon dried rosemary, crushed

½ teaspoon dried savory, crushed

¼ teaspoon pepper

2½ to 3 pounds meaty chicken pieces (breasts, thighs, and drumsticks)

Prep time: 10 minutes
Grilling time: 35 minutes

NUTRITION FACTS PER SERVING:

113 calories
2 g total fat
1 g saturated fat
50 mg cholesterol
312 mg sodium
0 g carbohydrate
0 g fiber
21 g protein

DIRECTIONS

1. In a small bowl combine salt, thyme, rosemary, savory, and pepper. Sprinkle mixture evenly over chicken; rub in with your fingers.

2. Grill chicken, bone side up, on the lightly greased rack of an uncovered grill directly over medium heat for 35 to 45 minutes or until chicken is tender and no longer pink, turning once halfway through cooking. Makes 6 servings.

chicken & banana curry

INGREDIENTS

- 8 ounces skinless, boneless chicken thighs or breast halves
- ¾ cup sliced green onions
- 3 to 4 teaspoons curry powder
- 1 tablespoon margarine or butter
- ¼ cup apricot preserves
- ⅓ cup mixed dried fruit bits
- ⅓ cup water
- 1½ cups plain low-fat yogurt
- 2 tablespoons cornstarch
- 1 medium banana, sliced
- Hot cooked rice

Cultures all over the world love curries. These mélanges of meat, vegetables, and fruit are seasoned with curry powder, a blend of up to 20 spices that can vary greatly in the degree of fire it gives to its namesake dish.

Start to finish: 20 minutes

DIRECTIONS

1. Cut chicken into 1-inch pieces. In a large nonstick skillet cook ½ cup of the green onions and the curry powder in hot margarine over medium-high heat for 1 minute. Push green onion mixture to side of skillet. Add chicken; cook and stir for 3 to 4 minutes or until no longer pink. Reduce heat.

2. Snip any large pieces of preserves. Stir preserves, fruit bits, and water into chicken mixture. Stir together yogurt and cornstarch; stir into chicken mixture. Cook and stir until thickened and bubbly. Cook and stir for 2 minutes more.

3. Stir in banana. Season to taste with salt. Serve over rice and sprinkle with the remaining ¼ cup green onions. Makes 4 servings.

NUTRITION FACTS PER SERVING:

374 calories
8 g total fat
2 g saturated fat
32 mg cholesterol
167 mg sodium
62 g carbohydrate
1 g fiber
16 g protein

sesame-ginger barbecued chicken

This Asian-style barbecue sauce spiked with Oriental chili sauce is so good, you'll definitely want to warm up the extra and pass it at the table with the chicken. Watch closely—or the bowl may be empty by the time it gets to you!

INGREDIENTS

⅓ cup bottled plum sauce or sweet and sour sauce

¼ cup water

3 tablespoons hoisin sauce

1½ teaspoons sesame seed (toasted, if desired)

1 clove garlic, minced

1 teaspoon grated fresh ginger or ¼ teaspoon ground ginger

¼ to ½ teaspoon Oriental chili sauce or several dashes bottled hot pepper sauce

6 small skinless, boneless chicken breast halves and/or thighs (about 1½ pounds total)

Here's a simple way to test the approximate temperature of your coals. Hold your hand, palm side down, at the spot where the food will cook for as long as it is comfortable. Count "one thousand one, one thousand two," etc. Two seconds means the coals are hot, three is medium-hot, four is medium, five is medium-low, and six is low.

Prep time: 10 minutes
Grilling time: 12 minutes

DIRECTIONS

1. For sauce, in a small saucepan combine all of the ingredients except the chicken. Bring to boiling over medium heat, stirring frequently; reduce heat. Simmer, covered, for 3 minutes. Set aside.

2. Grill chicken on the lightly greased rack of an uncovered grill directly over medium heat for 12 to 15 minutes or until chicken is tender and no longer pink, turning once and brushing once or twice with sauce during the last 5 minutes of grilling.

3. In a small saucepan heat the remaining sauce until bubbly; pass with chicken. Makes 6 servings.

NUTRITION FACTS PER SERVING:

166 calories
4 g total fat
1 g saturated fat
59 mg cholesterol
216 mg sodium
9 g carbohydrate
0 g fiber
22 g protein

braised chicken thighs with peppers & olives

INGREDIENTS

- 12 skinless, boneless chicken thighs (2 to 2½ pounds total)
- 2 tablespoons olive oil
- 1 large onion, chopped
- 1 medium red sweet pepper, cut into thin strips
- 3 cloves garlic, minced
- 1 cup uncooked long-grain rice
- ¼ teaspoon thread saffron, crushed, or ⅛ teaspoon ground saffron
- 1½ cups water
- ½ cup pimiento-stuffed green olives, halved
- ½ cup dry white wine, dry vermouth, or chicken broth
  Lemon wedges

Saffron colors this Spanish dish a sunny yellow. This prized spice is actually the dried stigmas of the crocus flower, which must be handpicked. Food-trivia lovers: About 250,000 stigmas make a pound. The pungent taste is well worth the high price.

Start to finish: 45 minutes

DIRECTIONS

1. Sprinkle the chicken with salt and black pepper. In a 12-inch skillet heat olive oil over medium-high heat. Add the chicken and cook about 10 minutes or until browned, turning once. Remove the chicken; reserve 1 tablespoon drippings in skillet.

2. Add the onion, sweet pepper, and garlic to skillet. Cook and stir for 4 to 5 minutes or until vegetables are tender. Stir in rice and saffron; add water, olives, and wine. Bring to boiling.

Return the chicken to skillet; reduce heat. Simmer, covered, about 25 minutes or until chicken is no longer pink and rice is tender. Serve with lemon wedges. Makes 6 servings.

NUTRITION FACTS PER SERVING:

328 calories
11 g total fat
3 g saturated fat
73 mg cholesterol
338 mg sodium
28 g carbohydrate
1 g fiber
24 g protein

49

chicken souvlaki

What the kabob is to the Middle East, skewered souvlaki is to Greece. Rosemary and thyme, which cover the hillsides of the Greek Islands, add authentic flavor to the marinade. Use a sprig of rosemary to brush the marinade on the assorted vegetables.

INGREDIENTS

- 1 pound skinless, boneless chicken thighs or breast halves
- 1/3 cup vinegar and oil salad dressing
- 1 teaspoon finely shredded lemon peel
- 1 tablespoon lemon juice
- 1 teaspoon snipped fresh rosemary or 1/4 teaspoon dried rosemary, crushed
- 1 teaspoon snipped fresh thyme or 1/4 teaspoon dried thyme, crushed
- 2 small green sweet peppers, cut into 1-inch pieces
- 1 medium onion, cut into 8 wedges
- 3 cups hot cooked rice

Presenting the chicken and vegetables

on fresh rosemary skewers will add a special touch to your meal. To use rosemary skewers, soak long stalks of fresh rosemary in water about 30 minutes to prevent them from burning. Thread the chicken and vegetables on the stalks, removing some of the leaves, and broil or grill the kabobs.

Prep time: 25 minutes
Marinating time: 3 hours
Broiling time: 10 minutes

DIRECTIONS

1. Cut chicken into 1-inch pieces. Place chicken in a plastic bag set in a shallow bowl. For marinade, in a small bowl combine salad dressing, lemon peel, lemon juice, rosemary, and thyme. Pour over chicken; close bag. Marinate in refrigerator for 3 to 24 hours, turning bag occasionally.

2. Drain chicken, reserving marinade. On eight 8-inch skewers alternately thread chicken, green peppers, and onion. Brush the peppers and onion with the reserved marinade. Broil kabobs on the unheated rack of a broiler pan 3 to 4 inches from the heat for 10 to 12 minutes or until chicken is tender and no longer pink, turning once halfway through cooking. (Or, grill on the lightly greased rack of an uncovered grill directly over medium heat for 10 to 12 minutes, turning once halfway through cooking.) Serve with rice. Makes 4 servings.

NUTRITION FACTS PER SERVING:

392 calories
17 g total fat
3 g saturated fat
54 mg cholesterol
337 mg sodium
41 g carbohydrate
1 g fiber
20 g protein

INGREDIENTS

- 2 cups mesquite wood chips
- 12 ounces skinless, boneless chicken breast halves
- 1 tablespoon cooking oil
- 1 tablespoon Worcestershire sauce
- 1 teaspoon snipped fresh thyme
- ¼ teaspoon pepper
- ½ of an 8-ounce tub plain cream cheese
- 2 oil-packed dried tomatoes, drained and finely chopped
- 2 tablespoons chopped pine nuts or almonds (optional)
- 4 8- or 9-inch plain, tomato, and/or spinach flour tortillas
- 16 fresh basil leaves, cut into strips

smoky chicken wraps

It's easy to get a grip on dinner when it's mesquite-smoked chicken all wrapped up in a flour tortilla that's slathered with tomato-and-pine nut cream cheese. For variety, try flavored tortillas, such as tomato or spinach.

Prep time: 20 minutes
Marinating time: 15 minutes
Grilling time: 10 minutes

DIRECTIONS

1. At least 1 hour before grilling, soak wood chips in enough water to cover. Place chicken in a shallow dish. For marinade, combine oil, Worcestershire sauce, thyme, and pepper. Pour over the chicken. Cover and marinate at room temperature for 15 minutes.

2. In a small bowl stir together cream cheese, dried tomatoes, and, if desired, nuts. If necessary, stir in enough water to make of spreading consistency. Season to taste with salt and pepper; set aside. Wrap the tortillas in heavy foil.

3. Drain wood chips. In a charcoal grill with a cover arrange medium-hot coals in bottom of grill. Sprinkle wood chips over coals. (For a gas grill, add wood chips according to manufacturer's directions). Place chicken on a lightly greased grill rack directly over coals. Cover and grill for 10 to 12 minutes or until chicken is tender and no longer pink, turning chicken once and adding tortillas halfway through cooking.

4. Transfer chicken to a cutting board; cool slightly. Cut into thin slices. Spread the cream cheese mixture over tortillas; sprinkle with basil. Divide the chicken among tortillas; roll up. Makes 4 servings.

NUTRITION FACTS PER SERVING:

454 calories
21 g total fat
6 g saturated fat
77 mg cholesterol
798 mg sodium
42 g carbohydrate
1 g fiber
26 g protein

thai chicken wraps

Join the wrap rage with this all-in-one meal of Pacific Rim flavors: sautéed chicken, a confetti of gingered vegetables, and a sweet and savory peanut sauce.

6 8- to 10-inch plain, tomato, and/or spinach flour tortillas
½ teaspoon garlic salt
¼ to ½ teaspoon pepper
12 ounces skinless, boneless chicken breast strips for stir-frying

1 tablespoon cooking oil
4 cups packaged shredded broccoli (broccoli slaw mix)
1 medium red onion, cut into thin wedges
1 teaspoon grated fresh ginger
1 recipe Peanut Sauce

Start to finish: 20 minutes

DIRECTIONS

1. Wrap tortillas in paper towels. Microwave on 100% power (high) for 30 seconds to soften. (Or, wrap tortillas in foil. Heat in a 350° oven for 10 minutes.)

2. Meanwhile, in a medium bowl combine garlic salt and pepper. Add chicken; toss to coat evenly. In a large skillet cook and stir the seasoned chicken in hot oil over medium-high heat for 2 to 3 minutes or until no longer pink. Remove from skillet; keep warm. Add the broccoli, onion, and ginger to skillet. Cook and stir for 2 to 3 minutes or until vegetables are crisp-tender.

3. To assemble, spread each tortilla with about 1 tablespoon peanut sauce. Top with chicken strips and vegetable mixture. Roll up each tortilla. Serve wraps immediately with remaining sauce. Makes 6 servings.

Peanut Sauce: In a small saucepan combine ¼ cup sugar, ¼ cup creamy peanut butter, 3 tablespoons soy sauce, 3 tablespoons water, 2 tablespoons cooking oil, and 1 teaspoon bottled minced garlic. Heat and stir until sugar is dissolved. Makes about ⅔ cup.

NUTRITION FACTS PER SERVING:

330 calories
16 g total fat
3 g saturated fat
30 mg cholesterol
911 mg sodium
30 g carbohydrate
3 g fiber
17 g protein

INGREDIENTS

- 6 ounces wide rice noodles or dried egg noodles
- 4 teaspoons cooking oil
- 2 cloves garlic, minced
- 1 pound Chinese long beans or whole green beans, cut into 3-inch pieces
- ¼ cup water

- 12 ounces skinless, boneless chicken breast halves, cut into thin strips
- 1 teaspoon Cajun seasoning or other spicy seasoning blend
- 2 medium tomatoes, cut into thin wedges
- 2 tablespoons raspberry vinegar

chicken, long beans, & tomato stir-fry

If you think good taste is hard to measure, consider Chinese long beans. A star of Asian stir-fries, these dark green, pencil-thin legumes average 1½ feet of meaty, crunchy flavor. Many supermarket produce sections stock them.

Start to finish: 30 minutes

DIRECTIONS

1. Cook rice noodles in boiling, lightly salted water for 3 to 5 minutes or until tender. Or, cook egg noodles according to package directions. Drain noodles and keep warm.

2. Meanwhile, pour 2 teaspoons of the oil into a large skillet. Preheat over medium-high heat. Stir-fry the garlic in hot oil for 15 seconds. Add beans; stir-fry for 2 minutes. Carefully add water to skillet; reduce heat to low. Simmer, covered, for 6 to 8 minutes or until beans are crisp-tender. Remove beans from skillet.

3. Toss chicken with Cajun seasoning. Add the remaining 2 teaspoons oil to skillet. Add chicken; stir-fry for 2 to 3 minutes or until no longer pink. Stir in beans, tomatoes, and vinegar; heat through. Serve over noodles. Makes 4 servings.

NUTRITION FACTS PER SERVING:

361 calories
5 g total fat
1 g saturated fat
45 mg cholesterol
334 mg sodium
54 g carbohydrate
5 g fiber
25 g protein

53

hawaiian-style barbecue pizza

Deli-roasted chicken, a bread shell, and chunks of already peeled pineapple make assembling this pizza a breeze. If you like your food on the hotter side, look for a spicy barbecue sauce.

INGREDIENTS

1   12-inch Italian bread shell (Boboli)

½   cup barbecue sauce

1   cup shredded pizza cheese

1   to 1½ cups deli-roasted chicken cut into strips or chunks (about ½ of a chicken)

1   cup fresh pineapple chunks

1   papaya, peeled, seeded, and sliced

1   medium green sweet pepper, cut into thin strips

¼   of a small red or yellow onion, thinly sliced and separated into rings

A fun way to entertain is to throw a pizza gathering where your guests get involved in layering on the ingredients. Italian bread shells and focaccia work well as a base. Offer traditional sauces and toppings as well as more unique ingredients, and consider pesto, peanut sauce, salsa, or refrigerated alfredo sauce. Fun toppers include smoked chicken or salmon, shrimp, cooked chorizo sausage, cooked asparagus, plum tomatoes, artichoke hearts, basil leaves, oil-packed dried tomatoes, kalamata olives, and feta cheese.

Prep time: 20 minutes
Baking time: 10 minutes

DIRECTIONS

1. Place bread shell on an ungreased baking sheet. Spread with barbecue sauce. Sprinkle with ½ cup of the cheese. Arrange the chicken, pineapple, papaya, green pepper, and onion on top. Sprinkle with the remaining ½ cup cheese.

2. Bake in a 425° oven about 10 minutes or until heated through. Makes 4 servings.

NUTRITION FACTS PER SERVING:

513 calories
15 g total fat
4 g saturated fat
55 mg cholesterol
1,040 mg sodium
65 g carbohydrate
4 g fiber
32 g protein

INGREDIENTS

- 1 8- to 10-inch tomato or onion Italian flatbread (focaccia) or 1 loaf sourdough bread
- 3 to 4 tablespoons light mayonnaise dressing or salad dressing
- 1 to 2 tablespoons shredded fresh basil
- 1½ cups packaged prewashed spinach
- 1½ cups sliced or shredded deli-cooked rotisserie chicken
- ½ of a 7-ounce jar roasted red sweet peppers, drained and cut into strips (about ½ cup)

fabulous focaccia sandwiches

Perfect picnic food in a flash, these hearty sandwiches of juicy rotisserie chicken, herbed mayonnaise, and vegetables on chewy focaccia require only fresh fruit and a bottle of chilled white wine to make an idyllic alfresco meal.

Start to finish: 15 minutes

DIRECTIONS

1. Using a long serrated knife, cut the bread in half horizontally. In a small bowl stir together mayonnaise dressing and basil. Spread cut sides of bread halves with mayonnaise mixture.

2. Layer spinach, chicken, and roasted sweet peppers between bread halves. Cut sandwich into quarters. Makes 4 servings.

NUTRITION FACTS PER SERVING:

370 calories
11 g total fat
4 g saturated fat
51 mg cholesterol
148 mg sodium
43 g carbohydrate
4 g fiber
25 g protein

stuffed turkey tenderloins

There's more than one way to stuff a turkey. Tender spinach and tangy goat cheese make a melt-in-your-mouth filling in these turkey tenderloins. When sliced, the rosy-red, spicy crust on the meat yields to a juicy, tender interior.

INGREDIENTS

- 2 8-ounce turkey breast tenderloins
- 2 cups chopped spinach leaves
- 3 ounces semisoft goat cheese (chèvre) or feta cheese, crumbled (about ¾ cup)
- ½ teaspoon black pepper
- 1 tablespoon olive oil
- 1 teaspoon paprika
- ½ teaspoon salt
- ⅛ to ¼ teaspoon ground red pepper

Prep time: 15 minutes
Grilling time: 16 minutes

DIRECTIONS

1. Make a pocket in each turkey tenderloin by cutting lengthwise from one side almost to, but not through, the opposite side; set aside. In a bowl combine the spinach, cheese, and black pepper. Spoon the spinach mixture into pockets. Tie 100% cotton kitchen string around each tenderloin in 3 or 4 places to hold in the stuffing.

2. In a small bowl combine oil, paprika, salt, and ground red pepper; brush evenly over tenderloins.

3. Grill on the lightly greased rack of an uncovered grill directly over medium heat for 16 to 20 minutes or until turkey is tender and no longer pink in center of the thickest part, turning once halfway through cooking. Remove and discard strings; slice tenderloins crosswise. Makes 4 servings.

NUTRITION FACTS PER SERVING:

220 calories
12 g total fat
4 g saturated fat
68 mg cholesterol
458 mg sodium
1 g carbohydrate
1 g fiber
26 g protein

INGREDIENTS

- 1 beaten egg
- ¼ cup fine dry bread crumbs
- 2 tablespoons snipped fresh cilantro
- 2 teaspoons grated fresh ginger
- 1 clove garlic, minced
- ½ teaspoon salt
- ½ teaspoon curry powder
- ¼ teaspoon freshly ground pepper
- 1 pound uncooked ground turkey
- 1 recipe Curry Catsup
- 2 large pita bread rounds (optional)

turkey burgers with fresh curry catsup

America's favorite condiment goes haute cuisine! Plain old catsup gets a lift from meaty tomatoes, cilantro, and curry powder to dress up a burger flavored with ginger, garlic, and more curry. Lightly grilled pita bread fills in for a more ordinary bun.

Prep time: 20 minutes
Grilling time: 14 minutes

DIRECTIONS

1. In a large bowl combine egg, bread crumbs, cilantro, ginger, garlic, salt, curry powder, and pepper. Add turkey and mix well. Form turkey mixture into four ¾-inch-thick patties. (If the mixture is sticky, moisten hands with water.)

2. Grill burgers on the lightly greased rack of an uncovered grill directly over medium heat for 14 to 18 minutes or until turkey is no longer pink, turning once halfway through cooking.

3. To serve, spoon the Curry Catsup over burgers. (Or, toast pita rounds on grill rack next to burgers the last 2 to 4 minutes of grilling, turning once. Cut rounds in half; place a burger in each pita half and top with Curry Catsup.) Makes 4 servings.

Curry Catsup: Chop 4 medium plum tomatoes. In a medium saucepan combine tomatoes, ½ cup catsup, 3 tablespoons finely chopped onion, 2 tablespoons snipped fresh cilantro, and 2 teaspoons curry powder. Bring to boiling; reduce heat. Simmer, covered, for 5 minutes, stirring occasionally. Season to taste with salt and pepper.

NUTRITION FACTS PER SERVING:

407 calories
11 g total fat
3 g saturated fat
95 mg cholesterol
1,113 mg sodium
52 g carbohydrate
2 g fiber
24 g protein

pineapple-rum turkey kabobs

Lemongrass—an essential ingredient in Indonesian and Thai cooking—imparts a woodsy, lemony flavor to the marinade for these kabobs. If you can't find lemongrass at your grocery store, look for it at almost any Asian market.

INGREDIENTS

- 12 ounces turkey breast tenderloin steaks or boneless turkey breast
- ⅓ cup unsweetened pineapple juice
- 3 tablespoons rum or unsweetened pineapple juice
- 1 tablespoon brown sugar
- 1 tablespoon finely chopped lemongrass or 2 teaspoons finely shredded lemon peel
- 1 tablespoon olive oil
- 1 medium red onion, cut into thin wedges
- 2 nectarines or 3 plums, pitted and cut into thick slices
- 1½ cups fresh or canned pineapple chunks
  Hot cooked rice (optional)
  Finely shredded lemon peel (optional)

Prep time: 15 minutes
Marinating time: 4 hours
Grilling time: 12 minutes

DIRECTIONS

1. Cut turkey into 1-inch cubes. Place turkey in a plastic bag set in a shallow dish. For marinade, combine the ⅓ cup pineapple juice, the rum, brown sugar, lemongrass, and oil. Pour over turkey; close bag. Marinate in refrigerator for 4 to 24 hours, turning bag occasionally.

2. Drain turkey, reserving marinade. On four 12-inch skewers alternately thread turkey and onion. Grill kabobs on the lightly greased rack of an uncovered grill directly over medium heat for 12 to 14 minutes or until turkey is no longer pink, turning once and brushing occasionally with marinade up to the last 5 minutes of grilling.

3. Meanwhile, on four 12-inch skewers alternately thread the nectarines and pineapple. Place on grill rack next to turkey kabobs the last 5 minutes of grilling, turning and brushing once with marinade halfway through cooking. If desired, toss hot cooked rice with lemon peel. Serve turkey and fruit kabobs over rice. Makes 4 servings.

NUTRITION FACTS PER SERVING:

229 calories
6 g total fat
1 g saturated fat
37 mg cholesterol
36 mg sodium
23 g carbohydrate
2 g fiber
17 g protein

INGREDIENTS

½ cup bottled onion-hickory
   barbecue sauce

1 small fresh jalapeño pepper,
   seeded and finely chopped
   (see tip, page 158)

1 tablespoon tahini (sesame
   butter)

4 tomatillos, husked and halved
   lengthwise, or ½ cup salsa
   verde

2 turkey breast tenderloins (about
   1 pound total)

4 French-style rolls, split
   Spinach leaves

barbecued turkey tenderloins

Southern barbecue goes gourmet! These substantial sandwiches feature spicy grilled turkey tucked into crusty French rolls with grilled tomatillos and robust spinach. Try accompanying them with sweet potato chips, a tasty alternative to regular chips.

Prep time: 10 minutes
Grilling time: 20 minutes

DIRECTIONS

1. For sauce, in a small bowl combine barbecue sauce, jalapeño pepper, and tahini. Transfer half of the sauce to another bowl for basting. Reserve remaining sauce until ready to serve. On two 8- to 10-inch skewers thread tomatillos, if using. Set aside.

2. Brush both sides of turkey with basting sauce. Grill turkey on the lightly greased rack of an uncovered grill directly over medium heat about 20 minutes or until the turkey is tender and no longer pink, turning and brushing once with basting sauce halfway through cooking.

3. Place tomatillos on grill rack next to turkey the last 8 minutes of grilling or until tender, turning once. Thinly slice turkey; chop tomatillos. Toast split rolls on the grill rack next to turkey the last 1 minute of grilling.

4. To serve, fill the toasted rolls with a few spinach leaves, the grilled turkey, and tomatillos or salsa verde. Spoon on the reserved sauce. Makes 4 servings.

Tahini is a thick paste that is made by crushing sesame seeds. It is most often used in Middle Eastern dishes and can be found in the ethnic foods section of most supermarkets.

NUTRITION FACTS PER SERVING:

378 calories
8 g total fat
2 g saturated fat
50 mg cholesterol
776 mg sodium
45 g carbohydrate
1 g fiber
30 g protein

59

southwest chicken salad

Grilling lends sweet oranges a pleasing smoky flavor in this refreshingly different chicken salad. To make a side salad to serve with your favorite grilled meats, poultry, or fish, simply omit the chicken.

INGREDIENTS

½ cup bottled poppy seed salad dressing

1 small fresh jalapeño pepper, seeded and finely chopped (see tip, page 158)

½ teaspoon finely shredded orange peel

4 medium skinless, boneless chicken breast halves (about 1 pound total)

2 oranges, peeled and sliced ½ inch thick

1 red sweet pepper, quartered

8 cups torn mixed salad greens

1 small jicama, peeled and cut into thin bite-size strips

Prep time: 15 minutes
Grilling time: 12 minutes

DIRECTIONS

1. In a small bowl combine the salad dressing, jalapeño pepper, and orange peel. Remove 1 tablespoon of the dressing mixture. Brush the chicken, orange slices, and sweet pepper with the 1 tablespoon mixture.

2. Grill the chicken, orange slices, and sweet pepper on the lightly greased rack of an uncovered grill directly over medium heat for 12 to 15 minutes or until chicken is tender and no longer pink, turning once halfway through cooking. Transfer chicken, orange slices, and sweet pepper to a cutting board; cool slightly. Cut chicken and sweet pepper into bite-size strips; quarter orange slices.

3. Meanwhile, in a large salad bowl toss together the greens and jicama. Add the chicken, oranges, and sweet pepper to the salad bowl; drizzle with the reserved dressing mixture. Season to taste with black pepper. Makes 4 servings.

NUTRITION FACTS PER SERVING:

339 calories
18 g total fat
3 g saturated fat
59 mg cholesterol
194 mg sodium
22 g carbohydrate
3 g fiber
24 g protein

INGREDIENTS

- 6 cups torn mixed salad greens or mesclun (about 8 ounces)
- 10 to 12 ounces roasted or grilled chicken breast, sliced
- ¾ cup bottled reduced-calorie or regular blue cheese salad dressing
- 2 ripe pears, cored and sliced

chicken, pear, & blue cheese salad

The pairing of mellow pears and tangy blue cheese is naturally fresh and simple. Combine this classic twosome with packaged assorted greens and rotisserie chicken from the deli, and you've got a dinner that's naturally elegant as well.

Start to finish: 15 minutes

DIRECTIONS

1. In a large bowl combine the salad greens, chicken, and salad dressing; toss gently to coat. Divide among 4 salad bowls or dinner plates.

2. Arrange pear slices on top of salads. If desired, sprinkle with freshly ground pepper. Makes 4 servings.

NUTRITION FACTS PER SERVING:

208 calories
6 g total fat
2 g saturated fat
72 mg cholesterol
591 mg sodium
18 g carbohydrate
3 g fiber
23 g protein

sesame chicken kabob salad

Kabobs in a microwave? Yes, indeed. Up-to-the-minute with Asian condiments such as sesame oil and plum sauce, these kabobs have real eye appeal teamed with slender enoki mushrooms and red radishes.

INGREDIENTS

1	pound skinless, boneless chicken breast halves
1	recipe Sesame Dressing
1	tablespoon bottled plum sauce or chili sauce
16	sugar snap peas, sliced lengthwise
2	cups chopped red cabbage

2	cups sliced bok choy or iceberg lettuce
16	fresh pineapple wedges
½	cup fresh enoki mushrooms (1 ounce)
½	cup cut-up radishes
	Sesame seed, toasted (optional)
	Savoy cabbage leaves (optional)

Start to finish: 30 minutes

DIRECTIONS

1. Cut each chicken breast half lengthwise into 4 strips. Thread 2 of the chicken strips on each of eight 6-inch wooden skewers. Place in a 2-quart rectangular microwave-safe baking dish.

2. Combine 2 tablespoons of the Sesame Dressing and the plum sauce; brush over kabobs. Cover dish with waxed paper and microwave on 100% power (high) for 2 minutes. Turn kabobs over, rearrange in dish, and brush again with the dressing mixture. Microwave for 2 to

4 minutes more or until chicken is no longer pink.

3. Meanwhile, if desired, remove strings and tips from snap peas. Slice lengthwise; set aside. Combine the red cabbage and bok choy; divide among 4 salad bowls or dinner plates. Top with the kabobs, snap peas, pineapple, mushrooms, and radishes. Drizzle Sesame Dressing over

salads. If desired, sprinkle with sesame seed and garnish with savoy cabbage. Makes 4 servings.

Sesame Dressing: In a screw-top jar combine 3 tablespoons salad oil, 3 tablespoons rice or white wine vinegar, 1 tablespoon toasted sesame oil, 1 tablespoon soy sauce, ½ teaspoon dry mustard, and ¼ teaspoon crushed red pepper. Cover; shake well.

NUTRITION FACTS PER SERVING:

323 calories
17 g total fat
3 g saturated fat
59 mg cholesterol
324 mg sodium
19 g carbohydrate
3 g fiber
24 g protein

62

INGREDIENTS

- 8 ounces skinless, boneless chicken breast halves
- ¼ cup olive oil or salad oil
- 2 tablespoons balsamic vinegar
- 1 clove garlic, minced
- ¼ teaspoon salt
- ¼ teaspoon pepper
- ¼ cup finely chopped pecans, toasted (see tip)
- 1 4-ounce log semisoft goat cheese (chèvre), cut into ¼-inch slices
- 8 cups mesclun
- 2 medium pears or apples, thinly sliced

chicken & pears with pecan goat cheese

Goat cheese, also known as chèvre, is a popular selection at the cheese shop, thanks to its distinctive tang that plays so well against fruit, nuts, and the bouquet of garden greens known as mesclun. This salad has them all, plus slices of juicy grilled chicken.

Start to finish: 30 minutes

DIRECTIONS

1. Broil chicken on the unheated rack of a broiler pan 4 to 5 inches from the heat for 12 to 15 minutes or until chicken is tender and no longer pink, turning once halfway through cooking.

(Or, grill on the lightly greased rack of an uncovered grill directly over medium heat for 12 to 15 minutes, turning once halfway through cooking.) Cut chicken breasts diagonally into thin slices.

2. Meanwhile, for dressing, in a screw-top jar combine oil, vinegar, garlic, salt, and pepper. Cover and shake well; set aside. Press toasted pecans onto one side of each cheese slice.

3. Divide mesclun among 4 dinner plates. Arrange chicken, pears, and cheese on top of mesclun. Drizzle with dressing. Makes 4 servings.

To toast nuts,

spread them in a single layer in a shallow baking pan. Bake in a 350° oven for 5 to 10 minutes or until light golden brown, watching carefully and stirring once or twice so the nuts don't burn.

NUTRITION FACTS PER SERVING:

389 calories
28 g total fat
7 g saturated fat
55 mg cholesterol
337 mg sodium
18 g carbohydrate
4 g fiber
18 g protein

63

cool-as-a-cucumber chicken salad

The cool in this dish includes its presentation. Shredded chicken surrounds a mound of cubed melon and vegetables, enhanced by a bracing lime-herb dressing. Just the antidote for a sultry day.

INGREDIENTS

- 2 cups cubed cantaloupe and/or honeydew melon
- 1 cup very finely chopped cucumber
- 1 cup very finely chopped zucchini
- ¼ cup thinly sliced green onions
- ⅓ cup lime juice
- 2 tablespoons salad oil
- 2 tablespoons water
- 2 tablespoons snipped fresh cilantro or mint
- 1 tablespoon sugar
- ⅛ teaspoon white pepper
- 4 cups shredded leaf lettuce
- 2 cups shredded cooked chicken (10 ounces)

When a recipe calls for cooked chicken,
you can purchase a deli-roasted chicken. Or, use a package of frozen chopped cooked chicken. A cooked whole chicken will yield 1½ to 2 cups boneless shredded or chopped meat. If you have more time, poach chicken breasts. For 2 cups cut-up cooked chicken, simmer 12 ounces skinless, boneless chicken breasts, covered, in 1½ cups water for 12 to 14 minutes or until no longer pink. Drain well and cut up.

Start to finish: 25 minutes

DIRECTIONS

1. In a large bowl toss together melon, cucumber, zucchini, and green onions.

2. For dressing, in a screw-top jar combine lime juice, oil, water, cilantro, sugar, and white pepper. Cover and shake well. Drizzle ½ cup of the dressing over the melon mixture; toss gently to coat.

3. Divide the lettuce among 4 dinner plates. Top with melon mixture. Arrange chicken around edges of plates. Drizzle remaining dressing over chicken. Makes 4 servings.

NUTRITION FACTS PER SERVING:

268 calories
13 g total fat
3 g saturated fat
68 mg cholesterol
79 mg sodium
15 g carbohydrate
2 g fiber
24 g protein

INGREDIENTS

- ¼ cup mango chutney, snipped
- 2 tablespoons light mayonnaise dressing or plain low-fat yogurt
- 1 teaspoon curry powder
- 2 cups shredded or chopped deli-roasted chicken or turkey breast
- 1 cup seedless red grapes, halved
- ¼ cup sliced or slivered almonds, toasted (see tip, page 63)
- Lettuce leaves
- Fresh sweet cherries (optional)

chutney-chicken salad

Curry powder and sweet-hot mango chutney add exotic touches to classic chicken salad with red grapes. Serve it on top of full-flavored salad greens with a side of cherries, or try it as a sandwich filling for croissants or wraps.

Start to finish: 15 minutes

DIRECTIONS

1. In a large bowl combine the chutney, mayonnaise dressing, and curry powder. Add chicken, grapes, and toasted almonds; toss gently to coat.

2. Serve chicken mixture on lettuce leaves. If desired, garnish with cherries. Makes 4 servings.

NUTRITION FACTS PER SERVING:

311 calories
16 g total fat
4 g saturated fat
76 mg cholesterol
118 mg sodium
20 g carbohydrate
2 g fiber
21 g protein

poached chicken & pasta with pesto dressing

What a clever idea: Cut down on pans used in the kitchen by poaching cubed chicken in the same pot with pasta. Once cooked, they're tossed again with a creamy, herb-flecked dressing quickly made with sour cream and store-bought pesto.

INGREDIENTS

- 12 ounces skinless, boneless chicken breast halves
- 6 ounces dried wagon-wheel macaroni or rotini pasta
- ½ cup fat-free dairy sour cream
- ¼ cup pesto
- 1 cup chopped fresh vegetables (such as red, yellow, or green sweet pepper; broccoli flowerets; zucchini; and/or cucumber)
- 1 small tomato, chopped
- ¼ cup pine nuts or chopped walnuts, toasted (see tip, page 63) (optional)

Start to finish: 30 minutes

DIRECTIONS

1. Cut chicken into 1-inch pieces; set aside.

2. Cook pasta according to package directions, adding chicken to the water with pasta the last 5 to 6 minutes of cooking; drain pasta and chicken in colander. Rinse with cold water; drain again.

3. In a large salad bowl combine sour cream and pesto. Add pasta mixture, chopped vegetables, and tomato; toss gently to coat. If desired, sprinkle with nuts. Makes 4 servings.

NUTRITION FACTS PER SERVING:

404 calories
13 g total fat
1 g saturated fat
47 mg cholesterol
183 mg sodium
43 g carbohydrate
1 g fiber
26 g protein

INGREDIENTS

- 1 3-ounce package chicken-flavor ramen noodles
- ¼ cup rice vinegar or white wine vinegar
- 2 tablespoons orange juice
- 2 tablespoons salad oil
  Few dashes bottled hot pepper sauce
- 6 cups torn mixed salad greens

- 2 cups fresh vegetables (such as bean sprouts; halved pea pods; and/or sliced carrots, yellow summer squash, zucchini, cucumber, and/or onions)
- 2 oranges, peeled, halved lengthwise, and thinly sliced
- 12 ounces skinless, boneless chicken breast halves
- 2 tablespoons cooking oil

teriyaki chicken noodle salad

This tasty chicken salad is "fast food" in the best possible sense. The crunchy noodles and mixture of Asian spices that enliven the dressing come ready-to-use in a package of ramen-style soup.

Start to finish: 30 minutes

DIRECTIONS

1. For dressing, in a screw-top jar combine the flavor packet from the ramen noodles, vinegar, orange juice, salad oil, and hot pepper sauce. Cover and shake well; set aside.

2. In a large salad bowl combine the salad greens, vegetables, and orange slices; toss gently to combine. Break ramen noodles into pieces; add to salad. Cover and refrigerate up to 1 hour.

3. Meanwhile, cut chicken into thin bite-size strips. Pour cooking oil into a wok or large skillet. Preheat over medium-high heat. Stir-fry chicken in hot oil for 2 to 3 minutes or until chicken is no longer pink.

4. While the chicken is cooking, pour the dressing over the salad mixture; toss gently to coat. Let stand about 5 minutes to soften noodles, tossing occasionally.

5. Add the chicken and pan juices to salad; toss gently to combine. If desired, sprinkle with coarsely ground pepper. Serve immediately. Makes 4 servings.

NUTRITION FACTS PER SERVING:

351 calories
17 g total fat
3 g saturated fat
45 mg cholesterol
521 mg sodium
30 g carbohydrate
4 g fiber
21 g protein

citrusy chicken salad

Brown-skinned jicama tastes like a cross between an apple and a water chestnut. Long used in Mexican cooking, it traverses the globe to add snap to a bright-colored, cumin-flavored salad with Mediterranean credentials.

INGREDIENTS

- ⅓ cup frozen orange juice concentrate, thawed
- ¼ cup olive oil
- 2 to 3 tablespoons white wine vinegar or white vinegar
- 1 teaspoon ground cumin
- ⅛ teaspoon ground red pepper
- 4 cups torn mixed salad greens
- 10 ounces cooked chicken or turkey, cut into bite-size pieces (2 cups)
- 2 medium oranges, peeled and sectioned
- 1 cup jicama cut into thin bite-size strips
- 1 medium red sweet pepper, cut into rings

Start to finish: 25 minutes

DIRECTIONS

1. For dressing, in a small bowl stir together orange juice concentrate, olive oil, vinegar, cumin, and ground red pepper. Set aside.

2. In a large salad bowl toss together salad greens, chicken, oranges, jicama, and sweet pepper. Pour dressing over salad; toss gently to coat. Makes 4 servings.

NUTRITION FACTS PER SERVING:

348 calories
20 g total fat
3 g saturated fat
68 mg cholesterol
73 mg sodium
20 g carbohydrate
2 g fiber
24 g protein

INGREDIENTS

- 2 medium oranges or one 11-ounce can mandarin orange sections, drained
- 3 cups cubed cooked chicken or turkey (about 1 pound)
- 2 cups seedless red grapes, halved
- 1 8-ounce can sliced water chestnuts, drained
- 1 cup thinly sliced celery
- ⅓ cup light mayonnaise dressing or salad dressing
- ⅓ cup lemon low-fat yogurt
- 2 teaspoons soy sauce
- 1 teaspoon curry powder

curried chicken salad

Ladies' luncheons have changed, and so has chicken salad. Today's version is a riot of color—red grapes, green celery, orange slices—and looks to the East for its flavorings of soy sauce and curry.

Prep time: 30 minutes
Chilling time: 4 hours

DIRECTIONS

1. If using fresh oranges, peel and slice; halve or quarter each slice. In a large bowl combine the oranges, chicken, grapes, water chestnuts, and celery.

2. For dressing, in a small bowl stir together the mayonnaise dressing, yogurt, soy sauce, and curry powder. Pour dressing over chicken mixture; toss gently to coat. Cover and refrigerate for 4 to 24 hours. Makes 6 servings.

NUTRITION FACTS PER SERVING:

275 calories
11 g total fat
3 g saturated fat
68 mg cholesterol
299 mg sodium
22 g carbohydrate
2 g fiber
24 g protein

69

scarlet salad

Beets are such an under-appreciated resource. Give them their due in this variation on a salad niçoise. When beets are combined with colorful asparagus, baby corn, and pea pods, it takes only a little imagination to create stunning arrangements on the plates.

INGREDIENTS

- 12 ounces tiny new potatoes, thinly sliced
- 12 ounces asparagus spears, trimmed
- 6 cups torn mixed salad greens
- 1½ cups chopped cooked chicken or turkey (about 8 ounces)
- 1 14-ounce can baby corn, drained
- 1 8-ounce can sliced beets, drained
- 1 cup fresh pea pods, strings and tips removed
- ⅓ cup chopped red onion
- ¼ teaspoon cracked pepper
- ⅓ cup bottled red wine vinaigrette or other vinaigrette salad dressing

The rich array of salad greens on the market these days allows cooks to select varieties for color, and piquant and sweet tastes. Consider compact smooth-textured Bibb, light-green Boston, crunchy loaf-shaped romaine, and red and green leaf lettuce. They mix nicely with specialty greens such as peppery watercress, tangy arugula, bitter radicchio, and colorful Swiss chard. Prewashed and cut greens, packaged in plastic bags, have expanded our choices and sliced salad preparation time to seconds.

Start to finish: 30 minutes

DIRECTIONS

1. In a large covered saucepan cook potatoes in a small amount of boiling water for 10 minutes. Add asparagus spears to saucepan. Cover and cook for 2 to 4 minutes more or until potatoes are tender and asparagus is crisp-tender; drain. If desired, cover and refrigerate vegetables up to 24 hours.

2. To serve, divide salad greens among 4 dinner plates. Arrange potatoes, asparagus, chicken, baby corn, beets, and pea pods on top of greens. Sprinkle with chopped onion and pepper. Drizzle dressing over salads. Makes 4 servings.

NUTRITION FACTS PER SERVING:

355 calories
14 g total fat
3 g saturated fat
51 mg cholesterol
574 mg sodium
34 g carbohydrate
6 g fiber
23 g protein

INGREDIENTS

10 cups torn romaine

1 15-ounce can black beans, rinsed and drained

1½ cups chopped cooked chicken or turkey (about 8 ounces)

1½ cups red and/or yellow cherry tomatoes, halved

½ cup bottled reduced-calorie Caesar salad dressing

2 teaspoons chili powder

½ teaspoon ground cumin

½ cup broken tortilla chips

2 tablespoons snipped fresh cilantro or parsley

Fresh cilantro sprigs (optional)

southwestern chicken & black bean salad

Fusion cooking conquers two continents in this global collaboration of Caesar dressing and a Mexican ingredient list of black beans, tortilla chips, chili powder, and cilantro.

Start to finish: 25 minutes

DIRECTIONS

1. In a large bowl combine the romaine, black beans, chicken, and tomatoes.

2. For dressing, in a small bowl whisk together salad dressing, chili powder, and cumin. Pour dressing over salad; toss gently to coat. Sprinkle with tortilla chips and snipped cilantro. If desired, garnish with cilantro sprigs. Makes 4 servings.

NUTRITION FACTS PER SERVING:

295 calories
10 g total fat
1 g saturated fat
55 mg cholesterol
913 mg sodium
26 g carbohydrate
9 g fiber
27 g protein

strawberry vinaigrette with turkey

An enduring combination is the mix of hot and sweet. See what the fuss is about with a dressing that combines sweet strawberries and pungent cracked pepper. It gives chicken salad a wake-up call.

INGREDIENTS

8 cups mesclun or 6 cups torn romaine and 2 cups torn curly endive, chicory, or escarole

2½ cups cooked turkey or chicken cut into thin bite-size strips (12 ounces)

2 cups sliced, peeled kiwi fruit and/or sliced star fruit (carambola)

1½ cups fresh enoki mushrooms (3 ounces)

1 cup red cherry tomatoes and/or yellow baby pear tomatoes, halved

1 recipe Strawberry-Peppercorn Vinaigrette

Start to finish: 25 minutes

DIRECTIONS

1. Divide mesclun among 4 dinner plates. Top each with turkey, kiwi fruit, mushrooms, and tomatoes.

2. Drizzle the Strawberry-Peppercorn Vinaigrette over salads; toss gently to coat. Makes 4 servings.

Strawberry-Peppercorn Vinaigrette: In a food processor bowl or blender container combine 1 cup cut-up fresh or frozen strawberries (thaw frozen strawberries), 2 tablespoons red wine vinegar, and ⅛ teaspoon cracked pepper. Cover and process or blend until smooth.

NUTRITION FACTS PER SERVING:

251 calories
8 g total fat
2 g saturated fat
84 mg cholesterol
102 mg sodium
15 g carbohydrate
5 g fiber
31 g protein

turkey & pasta salad

It's Waldorf salad with a twist! This delicious version builds on the classic, but goes modern with smoked turkey, raspberries, and curly rotini pasta—and lightens up with a low-fat dressing.

INGREDIENTS

- 6 ounces dried rotini or radiatore pasta
- 1 medium apple, chopped
- 1 tablespoon lime or lemon juice
- 8 ounces smoked turkey breast, cut into bite-size pieces
- 1 cup raspberries or strawberries, cut into quarters
- ½ cup sliced celery
- ¼ cup plain fat-free yogurt
- 2 tablespoons fat-free mayonnaise dressing or salad dressing
- 2 tablespoons fat-free milk
- 4 teaspoons Dijon-style mustard
- 1 tablespoon snipped fresh marjoram
- ¼ teaspoon celery seed

Start to finish: 25 minutes

DIRECTIONS

1. Cook pasta according to package directions; drain in colander. Rinse with cold water; drain again.

2. In a large bowl toss chopped apple with lime juice. Add the pasta, turkey, raspberries, and celery; toss gently to combine.

3. For dressing, in a small bowl combine the yogurt, mayonnaise dressing, milk, Dijon mustard, marjoram, and celery seed. Drizzle the dressing over pasta mixture; toss gently to coat. Makes 4 servings.

NUTRITION FACTS PER SERVING:

278 calories
2 g total fat
0 g saturated fat
25 mg cholesterol
820 mg sodium
45 g carbohydrate
3 g fiber
19 g protein

73

border grilled turkey salad

Try a refreshing new twist on taco salad. Chili-and-lime-flavored strips of grilled turkey are served over crisp greens and drizzled with a hot pepper-spiced, dried tomato vinaigrette. It's all topped off with crunchy crumbled tortilla chips.

INGREDIENTS

- 4 turkey breast tenderloin steaks (about 1 pound total)
- ¼ cup lime juice
- 1 teaspoon chili powder
- 1 teaspoon bottled minced garlic
- ¾ cup bottled dried tomato vinaigrette salad dressing
- 1 medium fresh jalapeño pepper, seeded and finely chopped (see tip, page 158)
- 4 cups torn mixed salad greens
- 1 cup peeled, seeded, and chopped cucumber or peeled and chopped jicama
- 1 large tomato, coarsely chopped
- 8 baked tortilla chips, broken into bite-size pieces

If you can't find bottled dried tomato vinaigrette salad dressing, substitute ⅔ cup bottled red wine vinaigrette salad dressing and 2 tablespoons snipped, drained oil-packed dried tomatoes.

Prep time: 15 minutes
Marinating time: 30 minutes
Grilling time: 12 minutes

DIRECTIONS

1. Place turkey in a plastic bag set in a shallow dish. For marinade, combine the lime juice, chili powder, and garlic. Pour over turkey; close bag. Marinate in refrigerator at least 30 minutes or up to 3 hours, turning bag occasionally.

2. Drain turkey, reserving marinade. Grill turkey on the lightly greased rack of an uncovered grill directly over medium heat for 12 to 15 minutes or until turkey is tender and no longer pink, turning once and brushing occasionally with marinade up to the last 5 minutes of grilling. Cut turkey into bite-size strips.

3. Meanwhile, for dressing, in a small bowl stir together tomato vinaigrette and jalapeño pepper. In a large bowl combine salad greens, cucumber, and tomato; toss gently to combine. Divide greens mixture among 4 dinner plates; arrange turkey on top of greens. Drizzle with dressing and sprinkle with tortilla chips. Makes 4 servings.

NUTRITION FACTS PER SERVING:

363 calories
19 g total fat
3 g saturated fat
79 mg cholesterol
402 mg sodium
13 g carbohydrate
2 g fiber
36 g protein

INGREDIENTS

- 4 turkey breast tenderloin steaks (about 1 pound total)
- 1 teaspoon olive oil
- 2 peaches, pitted and cut up
- 2 plums, pitted and sliced
- 2 tablespoons lemon juice
- ½ cup lemon low-fat yogurt
- 2 tablespoons thinly sliced green onion
- ¼ teaspoon poppy seed
  Mixed salad greens

turkey-peach salad

Fresh fruit and poultry are a pleasing pair with a natural lightness. Here, juicy grilled turkey breast, peaches, and plums are artfully served in a hollowed-out peach "bowl" and drizzled with a light-as-air lemon-poppy seed dressing made with yogurt.

toss gently to coat. For dressing, in a small bowl combine the yogurt, green onion, and poppy seed. If necessary, stir in 1 to 2 teaspoons additional lemon juice to make of drizzling consistency.

3. Divide greens among 4 dinner plates. (For peach bowls, see tip, right.) Arrange turkey and fruit on top of greens. Drizzle with dressing. Makes 4 servings.

To serve the salad in peach bowls, cut 2 large peaches in half crosswise; remove pits. Using a spoon, scoop out some of the pulp to create shallow "bowls." Place on top of salad greens and spoon turkey and fruit into peach halves. Drizzle with dressing.

Start to finish: 30 minutes

DIRECTIONS

1. Rub both sides of turkey with oil. Sprinkle with salt and pepper. Grill turkey on the rack of an uncovered grill directly over medium heat for 12 to 15 minutes or until turkey is tender and no longer pink, turning once halfway through cooking. Cut turkey into bite-size pieces.

2. Meanwhile, in a medium bowl combine the peaches and plums. Add lemon juice;

NUTRITION FACTS PER SERVING:

209 calories
4 g total fat
1 g saturated fat
51 mg cholesterol
96 mg sodium
20 g carbohydrate
2 g fiber
24 g protein

broiled turkey salad with pineapple wedges

Want to intensify the sweet goodness of pineapple? Let it sizzle under a broiler and enjoy its caramelized flavor. Add warm strips of turkey and refreshing jicama for an arresting lineup that goes beyond the usual suspects.

INGREDIENTS

Nonstick cooking spray
1 pound turkey breast tenderloin steaks
12 fresh pineapple wedges
6 cups shredded lettuce
1 cup jicama cut into thin bite-size strips

1 cup coarsely shredded carrots
1 6-ounce carton tropical or pineapple fat-free yogurt
2 tablespoons pineapple juice or orange juice
½ teaspoon curry powder
Dash pepper

Start to finish: 25 minutes

DIRECTIONS

1. Coat the unheated rack of a broiler pan with cooking spray. Arrange turkey and pineapple wedges on rack. Broil 4 to 5 inches from the heat for 8 to 10 minutes or until turkey is tender and no longer pink, turning turkey and pineapple once halfway through cooking. Cool slightly; cut turkey into bite-size strips.

2. Divide the lettuce among 4 dinner plates. Arrange the turkey, pineapple, jicama, and carrots on top of lettuce.

3. For dressing, stir together yogurt, pineapple juice, curry powder, and pepper. Drizzle dressing over salads. Makes 4 servings.

NUTRITION FACTS PER SERVING:

221 calories
4 g total fat
1 g saturated fat
61 mg cholesterol
95 mg sodium
21 g carbohydrate
2 g fiber
25 g protein

INGREDIENTS

- 1 **pound sweet potatoes or yams, peeled and cut into ½-inch pieces (3 cups)**
- 1 **small onion, cut into thin wedges**
- 2 **tablespoons margarine or butter**
- 1 **pound cooked smoked turkey sausage, cut diagonally into ½-inch slices**
- 2 **medium cooking apples, cut into wedges**
- ½ **cup bottled sweet and sour sauce**
- ½ **teaspoon caraway seed**
- 6 **cups torn spinach**

warm sweet potato, apple, & sausage salad

This main dish conjures up crisp autumn days and a fall bounty of sweet potatoes and apples. Leafy raw spinach provides a nutrient-rich base for a hearty salad that includes smoked turkey sausage.

Start to finish: 30 minutes

DIRECTIONS

1. In a large skillet cook sweet potatoes and onion in hot margarine over medium heat about 10 minutes or until tender, stirring occasionally.

2. Stir in sausage, apples, sweet and sour sauce, and caraway seed. Cook, covered, about 3 minutes or until apples are tender and sausage is heated through, stirring occasionally. (If mixture seems thick, add water, 1 tablespoon at a time, to make desired consistency.)

3. Place spinach on a large serving platter. Top with sweet potato mixture. Makes 4 servings.

NUTRITION FACTS PER SERVING:

415 calories
14 g total fat
3 g saturated fat
72 mg cholesterol
196 mg sodium
50 g carbohydrate
7 g fiber
24 g protein

blt salad with crostini

BLTs have been a part of the American food experience for decades, but crostini, savory grilled bread slices topped with tomato and garlic, is a more recent addition to our dining vocabulary and an inspired sidekick to the legendary combo.

INGREDIENTS

- ⅓ cup fat-free mayonnaise dressing or salad dressing
- ¼ cup milk
- 2 tablespoons chopped, drained oil-packed dried tomatoes
- 1 clove garlic, minced
- 12 thin slices baguette-style French bread
- 6 cups torn mixed salad greens

- 3 plum tomatoes, seeded and chopped (1 cup)
- 1 small cucumber, halved lengthwise and thinly sliced
- ½ cup cubed Muenster or mozzarella cheese (2 ounces)
- 8 slices turkey bacon, crisp-cooked, drained, and crumbled

Start to finish: 30 minutes

DIRECTIONS

1. For dressing, in a blender container or food processor bowl combine mayonnaise dressing, milk, dried tomatoes, and garlic. Cover and blend or process until tomatoes and garlic are finely chopped. Set aside.

2. Place bread slices on a baking sheet. Bake in a 450° oven about 5 minutes or until toasted. Turn slices over; spread with some of the dressing. Bake for 3 minutes more. Set aside.

3. Meanwhile, in a large bowl toss together salad greens, chopped tomato, cucumber, cheese, and bacon. Drizzle with dressing; toss gently to coat. Serve with toasted bread slices. Makes 4 servings.

NUTRITION FACTS PER SERVING:

236 calories
12 g total fat
5 g saturated fat
33 mg cholesterol
913 mg sodium
22 g carbohydrate
2 g fiber
13 g protein

INGREDIENTS

- 1 large onion, finely chopped
- 4 cloves garlic, minced
- 1 tablespoon olive oil or cooking oil
- 12 ounces skinless, boneless chicken breast halves, cut into bite-size strips
- 1 14½-ounce can chicken broth
- 2 teaspoons chopped canned chipotle peppers in adobo sauce
- ½ teaspoon sugar
- ¼ teaspoon salt
- 2 cups chopped tomatoes or one 14½-ounce can low-sodium diced tomatoes
- ¼ cup snipped fresh cilantro

chipotle chile pepper soup

If you have never tried chipotle (chih-POHT-lay) peppers, jalapeño peppers that have been smoked, here's your chance. As well as adding the heat, these peppers add a pleasant smoked flavor.

Start to finish: 35 minutes

DIRECTIONS

1. In a Dutch oven cook onion and garlic in hot oil over medium-high heat about 4 minutes or until tender. Add chicken; cook for 2 minutes. Stir in chicken broth, chipotle peppers, sugar, and salt.

2. Bring to boiling; reduce heat. Simmer, uncovered, for 15 minutes. Remove from heat. Stir in the tomatoes and the snipped cilantro. Makes 3 servings.

NUTRITION FACTS PER SERVING:

246 calories
9 g total fat
2 g saturated fat
60 mg cholesterol
735 mg sodium
14 g carbohydrate
3 g fiber
26 g protein

Keep soup garnishes simple. A sprinkling of snipped fresh herbs or sliced green onions adds nice color to any soup, while croutons offer a little crunch. A slice of lemon, a little grated cheese, a few chopped nuts, sieved cooked egg white or yolk, or shredded radishes add complementary color to many soups.

mushroom medley soup

If you're used to mushroom soup from a can, you're in for a tasty surprise. You can prepare this soup conveniently. For speed, use presliced button mushrooms from the produce aisle of your market; if you have the time, select a variety of fresh mushrooms.

INGREDIENTS

2 medium onions, cut up

2 large cloves garlic

2 medium carrots, cut up

2 tablespoons olive oil

6 cups sliced fresh mushrooms
(such as button, cremini, porcini, oyster, and/or baby portobello mushrooms) (about 1 pound)

6 cups chicken broth

1 7½-ounce can tomatoes, cut up

2 bay leaves

2 fresh savory sprigs

¾ cup dried orzo pasta (rosamarina)

2 cups shredded cooked chicken

¼ cup shredded Parmesan cheese

¼ cup snipped fresh Italian flat-leaf parsley

Orzo or rosamarina (a tiny pasta that looks like long grains of rice) is ideal for soups or as a side dish in place of rice. If you like, you may substitute dried tiny bow-tie or ditalini pasta.

Start to finish: 40 minutes

DIRECTIONS

1. In a food processor bowl combine onions and garlic. Cover and process until finely chopped. Remove from bowl. Repeat with carrots until finely chopped. (Or, finely chop vegetables by hand.)

2. In a 4-quart Dutch oven heat olive oil over medium heat. Add the onion mixture, carrots, and mushrooms. Cook about 5 minutes or until tender. Add chicken broth, undrained tomatoes, bay leaves, and savory. Bring to boiling. Stir in the pasta; reduce heat. Simmer, covered, for 10 to 12 minutes or until pasta is tender but still firm, stirring occasionally. Stir in chicken; heat through. Remove bay leaves and savory sprigs. Season to taste with salt and pepper.

3. Ladle into soup bowls. Sprinkle each serving with Parmesan cheese and parsley. Makes 6 to 8 servings.

NUTRITION FACTS PER SERVING:

296 calories
12 g total fat
2 g saturated fat
49 mg cholesterol
971 mg sodium
22 g carbohydrate
3 g fiber
26 g protein

INGREDIENTS

- 2 cups water
- 1 14½-ounce can reduced-sodium chicken broth
- 1 yellow summer squash
- 6 cups torn beet greens, turnip greens, or spinach
- 1 medium green sweet pepper, coarsely chopped
- 1 cup dried cheese-filled tortellini
- 1 medium onion, cut into thin wedges
- 1 medium carrot, sliced
- 1½ teaspoons snipped fresh rosemary
- ½ teaspoon salt-free seasoning blend
- ¼ teaspoon black pepper
- 2 cups chopped cooked chicken
- 1 tablespoon snipped fresh basil

chicken stew with tortellini

Dress up leftover chicken by stirring it into this easy-to-prepare stew. Chunks of yellow squash and sweet pepper accompany plump tortellini and beet greens.

Start to finish: 35 minutes

DIRECTIONS

1. In a Dutch oven bring water and chicken broth to boiling. Meanwhile, halve summer squash lengthwise and cut into ½-inch slices. Add squash, greens, sweet pepper, tortellini, onion, carrot, rosemary, seasoning blend, and black pepper to Dutch oven.

2. Return to boiling; reduce heat. Simmer, covered, about 15 minutes or until pasta and vegetables are nearly tender.

3. Stir in chicken. Cook, covered, about 5 minutes more or until pasta and vegetables are tender. Stir in basil. Makes 6 servings.

NUTRITION FACTS PER SERVING:

234 calories
6 g total fat
1 g saturated fat
45 mg cholesterol
530 mg sodium
22 g carbohydrate
3 g fiber
22 g protein

spring vegetable stew

Spring has sprung—and so has supper. Pick the tiniest and tenderest leeks, asparagus, new potatoes, baby carrots, squash, or green beans to brighten this creamy potage.

INGREDIENTS

2½ cups spring vegetables (such as sliced leeks, zucchini, and/or yellow summer squash; cut asparagus and/or green beans; cubed new potatoes; and/or halved baby carrots)

1 teaspoon olive oil or cooking oil

1 cup reduced-sodium chicken broth

½ cup refrigerated light alfredo sauce

1 teaspoon snipped fresh tarragon or thyme

1 cup cubed smoked or roasted chicken (5 ounces)

¼ cup finely shredded smoked Jarlsberg or Parmesan cheese (1 ounce)

When choosing a mix of veggies

for Spring Vegetable Stew, pick your favorites, keeping an eye out for a balance of color and texture (bright green asparagus with vivid orange carrots, for instance, or creamy new potatoes with crisp-tender green beans). For added convenience, look for precut vegetables at your market's salad bar or a stir-fry mix in the produce department.

Start to finish: 20 minutes

DIRECTIONS

1. In a large saucepan cook and stir vegetables in hot oil over medium-high heat for 3 minutes. Stir in the broth, alfredo sauce, and tarragon.

2. Bring to boiling; reduce heat. Simmer, covered, about 5 minutes or until vegetables are tender. Stir in the chicken; cook and stir until heated through. Ladle into soup bowls. Sprinkle each serving with cheese. Makes 3 servings.

NUTRITION FACTS PER SERVING:

324 calories
18 g total fat
8 g saturated fat
63 mg cholesterol
962 mg sodium
25 g carbohydrate
3 g fiber
17 g protein

INGREDIENTS

2 14½-ounce cans chicken broth
1 cup water
¾ cup dried fine egg noodles
1 tablespoon soy sauce
1 teaspoon grated fresh ginger
⅛ teaspoon crushed red pepper
1 medium red sweet pepper, cut
   into ¾-inch pieces

1 medium carrot, chopped
⅓ cup thinly sliced green onions
1 cup chopped cooked chicken or
   turkey (5 ounces)
1 cup fresh pea pods, halved
   crosswise, or ½ of a 6-ounce
   package frozen pea pods,
   thawed and halved crosswise

asian chicken noodle soup

Chicken soup is known universally as a comforting cure-all for the body and soul. Soy sauce, ginger, and pea pods add an Asian flair to this version of a classic favorite.

Start to finish: 20 minutes

DIRECTIONS

1. In a large saucepan combine chicken broth, water, noodles, soy sauce, ginger, and crushed red pepper. Bring to boiling. Stir in the sweet pepper, carrot, and green onions. Return to boiling; reduce heat. Simmer, covered, for 4 to 6 minutes or until vegetables are crisp-tender and noodles are tender.

2. Stir in chicken and pea pods. Simmer, uncovered, for 1 to 2 minutes more or until pea pods are crisp-tender. Makes 3 servings.

NUTRITION FACTS PER SERVING:

224 calories
6 g total fat
2 g saturated fat
58 mg cholesterol
1,280 mg sodium
17 g carbohydrate
2 g fiber
24 g protein

83

mexican chicken posole

In parts of Mexico, one day a week is designated as "posole day." Shops and businesses close early and people retire to temporary posole "restaurants" to enjoy a steaming bowl of this hearty soup. See what all the fuss is about—without all the fuss.

INGREDIENTS

- 12 ounces skinless, boneless chicken thighs or breast halves
- 3 to 4 teaspoons Mexican seasoning or chili powder
- 2 teaspoons cooking oil or olive oil
- 1 medium red or yellow sweet pepper, cut into bite-size pieces
- 2 14½-ounce cans reduced-sodium or regular chicken broth
- 1 15-ounce can hominy or black-eyed peas, rinsed and drained
- Fresh cilantro sprigs (optional)
- Salsa, light dairy sour cream, and/or lime wedges (optional)

Start to finish: 18 minutes

DIRECTIONS

1. Cut chicken into 1-inch pieces. Sprinkle chicken with Mexican seasoning; toss to coat evenly. In a large saucepan cook and stir the seasoned chicken in hot oil over medium-high heat for 3 minutes. Add sweet pepper; cook and stir about 1 minute more or until chicken is no longer pink.

2. Carefully add broth and hominy. Bring to boiling; reduce heat. Simmer, covered, about 3 minutes or until heated through.

3. Ladle into soup bowls. If desired, garnish with cilantro sprigs and serve with salsa, sour cream, and/or lime wedges. Makes 4 servings.

NUTRITION FACTS PER SERVING:

192 calories
8 g total fat
2 g saturated fat
41 mg cholesterol
905 mg sodium
14 g carbohydrate
1 g fiber
15 g protein

soup with mixed pastas

Finally, the perfect use for all those leftover pastas that don't add up to a meal. And because your pantry stock is ever-changing, this soup is different every time.

INGREDIENTS

- 4 cups reduced-sodium chicken broth
- 1 cup water
- 1 large onion, chopped
- 1 large carrot, chopped
- 4 cloves garlic, minced
- 3 bay leaves
- 4 ounces skinless, boneless chicken breast halves

- 1 teaspoon olive oil or cooking oil
- 2 ounces small dried pasta (such as rotini, ditalini, fusilli, wagon wheel or shell macaroni, and/or broken spaghetti)
- 1 tablespoon snipped fresh sage

Start to finish: 30 minutes

DIRECTIONS

1. In a large saucepan bring chicken broth and water to boiling. Add onion, carrot, garlic, and bay leaves; reduce heat. Simmer, uncovered, for 10 minutes.

2. Meanwhile, coarsely chop chicken. In a medium skillet heat oil over medium-high heat. Add chicken; cook and stir about 2 minutes or until browned.

3. Add chicken, pasta, and sage to broth mixture. Simmer, uncovered, for 8 to 10 minutes or until the larger pieces of pasta are tender but still firm. Remove bay leaves. Makes 3 servings.

NUTRITION FACTS PER SERVING:

220 calories
6 g total fat
1 g saturated fat
20 mg cholesterol
896 mg sodium
28 g carbohydrate
2 g fiber
14 g protein

chunky chicken chili

Chili connoisseurs, save your long-simmering recipes for weekends and enjoy this hearty bowl o' red when you have only minutes to spare. With just four ingredients, in no time you'll have a zesty, full-flavored chicken chili that's healthful, too.

INGREDIENTS

12 ounces skinless, boneless chicken thighs

Nonstick cooking spray

1½ cups frozen pepper stir-fry vegetables

2 15-ounce cans chili beans with spicy chili gravy

¾ cup salsa

The traditional chili toppings of

sour cream, cheese, and chopped raw onion have stood the test of time because they're good. But consider these more creative ways to crown your chili: chopped red, yellow, and orange sweet peppers; minced watercress, arugula, or fresh cilantro; snipped fresh chives or thinly sliced green onions; broken corn chips; crumbled, crisp-cooked bacon; corn relish or salsa; and/or crumbled queso fresco or feta cheese (plain or jalapeño-flavored).

Start to finish: 20 minutes

DIRECTIONS

1. Cut chicken into 1-inch pieces. Coat an unheated large saucepan with cooking spray. Add chicken and frozen vegetables. Cook and stir over medium-high heat until chicken is brown.

2. Stir in undrained chili beans and salsa. Bring to boiling; reduce heat. Simmer, uncovered, about 7 minutes or until chicken is no longer pink. Makes 4 servings.

NUTRITION FACTS PER SERVING:

332 calories
7 g total fat
2 g saturated fat
91 mg cholesterol
916 mg sodium
42 g carbohydrate
10 g fiber
24 g protein

INGREDIENTS

- 3 cloves garlic, minced
- 1 fresh jalapeño pepper, seeded and finely chopped (see tip, page 158)
- 1 tablespoon cooking oil
- 2 cups frozen small whole onions
- 1 cup reduced-sodium or regular chicken broth
- 2 teaspoons chili powder
- 1 teaspoon ground cumin
- 1 teaspoon dried oregano, crushed
- ¼ teaspoon salt
- ⅛ teaspoon white pepper
- ⅛ teaspoon ground red pepper
- 1 19-ounce can white kidney (cannellini) beans, rinsed and drained
- 1 cup chopped cooked chicken or turkey (5 ounces)
- 1 cup chopped tomatillos
- 2 cups hot cooked couscous or rice
- Red cabbage leaves (optional)

chicken chili with rice

Tomatillos often are referred to as Mexican green tomatoes because they resemble a small green tomato and are often used in Mexican cooking. They hint of a lemon and apple flavor. Tomatillos add a unique taste to salads, salsas, and this chunky soup.

Start to finish: 35 minutes

DIRECTIONS

1. In a large saucepan cook garlic and jalapeño pepper in hot oil for 30 seconds. Carefully stir in onions, chicken broth, chili powder, cumin, oregano, salt, white pepper, and red pepper.

2. Bring to boiling; reduce heat. Simmer, covered, for 20 minutes. Add beans, chicken, and tomatillos. Cook and stir until heated through. Serve over couscous. If desired, garnish with cabbage leaves. Makes 4 servings.

NUTRITION FACTS PER SERVING:

335 calories
8 g total fat
1 g saturated fat
34 mg cholesterol
417 mg sodium
51 g carbohydrate
8 g fiber
23 g protein

dilled spinach soup

The essence of summer in a bowl. Few things are as satisfying at the end of a warm summer day as sitting down to a refreshing cold soup seasoned with fragrant herbs. Pair it with purchased croissants and follow it with fresh peaches for dessert.

INGREDIENTS

9   cups packaged prewashed spinach (about 10 ounces)
2   cups milk
1   small onion, cut up
2   tablespoons snipped fresh dill
1   teaspoon lemon-pepper seasoning

2   8-ounce cartons plain fat-free yogurt
1   cup cubed cooked turkey or ham, or cooked small shrimp
    Edible flowers (such as nasturtiums) and/or slivered almonds, toasted (see tip, page 63) (optional)

Start to finish: 18 minutes

DIRECTIONS

1. In a blender container or food processor bowl combine about one-third of the spinach, 1 cup of the milk, the onion, dill, and lemon-pepper seasoning. Cover and blend or process until nearly smooth. Add another one-third of the spinach; cover and blend until smooth. Pour blended mixture into a serving bowl or large storage container.

2. In the blender container or food processor bowl combine the remaining spinach, remaining milk, and the yogurt. Cover and blend until nearly smooth. Stir into the mixture in serving bowl; stir in the turkey. Serve immediately or cover and store in the refrigerator up to 24 hours.

3. To serve, ladle into soup bowls. If desired, garnish each serving with edible flowers and/or toasted almonds. Makes 4 servings.

NUTRITION FACTS PER SERVING:

217 calories
6 g total fat
2 g saturated fat
45 mg cholesterol
508 mg sodium
18 g carbohydrate
2 g fiber
24 g protein

INGREDIENTS

- 6 ounces cooked smoked turkey sausage links
- 2 cups milk
- 1½ cups water
- 1 medium onion, chopped
- ½ cup chopped red or green sweet pepper
- ½ cup frozen whole kernel corn

- 2 teaspoons instant chicken bouillon granules
- 2 teaspoons snipped fresh marjoram or ½ teaspoon dried marjoram, crushed
- ¼ teaspoon black pepper
- 2 tablespoons all-purpose flour
- 1½ cups cooked wild or brown rice

turkey & wild rice chowder

If you yearn for the nutty flavor of wild rice, but time is short, substitute quick-cooking long grain and wild rice mix, omitting the seasoning packet.

Start to finish: 25 minutes

DIRECTIONS

1. Cut turkey sausage links in half lengthwise; cut into ½-inch slices. In a large saucepan combine the sausage, 1¾ cups of the milk, the water, onion, sweet pepper, corn, bouillon granules, dried marjoram (if using), and black pepper. Bring to boiling.

2. Meanwhile, combine flour and remaining ¼ cup milk. Stir into turkey mixture. Cook and stir until thickened and bubbly. Cook and stir for 1 minute more. Stir in the cooked rice and, if using, fresh marjoram; heat through. Makes 4 servings.

NUTRITION FACTS PER SERVING:

236 calories
7 g total fat
3 g saturated fat
40 mg cholesterol
742 mg sodium
30 g carbohydrate
2 g fiber
15 g protein

When you have the time— and to save time later—cook extra rice and save it. Place cooked rice in an airtight container and store it in the refrigerator for up to 1 week or in the freezer for up to 6 months. Generally, 1 cup of uncooked brown or white rice will yield 3 cups of cooked rice. One cup of wild rice will yield about 2⅔ cups of cooked wild rice.

Garlic Steaks with Nectarine-Onion Relish
See recipe, page 95

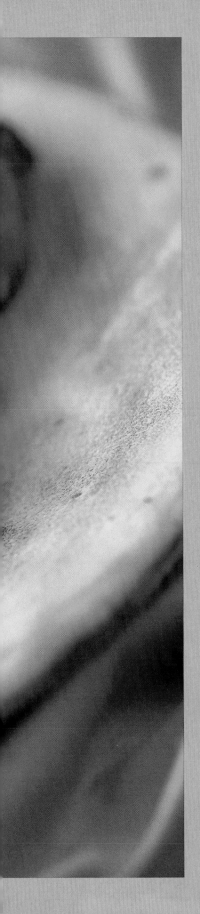

meats in minutes

Tenderloin Steaks with Arugula-Cornichon Relish 92
Lemony Flank Steak. 93
Bistro Beef & Mushrooms 94
Garlic Steaks with Nectarine-Onion Relish 95
Beef with Cucumber Raita 96
Sesame Beef 97
Spanish Meat Loaves 98
Sun-Dried Tomato Burgers 99
Beef & Avocado Tacos 100
Roasted Vegetable & Pastrami Panini 101
Veal Chops with Pesto-Stuffed Mushrooms 102
Pork Medallions with Fennel & Pancetta 103
Grilled Mustard-Glazed Pork 104
Pork Medallions with Cherry Sauce 105
Jamaican Pork Chops with Melon Salsa 106
Southwest Pork Chops with Corn Salsa 107
Pork Chops with Savory Mushroom Stuffing 108
Summer Pasta with Pork 109
Thai Pork & Vegetable Curry 110
Jamaican Pork & Sweet Potato Stir-Fry 111
Jamaican Pork Kabobs 112
Peach-Mustard Glazed Ham 113
Canadian Bacon Pizza 114
Sweet Potato Frittata with Fresh Cranberry Salsa . . 115
Grilled Italian Sausage with Sweet & Sour Peppers . . 116
Lamb Chops with Sweet Potato Chutney 117
Tuscan Lamb Chop Skillet 118
Apple-Glazed Lamb Chops 119
Tandoori-Style Lamb Chops 120
Greek-Inspired Lamb Pockets 121

Grilled Lambburger Roll-Ups 122
Spicy Steak & Ranch Salad 123
Beef & Curry Pinwheels on Spinach 124
Beef & Apple Salad 125
Beef & Fruit Salad 126
Flank Steak with Pineapple Salsa 127
Gingered Beef & Pasta Salad 128
Grilled Beef, Red Onion, & Blue Cheese Salad 129
Pork Salad with Cabbage Slaw 130
Peppered Pork & Apricot Salad 131
Thai Cobb Salad 132
Spinach, Ham, & Melon Salad 133
Red Beans & Grains 134
Muffuletta Salad 135
Greek Lamb Salad with Yogurt Dressing 136
Balsamic-Glazed Springtime Lamb Salad 137
Beef & Vegetable Ragout 138
Asian Beef & Noodle Bowl 139
Allspice Meatball Stew 140
Pork, Corn, & Three-Pepper Soup 141
Caribbean-Style Pork Stew 142
Gingered Pork & Cabbage Soup 143
Southern Ham Chowder 144
White Bean Soup with Sausage & Kale 145
Fennel-Asparagus Soup 146
Moroccan Lamb Tagine 147

tenderloin steaks with arugula-cornichon relish

Most guests love a good steak, but it's better yet with this caper and fresh-herb relish. Peppery arugula, a built-in salad, offers a pleasant bite. Serve the steaks with mashed potatoes. For dessert, Gingered Shortcake with Spiced Fruit (page 275).

INGREDIENTS

- 4 beef tenderloin steaks or 2 halved rib eye steaks, cut 1 inch thick (about 1 pound total)
- 1 tablespoon cracked pepper
- ½ teaspoon salt
- 3 tablespoons olive oil
- ⅓ cup snipped fresh Italian flat-leaf parsley
- 3 tablespoons finely chopped cornichons or sweet pickles
- 2 tablespoons capers, drained and coarsely chopped
- 1 medium green onion, chopped
- 1 tablespoon balsamic vinegar
- 3 cups torn arugula and/or torn mixed salad greens

Prep time: 20 minutes
Cooking time: 8 minutes

DIRECTIONS

1. Trim fat from steaks. Rub both sides of steaks with pepper and salt. In a large skillet heat 1 tablespoon of the olive oil over medium heat. Add steaks; cook until desired doneness, turning once halfway through cooking. (Allow 8 to 11 minutes for medium rare or 12 to 14 minutes for medium.)

2. Meanwhile, for relish, in a small bowl combine the remaining 2 tablespoons olive oil, the parsley, cornichons, capers, green onion, and vinegar. Set aside.

3. To serve, transfer steaks to a cutting board; cut into thin slices. Arrange arugula on 4 dinner plates. Top with the steak slices. Spoon the relish over steak and arugula. Makes 4 servings.

NUTRITION FACTS PER SERVING:

273 calories
18 g total fat
4 g saturated fat
64 mg cholesterol
460 mg sodium
6 g carbohydrate
1 g fiber
23 g protein

INGREDIENTS

1 1½-pound beef flank steak or boneless top sirloin steak
1 teaspoon finely shredded lemon peel
½ cup lemon juice
2 tablespoons sugar
2 tablespoons soy sauce
2 teaspoons snipped fresh oregano or ½ teaspoon dried oregano, crushed
⅛ teaspoon pepper
   Lemon slices (optional)
   Fresh oregano leaves (optional)

lemony flank steak

Though it's rare to utter the words "light" and "beef" in the same breath, this refreshingly different dish is undeniably both. Lots of zesty lemon flavors the super-lean flank steak or top sirloin. Serve it with a side of grilled or steamed asparagus.

Prep time: 15 minutes
Marinating time: 2 hours
Grilling time: 12 minutes

DIRECTIONS

1. Trim fat from steak. Score steak on both sides by making shallow cuts at 1-inch intervals in a diamond pattern. Place steak in a plastic bag set in a shallow dish. For marinade, combine the lemon peel, lemon juice, sugar, soy sauce, snipped fresh or dried oregano, and pepper. Pour over steak; close bag. Marinate in refrigerator at least 2 hours or overnight.

2. Drain steak, reserving marinade. Grill steak on the rack of an uncovered grill directly over medium heat until desired doneness, turning and brushing once with marinade halfway through cooking. (Allow 12 to 14 minutes for medium.)

3. To serve, thinly slice steak diagonally across the grain. If desired, garnish with lemon slices and fresh oregano leaves. Makes 3 servings.

NUTRITION FACTS PER SERVING:

267 calories
12 g total fat
5 g saturated fat
80 mg cholesterol
357 mg sodium
5 g carbohydrate
0 g fiber
33 g protein

93

bistro beef & mushrooms

Serve French bistro fare in a flash. The Burgundian flavors of Dijon mustard, red wine, and fresh thyme spark this hearty dish. Accompany the steaks with deli mashed potatoes and steamed and buttered haricots verts (tiny, slender green beans).

INGREDIENTS

- 4 beef tenderloin steaks, cut ¾ inch thick (about 1 pound total)
- 1 tablespoon Dijon-style mustard or coarse-grain brown mustard
- 2 tablespoons olive oil or roasted garlic olive oil
- 2 4-ounce packages sliced cremini, shiitake, or portobello mushrooms or one 8-ounce package sliced button mushrooms (about 3 cups)
- ⅓ cup dry red wine or sherry
- 1 tablespoon white wine Worcestershire sauce
- 2 teaspoons snipped fresh thyme

Start to finish: 20 minutes

DIRECTIONS

1. Trim fat from steaks. Spread mustard evenly over both sides of steaks. In a large skillet heat 1 tablespoon of the oil over medium heat. Add steaks; cook until desired doneness, turning once halfway through cooking. (Allow 7 to 10 minutes for medium rare or 10 to 12 minutes for medium.) Transfer steaks to a serving platter; keep warm.

2. Add the remaining 1 tablespoon oil to drippings in skillet. Add mushrooms; cook and stir for 4 minutes. Stir in wine, Worcestershire sauce, and thyme. Simmer, uncovered, for 3 minutes. Spoon over steaks. Makes 4 servings.

NUTRITION FACTS PER SERVING:

263 calories
14 g total fat
4 g saturated fat
64 mg cholesterol
176 mg sodium
5 g carbohydrate
1 g fiber
23 g protein

INGREDIENTS

- **4** boneless beef top loin steaks, cut 1 inch thick (1½ to 2 pounds total)
- **6** cloves garlic, thinly sliced
- **2** medium onions, coarsely chopped
- **1** teaspoon olive oil
- **2** tablespoons cider vinegar
- **1** tablespoon honey
- **1** medium nectarine, chopped
- **2** teaspoons snipped fresh applemint, pineapplemint, or spearmint
- Fresh applemint, pineapplemint, or spearmint sprigs (optional)

garlic steaks with nectarine-onion relish

What's better than the smell of steak on the grill in the summertime? The aroma of garlic-studded beef on the grill. The mint-scented relish features one of summer's favorite fruits. Serve this steak with some crusty bread to soak up the delicious juices.

Prep time: 25 minutes
Grilling time: 8 minutes

DIRECTIONS

1. Trim fat from steaks. With the point of a paring knife, make small slits in steaks. Insert half of the garlic into slits. Wrap steaks in plastic wrap; let stand at room temperature up to 20 minutes. (For more intense flavor, refrigerate up to 8 hours.) Sprinkle with salt and pepper.

2. Meanwhile, for relish, in a large nonstick skillet cook onions and remaining garlic in hot oil over medium heat about 10 minutes or until onions are a deep golden color (but not brown), stirring occasionally. Stir in vinegar and honey. Stir in nectarine and the snipped mint; heat relish through.

3. Grill steaks on the rack of an uncovered grill directly over medium heat until desired doneness, turning once halfway through cooking. (Allow 8 to 12 minutes for medium rare or 12 to 15 minutes for medium.) Serve the relish with steaks. If desired, garnish with mint sprigs. Makes 4 servings.

NUTRITION FACTS PER SERVING:

272 calories
9 g total fat
3 g saturated fat
97 mg cholesterol
108 mg sodium
13 g carbohydrate
1 g fiber
34 g protein

beef with cucumber raita

In the oft-fiery cuisine of India, a respite is offered in the form of a raita, a simple, cooling salad made with yogurt and fruits or vegetables. Snipped mint makes this raita particularly flavorful and refreshing.

INGREDIENTS

- 1   8-ounce carton plain fat-free or low-fat yogurt
- ¼   cup coarsely shredded unpeeled cucumber
- 1   tablespoon finely chopped red or yellow onion
- 1   tablespoon snipped fresh mint
- ¼   teaspoon sugar
- 1   pound boneless beef sirloin steak, cut 1 inch thick
- ½   teaspoon lemon-pepper seasoning
    Fresh mint leaves (optional)

Start to finish: 20 minutes

DIRECTIONS

1. For raita, in a small bowl combine yogurt, cucumber, onion, snipped mint, and sugar. Season to taste with salt and pepper; set aside.

2. Trim fat from steak. Sprinkle steak with lemon-pepper seasoning. Grill steak on the rack of an uncovered grill directly over medium heat until desired doneness, turning once halfway through cooking. (Allow 12 to 15 minutes for medium.) [Or, broil on the unheated rack of a broiler pan 3 to 4 inches from the heat, turning once halfway through cooking. (Allow 12 to 15 minutes for medium.)]

3. Cut steak across the grain into thin slices. If desired, arrange steak slices on mint leaves. Top with raita. Makes 4 servings.

NUTRITION FACTS PER SERVING:

237 calories
10 g total fat
4 g saturated fat
77 mg cholesterol
235 mg sodium
5 g carbohydrate
0 g fiber
29 g protein

INGREDIENTS

6 ounces wide rice noodles or
dried egg noodles

2 tablespoons cooking oil or
peanut oil

2 medium carrots, thinly sliced

2 stalks celery, cut into thin
bite-size strips

1 red sweet pepper, cut into thin
bite-size strips

12 ounces boneless beef sirloin
steak or top round steak, cut
into bite-size strips

1 tablespoon sesame seed

⅓ cup bottled stir-fry sauce

sesame beef

Get a jump on dinner. Slice the vegetables and beef ahead and refrigerate airtight. Minutes before mealtime, swirl them in a wok or skillet and serve up swiftly with Chinese rice noodles.

Start to finish: 30 minutes

DIRECTIONS

1. Cook rice noodles in boiling, lightly salted water for 3 to 5 minutes or just until tender. Or, cook egg noodles according to package directions. Drain noodles and keep warm.

2. Meanwhile, pour 1 tablespoon of the oil into a wok or large skillet. Preheat over medium-high heat. Stir-fry carrots in hot oil for 2 minutes. Add celery and sweet pepper; stir-fry for 1 to 2 minutes more or until vegetables are crisp-tender. Remove from wok.

3. Add the remaining oil to wok. Add beef; stir-fry for 2 minutes. Sprinkle sesame seed over beef; continue to stir-fry about 1 minute more or until beef is slightly pink in center. Return vegetables to wok; add stir-fry sauce. Cook and stir for 1 to 2 minutes or until heated through. Serve over noodles. Makes 4 servings.

NUTRITION FACTS PER SERVING:

419 calories
16 g total fat
4 g saturated fat
57 mg cholesterol
590 mg sodium
47 g carbohydrate
2 g fiber
22 g protein

spanish meat loaves

Humble meat loaf goes haute cuisine, but retains its almost-universal appeal. These miniature loaves, flavored with pimiento-stuffed green olives and Italian flat-leaf parsley and glazed with sweet-hot jalapeño pepper jelly, will charm their way into your repertoire.

INGREDIENTS

- 1 beaten egg
- ¾ cup quick-cooking rolled oats
- ½ cup pimiento-stuffed green olives, sliced
- ¼ cup snipped Italian flat-leaf parsley or regular parsley
- ¼ cup tomato paste
- ¼ teaspoon pepper
- 1 pound lean ground beef
- ¼ cup jalapeño pepper jelly or apple jelly, melted
- 1 medium tomato, chopped
- ⅓ cup chunky salsa
- ¼ cup chopped seeded cucumber
- 2 tablespoons sliced pimiento-stuffed green olives (optional)
- Lettuce leaves
- 8 thin slices bread, toasted (optional)

Prep time: 15 minutes
Grilling time: 18 minutes

DIRECTIONS

1. In a medium bowl combine the egg, rolled oats, the ½ cup olives, the parsley, tomato paste, and pepper. Add the ground beef; mix well. Shape into four 4×2½×1-inch meat loaves.

2. Grill meat loaves on the rack of an uncovered grill directly over medium heat for 16 to 18 minutes or until meat is no longer pink, turning once halfway through cooking. Brush with jelly; grill for 2 minutes more.

3. Meanwhile, for relish, in a small bowl combine the tomato, salsa, cucumber, and, if desired, the 2 tablespoons olives. Divide the lettuce and, if desired, bread slices among 4 dinner plates. Top with the meat loaves and relish. Makes 4 servings.

NUTRITION FACTS PER SERVING:

362 calories
16 g total fat
5 g saturated fat
125 mg cholesterol
479 mg sodium
31 g carbohydrate
2 g fiber
26 g protein

INGREDIENTS

- 1 pound lean ground beef
- 1 tablespoon finely chopped, drained, oil-packed dried tomatoes
- 1 teaspoon finely shredded lemon or lime peel
- ½ teaspoon salt
- ¼ teaspoon black pepper
- ¼ cup light mayonnaise dressing or salad dressing
- 2 tablespoons snipped fresh basil
- 1 fresh jalapeño pepper, seeded and finely chopped (see tip, page 158)
- 4 onion hamburger buns
- 1 cup lightly packed arugula or spinach leaves

sun-dried tomato burgers

Burgers on the grill take on a whole new meaning when they're infused with fresh lemon, studded with dried tomatoes, and slathered with a basil mayonnaise dressing zipped up with a jalapeño pepper.

Prep time: 15 minutes
Grilling time: 12 minutes

DIRECTIONS

1. In a medium bowl combine the ground beef, tomatoes, lemon peel, salt, and black pepper; mix well. Shape into four ½-inch-thick patties. Grill patties on the rack of an uncovered grill directly over medium heat for 12 to 16 minutes or until meat is no longer pink, turning once halfway through cooking.

2. Meanwhile, in a small bowl combine mayonnaise dressing, basil, and jalapeño pepper. Toast buns, cut sides down, on grill rack next to burgers the last 1 to 2 minutes of grilling.

3. Place burgers on bottom halves of buns. Top with mayonnaise dressing mixture and arugula. Add bun tops. Makes 4 servings.

NUTRITION FACTS PER SERVING:

450 calories
20 g total fat
6 g saturated fat
71 mg cholesterol
784 mg sodium
40 g carbohydrate
2 g fiber
26 g protein

Warm summer evenings call for cooling drinks. Consider these:

- Sparkling water with fruit-juice cubes (orange, cranberry, mango, or papaya juice frozen in ice cube trays) and fresh mint.
- Spritzers made with sparkling water, cranberry juice, and a lime twist.
- Special iced teas, made with brewed green, herbal, or raspberry- or currant-flavored black tea.

99

beef & avocado tacos

Try the real flavors of Mexico with these soft tacos filled with grilled sirloin, peppers, and onion. True caballeros enjoy their tacos and burritos made with carne asada (grilled meat) and a little picante sauce.

INGREDIENTS

2   tablespoons lemon juice
1   avocado, seeded, peeled, and cut into ½-inch cubes
1   pound boneless beef sirloin or eye round steak, cut 1 inch thick
1   medium onion, cut into wedges

2   fresh cubanelle, Anaheim, or poblano peppers, cut into 1-inch squares (see tip, page 158)
1   tablespoon olive oil
½   cup picante sauce
2   cups shredded lettuce
4   7- to 8-inch flour tortillas
    Picante sauce (optional)

Prep time: 20 minutes
Grilling time: 10 minutes

DIRECTIONS

1. In a small bowl drizzle lemon juice over avocado; toss gently to coat. Set aside.

2. Trim fat from steak. Cut steak into 2×1-inch thin strips. On four 12-inch skewers thread steak, accordion-style. On four 12-inch skewers alternately thread onion and peppers. Brush vegetables with oil.

3. Grill kabobs on the rack of an uncovered grill directly over medium heat for 10 to 12 minutes or until steak is desired doneness, turning kabobs once and brushing occasionally with the ½ cup picante sauce up to the last 5 minutes of grilling.

4. To serve, divide steak, onion, peppers, avocado, and lettuce among the tortillas. Fold the tortillas over filling. If desired, serve with additional picante sauce. Makes 4 servings.

NUTRITION FACTS PER SERVING:

425 calories
24 g total fat
6 g saturated fat
76 mg cholesterol
403 mg sodium
24 g carbohydrate
3 g fiber
30 g protein

INGREDIENTS

4 thin slices provolone cheese
   (2 ounces)
8 ½-inch-thick slices sourdough or
   Vienna bread

1 cup roasted or grilled vegetables
   from the deli or deli-
   marinated vegetables,
   coarsely chopped
4 thin slices pastrami (3 ounces)
1 tablespoon olive oil or
   basil-flavored olive oil

roasted vegetable & pastrami panini

To Italians, panini simply means sandwiches. To American chefs, panini is a trendy title for selling the same. Serve these provolone, vegetable, and pastrami melts with seasonal fruit.

Start to finish: 15 minutes

DIRECTIONS

1. Place a cheese slice on 4 of the bread slices. Spread vegetables evenly over cheese. Top with pastrami and remaining bread slices. Brush outsides of sandwiches with oil.

2. Preheat a large nonstick skillet or griddle over medium heat. Add the sandwiches; cook for 4 to 6 minutes or until sandwiches are golden brown and cheese is melted, turning once halfway through cooking. Halve sandwiches. Makes 4 servings.

Opt to cook these Italian-style sandwiches in a preheated waffle iron brushed with oil for a special textured effect.

NUTRITION FACTS PER SERVING:

254 calories
9 g total fat
3 g saturated fat
30 mg cholesterol
658 mg sodium
30 g carbohydrate
1 g fiber
13 g protein

veal chops with pesto-stuffed mushrooms

INGREDIENTS

4 veal loin chops, cut ¾ inch thick (about 1¼ pounds total)

¼ cup dry white wine

3 large cloves garlic, minced

1 tablespoon snipped fresh sage or thyme

1 tablespoon white wine Worcestershire sauce

1 tablespoon olive oil

8 large fresh mushrooms (2 to 2½ inches in diameter)

2 to 3 tablespoons pesto

Short on time tonight? Briefly soak tender veal chops in a white wine-sage marinade and toss them on the grill. Short on time tomorrow? Marinate the meat overnight for a dinner in no time and for more flavorful chops, too.

Prep time: 10 minutes
Marinating time: 15 minutes
Grilling time: 12 minutes

DIRECTIONS

1. Trim fat from chops. Place chops in a plastic bag set in a shallow dish. For marinade, in a small bowl combine wine, garlic, sage, Worcestershire sauce, and oil. Pour over chops; close bag. Marinate at room temperature for 15 minutes. (Or, marinate in refrigerator up to 24 hours, turning bag occasionally.)

2. Drain chops, reserving marinade. Sprinkle chops with freshly ground pepper. Grill chops on the rack of an uncovered grill directly over medium heat until desired doneness, turning and brushing once with marinade halfway through cooking. (Allow 12 to 14 minutes for medium rare or 15 to 17 minutes for medium.)

3. Meanwhile, carefully remove the stems from mushrooms; chop stems for another use or discard. Brush mushroom caps with reserved marinade. Place mushrooms, rounded sides up, on grill rack; grill for 4 minutes. Turn rounded sides down; spoon some pesto into each mushroom. Grill about 4 minutes more or until heated through. Serve the mushrooms with chops. Makes 4 servings.

NUTRITION FACTS PER SERVING:

285 calories
16 g total fat
2 g saturated fat
100 mg cholesterol
157 mg sodium
4 g carbohydrate
1 g fiber
28 g protein

pork medallions with fennel & pancetta

A little gourmet, a little down-home. Coin-shaped pieces of meat and onions experience a bistro-style revival with fennel, Italian bacon, and sage-cream sauce. Round out your meal with steamed green beans and frozen cooked winter squash.

INGREDIENTS

- 1   12-ounce pork tenderloin
- ¼   cup all-purpose flour
-     Dash salt
-     Dash pepper
- 2   tablespoons olive oil
- 2   ounces pancetta (Italian bacon) or bacon, finely chopped
- 2   fennel bulbs, trimmed and cut into ¼-inch slices
- 1   small onion, thinly sliced
- 2   cloves garlic, minced
- 2   tablespoons lemon juice
- ½   cup whipping cream

Start to finish: 30 minutes

DIRECTIONS

1. Trim fat from meat. Cut meat into 1-inch slices. Place each slice between 2 pieces of plastic wrap. Using the flat side of a meat mallet, pound the meat lightly to ¼-inch thickness. Remove plastic wrap. Combine flour, salt, and pepper. Coat meat with flour mixture. In a heavy large skillet heat olive oil over high heat (add more oil if necessary during cooking). Add meat, half at a time, and cook for 2 to 3 minutes or until meat is slightly pink in center, turning once halfway through cooking. Remove from skillet.

2. In the same skillet cook pancetta over medium-high heat until crisp. Add fennel, onion, and garlic and cook for 3 to 5 minutes or until crisp-tender. Add lemon juice; stir in cream. Bring to boiling; return meat to pan. Cook until the meat is heated through and the sauce is slightly thickened.

3. Transfer the meat to a serving platter. Spoon the sauce over the meat. Makes 4 servings.

NUTRITION FACTS PER SERVING:

341 calories
23 g total fat
10 g saturated fat
105 mg cholesterol
175 mg sodium
12 g carbohydrate
12 g fiber
22 g protein

103

grilled mustard-glazed pork

INGREDIENTS

- 2 12- to 14-ounce pork tenderloins
- ½ cup apple juice
- 2 large shallots, minced
- ¼ cup cider vinegar
- ¼ cup coarse-grain brown mustard
- 2 tablespoons olive oil
- 1 tablespoon brown sugar
- 1½ teaspoons soy sauce
- Dash pepper
- Snipped fresh chives (optional)

This express-lane dinner gives you time to slow down as soon as you walk in the door. Simply mix up the marinade and pour it over the pork. Let it sit in the refrigerator while you unwind. Grill about 20 minutes and dinner's done!

Marinating is great in two ways: it adds flavor and it tenderizes meats. Generally marinades are made with an acidic liquid (which has the tenderizing effect) such as wine, vinegar, or citrus juice, plus herbs and seasonings—and sometimes a little oil. The longer the meat spends luxuriating in the liquid, the more great flavor it will have.

Prep time: 10 minutes
Marinating time: 30 minutes
Grilling time: 23 minutes

DIRECTIONS

1. Trim fat from meat. Place meat in a plastic bag set in a shallow dish. For marinade, combine the apple juice, shallots, vinegar, mustard, oil, brown sugar, soy sauce, and pepper. Pour over meat; close bag. Marinate in refrigerator for 30 minutes, turning bag occasionally. Drain meat, reserving marinade.

2. In a charcoal grill with a cover arrange medium-hot coals around a drip pan. Place meat on grill rack directly over coals. Grill, uncovered, for 8 minutes, turning once to brown both sides. Position meat over drip pan. Cover and grill for 15 to 20 minutes more or until meat is slightly pink in center and juices run clear. (For a gas grill, place meat on grill rack over medium-hot heat. Cover and grill for 8 minutes, turning once. Adjust for indirect cooking; continue as directed.)

3. Meanwhile, for sauce, pour reserved marinade into a medium saucepan. Bring to boiling; reduce heat. Simmer, uncovered, about 8 minutes or until reduced to ⅔ cup. Slice the meat across the grain. Serve with the sauce. If desired, sprinkle with chives. Makes 6 servings.

NUTRITION FACTS PER SERVING:

215 calories
9 g total fat
2 g saturated fat
81 mg cholesterol
280 mg sodium
7 g carbohydrate
0 g fiber
26 g protein

INGREDIENTS

1   **pound pork tenderloin**
    Nonstick cooking spray

¾   **cup cranberry juice or apple**
    juice

2   **teaspoons spicy brown mustard**

1   **teaspoon cornstarch**

1   **cup sweet cherries (such as**
    Rainier or Bing), halved and
    pitted, or 1 cup frozen
    unsweetened pitted dark
    sweet cherries, thawed

pork medallions with cherry sauce

During the autumn months, pork is often prepared with fruit such as prunes or apples. These quick-seared medallions cloaked in a delightful sweet cherry sauce provide a whole new reason—and season—to pair pork with fruit.

Start to finish: 20 minutes

DIRECTIONS

1. Trim fat from meat. Cut meat into 1-inch slices. Place each slice between 2 pieces of plastic wrap. Using the heel of your hand, press slice into a ½-inch-thick medallion. Remove the plastic wrap. Sprinkle lightly with salt and freshly ground pepper.

2. Coat an unheated large nonstick skillet with cooking spray. Heat skillet over medium-high heat. Add meat; cook for 6 minutes or until meat is slightly pink in center and juices run clear, turning once halfway through cooking. Transfer to a serving platter; keep warm.

3. Combine the cranberry juice, mustard, and cornstarch; add to skillet. Cook and stir until thickened and bubbly. Cook and stir for 2 minutes more. Stir in cherries. Serve over meat. Makes 4 servings.

NUTRITION FACTS PER SERVING:

197 calories
5 g total fat
2 g saturated fat
81 mg cholesterol
127 mg sodium
12 g carbohydrate
0 g fiber
26 g protein

jamaican pork chops with melon salsa

The jerk cooks of Jamaica may use dry rubs or wet marinades, but the central ingredient in all jerk seasoning is allspice (along with fiery Scotch bonnet chilies and thyme), which grows in abundance on the sunny island.

INGREDIENTS

- 1 cup chopped honeydew melon
- 1 cup chopped cantaloupe
- 1 tablespoon snipped fresh mint
- 1 tablespoon honey
- 4 boneless pork top loin chops, cut ¾ to 1 inch thick
- 4 teaspoons purchased or homemade Jamaican jerk seasoning
-    Star anise and/or fresh mint sprigs (optional)

For homemade Jamaican jerk

seasoning, combine 1 teaspoon crushed red pepper; ½ teaspoon ground allspice; ¼ teaspoon curry powder; ¼ teaspoon coarsely ground black pepper; ⅛ teaspoon dried thyme, crushed; ⅛ teaspoon ground red pepper; and ⅛ teaspoon ground ginger.

Prep time: 15 minutes
Grilling time: 8 minutes

DIRECTIONS

1. For salsa, in a medium bowl combine honeydew, cantaloupe, snipped mint, and honey. Cover and refrigerate until ready to serve.

2. Trim fat from chops. Rub both sides of the chops with Jamaican jerk seasoning. Grill chops on the rack of an uncovered grill directly over medium heat for 8 to 12 minutes or until chops are slightly pink in center and juices run clear. Serve the salsa with chops. If desired, garnish with star anise and/or mint sprigs. Makes 4 servings.

NUTRITION FACTS PER SERVING:

189 calories
8 g total fat
3 g saturated fat
51 mg cholesterol
231 mg sodium
13 g carbohydrate
1 g fiber
17 g protein

southwest pork chops with corn salsa

INGREDIENTS

- ¼ cup white wine vinegar
- 3 tablespoons snipped fresh cilantro
- 1 teaspoon olive oil
- 1 cup fresh or frozen whole kernel corn
- 3 plum tomatoes, chopped
- ½ cup thinly sliced green onions

- 1 small fresh jalapeño pepper, seeded and minced (see tip, page 158)
- 4 center-cut pork loin chops, cut ¾ inch thick
- Cactus leaves (optional)
- Fresh cilantro sprigs (optional)

In late summer, when corn is at its sweetest and tomatoes are at their juiciest, these meaty pork chops crowned with a colorful, chunky salsa are unsurpassed for the freshest tastes of the season's best.

Prep time: 20 minutes
Grilling time: 8 minutes

DIRECTIONS

1. For sauce, in a small bowl combine 3 tablespoons of the vinegar, 1 tablespoon of the snipped cilantro, and the olive oil. For salsa, in a covered small saucepan cook fresh corn in a small amount of boiling water for 2 to 3 minutes or until corn is crisp-tender; drain. Or, thaw corn, if frozen. In a medium bowl combine the corn, tomatoes, green onions, jalapeño pepper, remaining vinegar, and remaining snipped cilantro. Set aside.

2. Trim fat from chops. Grill chops on the rack of an uncovered grill directly over medium heat for 8 to 11 minutes or until chops are slightly pink in center and juices run clear, turning once and brushing occasionally with sauce up to the last 5 minutes of grilling. If desired, arrange chops on cactus leaves and garnish with cilantro sprigs. Serve

NUTRITION FACTS PER SERVING:

201 calories
9 g total fat
3 g saturated fat
51 mg cholesterol
51 mg sodium
14 g carbohydrate
2 g fiber
18 g protein

pork chops with savory mushroom stuffing

There's a surprise inside the pocket of these boneless pork chops—a mouthwatering mushroom stuffing. Instead of white button mushrooms, try using brown cremini mushrooms for even more mushroom flavor.

INGREDIENTS

- 2 teaspoons olive oil
- 2 tablespoons thinly sliced green onion
- 1 8-ounce package fresh mushrooms, coarsely chopped
- 2 teaspoons snipped fresh rosemary or oregano
- ⅛ teaspoon salt
- ⅛ teaspoon pepper
- 4 boneless pork loin chops, cut 1 inch thick
- 2 teaspoons Worcestershire sauce

Prep time: 15 minutes
Grilling time: 20 minutes

DIRECTIONS

1. For stuffing, in a large skillet heat oil over medium heat. Add green onion and cook for 1 minute. Stir in mushrooms, rosemary, salt, and pepper. Cook and stir for 2 to 3 minutes more or until mushrooms are tender. Remove from heat.

2. Trim fat from chops. Make a pocket in each chop by cutting from fat side almost to, but not through, the opposite side. Spoon stuffing into pockets in chops. If necessary, secure with wooden toothpicks.

3. Brush chops with Worcestershire sauce. Season chops lightly with additional salt and pepper. Grill chops on the rack of an uncovered grill directly over medium heat about 20 minutes or until juices run clear, turning once halfway through cooking. To serve, remove toothpicks. Makes 4 servings.

NUTRITION FACTS PER SERVING:

241 calories
14 g total fat
4 g saturated fat
77 mg cholesterol
218 mg sodium
4 g carbohydrate
1 g fiber
25 g protein

INGREDIENTS

- ¼ cup dried tomatoes (not oil-packed)
- 2 tablespoons dried mushrooms (such as shiitake or porcini)
- 6 ounces dried trenne or bow-tie pasta
- 2 cups green beans cut into 1-inch pieces
- 1 medium yellow summer squash, halved lengthwise and sliced (1¼ cups)

- 1 cup milk
- ¾ cup chicken broth
- 1 green onion, sliced
- 1 tablespoon cornstarch
- ½ teaspoon lemon-pepper seasoning
- ¼ teaspoon salt
- 1 pound boneless pork loin chops, cut ¾ to 1 inch thick
- 1 tablespoon olive oil

summer pasta with pork

This colorful dish marries all the elements of a delicious warm-weather dinner. Tender, young green beans and summer squash, combined with a few pantry foods like dried mushrooms and tomatoes, means dinner al fresco is a few easy steps away.

Start to finish: 30 minutes

DIRECTIONS

1. Soak tomatoes and mushrooms in enough boiling water to cover for 5 minutes. Drain and snip, discarding mushroom stems. Set aside.

2. Cook pasta according to package directions, adding beans to the water with pasta. Add squash the last 2 minutes of cooking. Drain and keep warm.

3. Meanwhile, stir together the milk, chicken broth, onion, cornstarch, lemon-pepper seasoning, and salt; set aside. Trim fat from chops. Sprinkle chops lightly with additional salt and lemon-pepper seasoning. In a large skillet cook chops in hot oil over medium heat for 10 to 12 minutes or until chops are slightly pink in center and juices run clear, turning once halfway through cooking. Remove chops from skillet. Cut into thin bite-size strips. Keep warm.

4. For sauce, drain fat from skillet. Pour cornstarch mixture into skillet. Cook and stir until thickened and bubbly, scraping up any brown bits from bottom of skillet. Reduce heat; cook for 2 minutes more. Stir in mushrooms and tomatoes.

5. Divide pasta mixture among 4 dinner plates. Arrange meat strips on each serving; spoon sauce over all. Makes 4 servings.

NUTRITION FACTS PER SERVING:

453 calories
20 g total fat
8 g saturated fat
110 mg cholesterol
659 mg sodium
43 g carbohydrate
2 g fiber
26 g protein

thai pork & vegetable curry

Give a traditional Thai curry a new, cross-cultural spin by serving it over Italian orzo pasta instead of the usual rice. Prepared curry paste adds authentic flavor without fuss.

INGREDIENTS

1⅓ cups dried orzo pasta (rosamarina)

2 tablespoons cooking oil

12 ounces pork tenderloin or lean boneless pork, cut into bite-size pieces

8 ounces green beans, bias-sliced into 1½-inch pieces (2 cups)*

1 red sweet pepper, cut into thin bite-size strips

2 green onions, bias-sliced into ¼-inch pieces

1 14-ounce can reduced-fat unsweetened coconut milk

4 teaspoons bottled curry paste

2 teaspoons sugar

2 tablespoons lime juice

Along with Asian markets, many groceries now stock coconut milk and curry paste, two classic Thai ingredients. Sold in cans in regular and reduced-fat versions, coconut milk is a creamy blend of fresh coconut meat and water. Bottled curry paste blends herbs, spices, and fiery chilies.

Start to finish: 30 minutes

DIRECTIONS

1. Cook pasta according to package directions; drain. Meanwhile, pour 1 tablespoon of the oil into a large nonstick skillet. Preheat over medium-high heat. Stir-fry meat in hot oil for 3 to 4 minutes or until slightly pink in center. Remove from skillet.

2. Add the remaining 1 tablespoon oil to skillet. Add green beans; stir-fry for 3 minutes. Add sweet pepper and green onions; stir-fry about 2 minutes more or until vegetables are crisp-tender. Add coconut milk, curry paste, and sugar. Reduce heat to low, stirring until combined. Stir in cooked meat and lime juice; heat through. Serve immediately over pasta. Makes 4 servings.

*Note: One 9-ounce package of frozen cut green beans, thawed, may be substituted for the fresh beans. Add them to the skillet with sweet pepper and green onions; stir-fry as directed.

NUTRITION FACTS PER SERVING:

489 calories
18 g total fat
6 g saturated fat
60 mg cholesterol
79 mg sodium
55 g carbohydrate
1 g fiber
27 g protein

INGREDIENTS

- 1½ cups quick-cooking rice
- ¼ cup thinly sliced green onions
- 1 large sweet potato (about 12 ounces)
- 1 medium tart apple (such as Granny Smith), cored
- 12 ounces lean boneless pork strips for stir-frying
- 2 to 3 teaspoons purchased or homemade Jamaican jerk seasoning (see tip, page 106)
- 1 tablespoon cooking oil
- ⅓ cup apple juice or water

jamaican pork & sweet potato stir-fry

Take a vacation from the postwork, predinner rush with this Jamaica-inspired dish that features two of this easygoing island's favorite ingredients: lean pork and golden sweet potatoes. Pick up Jamaican jerk seasoning in the grocery store spice aisle or make your own seasoning.

Start to finish: 18 minutes

DIRECTIONS

1. Prepare rice according to package directions. Stir half of the green onions into cooked rice. Meanwhile, peel sweet potato. Cut in quarters lengthwise, then thinly slice crosswise. Place in a microwave-safe pie plate or shallow dish. Cover with vented plastic wrap. Microwave on 100% power (high) for 3 to 4 minutes or until tender, stirring once. Cut apple into 16 wedges.

2. Sprinkle meat strips with Jamaican jerk seasoning; toss to coat evenly. Pour oil into a wok or large skillet. Preheat over medium-high heat (add more oil if necessary during cooking). Stir-fry seasoned meat in hot oil for 2 minutes. Add apple and remaining green onions; stir-fry for 1 to 2 minutes or until meat is slightly pink in center.

3. Stir sweet potato and apple juice into meat mixture. Bring to boiling; reduce heat. Simmer, uncovered, for 1 minute more. Serve meat mixture over rice mixture. Makes 4 servings.

NUTRITION FACTS PER SERVING:

365 calories
9 g total fat
2 g saturated fat
38 mg cholesterol
131 mg sodium
54 g carbohydrate
3 g fiber
16 g protein

111

jamaican pork kabobs

Jamaican doesn't always mean jerk. These pork and vegetable kabobs get an island air from mango chutney and a liberal dose of Pickapeppa sauce, a much milder version of its famous relative, Tabasco. Cool the fire with slices of mango and lime.

INGREDIENTS

2 ears of corn, husked and cleaned

1 12- to 14-ounce pork tenderloin

1 small red onion, cut into ½-inch wedges

16 baby pattypan squash, about 1 inch in diameter, or 4 tomatillos, quartered

¼ cup mango chutney, finely chopped

3 tablespoons Pickapeppa sauce

1 tablespoon cooking oil

1 tablespoon water

Today's pork is leaner—and therefore lower in fat and calories—than ever before.
Because there is so little fat, pork requires extra attention when being cooked to ensure tender, juicy meat. Closely check timings and temperatures in the recipes. Cook chops from the loin and rib sections until slightly pink in center. Cook ground pork and less-tender cuts such as sirloin or loin blade chops until no longer pink.

Prep time: 15 minutes
Grilling time: 10 minutes

DIRECTIONS

1. Cut corn crosswise into 1-inch pieces. In a medium saucepan cook corn pieces in a small amount of boiling water for 3 minutes; drain. Rinse with cold water; drain again. Meanwhile, trim fat from meat. Cut meat into 1-inch slices. On long skewers alternately thread the meat, onion wedges, squash, and corn.

2. In a small bowl combine chutney, Pickapeppa sauce, oil, and water; set aside. Grill kabobs on the rack of an uncovered grill directly over medium heat for 10 to 12 minutes or until meat is slightly pink in center and

vegetables are tender, turning once and brushing occasionally with chutney mixture during the last 5 minutes of grilling. Makes 4 servings.

NUTRITION FACTS PER SERVING:

252 calories
7 g total fat
2 g saturated fat
60 mg cholesterol
127 mg sodium
27 g carbohydrate
3 g fiber
21 g protein

peach-mustard glazed ham

Head south to a sunnier clime at dinnertime. Juicy peaches and ham—two Southern specialties—make perfect partners in this sweet and smoky dish. Serve it with warm cornbread spread with butter and honey.

INGREDIENTS

2 tablespoons brown sugar

2 tablespoons spicy brown mustard

⅓ cup peach or apricot nectar

1 1-pound cooked ham slice, cut ¾ to 1 inch thick

4 medium peaches, peeled and halved lengthwise

2 small green and/or red sweet peppers, each cut crosswise into 4 rings

Prep time: 5 minutes
Grilling time: 12 minutes

DIRECTIONS

1. For glaze, in a bowl combine brown sugar and mustard. Gradually whisk in nectar until smooth.

2. To prevent ham from curling, make shallow cuts around the edge at 1-inch intervals. Brush one side of ham with glaze.

3. Grill ham, glazed-side down, on a greased rack of an uncovered grill directly over medium-hot heat for 6 minutes. Turn ham. Add peaches and peppers. Brush ham, peaches, and peppers with glaze. Grill for 6 to 10 minutes more or until heated through, brushing occasionally with glaze. Makes 4 servings.

NUTRITION FACTS PER SERVING:

284 calories
7 g total fat
2 g saturated fat
60 mg cholesterol
1,468 mg sodium
31 g carbohydrate
3 g fiber
26 g protein

113

canadian bacon pizza

Pizza—on the grill? You bet! The intense, direct heat of the grill approximates that of a wood-fired pizza oven, imparting the pie's veggies and cheese with a pleasing smoke flavor, the Canadian bacon with real sizzle, and the crust with a delightful crunch.

INGREDIENTS

- 1 6-ounce jar marinated artichoke hearts
- 4 6-inch Italian bread shells (Boboli)
- ½ cup shredded fontina or mozzarella cheese (2 ounces)
- 4 slices Canadian-style bacon, cut into strips (2 ounces)
- 2 plum tomatoes, sliced
- ¼ cup crumbled feta cheese (1 ounce)
- 1 green onion, thinly sliced
- 2 teaspoons snipped fresh oregano or basil

Prep time: 20 minutes
Grilling time: 8 minutes

DIRECTIONS

1. Drain artichoke hearts, reserving marinade. Halve artichoke hearts lengthwise; set aside.

2. Brush the bread shells with some of the reserved marinade. Sprinkle fontina cheese over shells. Divide artichoke hearts, Canadian bacon, tomatoes, feta cheese, green onion, and oregano among shells. Transfer the bread shells to a large piece of double-thickness foil.

3. In a grill with a cover place foil with bread shells on the rack directly over medium heat. Cover and grill about 8 minutes or until cheese is melted and pizza is heated through. Makes 4 servings.

NUTRITION FACTS PER SERVING:

465 calories
19 g total fat
6 g saturated fat
44 mg cholesterol
1,264 mg sodium
56 g carbohydrate
2 g fiber
23 g protein

INGREDIENTS

1 cup cranberries, coarsely chopped

¼ cup sugar

1 tablespoon water

⅓ cup chutney

¼ cup chopped red onion

1 tablespoon margarine or butter

1½ cups sliced and halved peeled sweet potato

¼ cup chopped red onion

2 ounces Canadian-style bacon, chopped (about ⅓ cup)

8 beaten eggs

sweet potato frittata with fresh cranberry salsa

Chutney, the traditional Indian relish that adds verve to this slightly sweet salsa, contains fruit (usually mangoes or limes), vinegar, sugar, and spices combined in proportions that play up contrasting flavors: sweet, sour, spicy, and piquant.

Start to finish: 25 minutes

DIRECTIONS

1. For cranberry salsa, in a small saucepan combine cranberries, sugar, and water. Bring to boiling, stirring occasionally. Remove from heat. Snip any large pieces of chutney. Stir chutney and ¼ cup onion into cranberry mixture. Set aside.

2. In a 10-inch skillet melt margarine over medium heat. Add sweet potato and ¼ cup onion. Cook, covered, for 4 to 5 minutes or until potato is almost tender, turning once. Sprinkle with chopped Canadian bacon.

3. Pour eggs over potato mixture. Cook, uncovered, over medium heat. As the eggs begin to set, run a spatula around edge of the skillet, lifting eggs so uncooked portion flows underneath. Continue cooking and lifting the edges until eggs are almost set (surface will be moist). Remove from heat.

4. Cover and let stand for 3 to 4 minutes or until top is set. Cut into wedges. Serve with warm cranberry salsa. Makes 4 servings.

NUTRITION FACTS PER SERVING:

359 calories
14 g total fat
4 g saturated fat
431 mg cholesterol
308 mg sodium
43 g carbohydrate
4 g fiber
16 g protein

grilled italian sausage with sweet & sour peppers

Sicilians love sweet and sour flavors and toss super-sweet raisins into their delicious meat and fish dishes with culinary abandon. Here, grilled Italian sausage is presented on a bed of tangy, yet sweet grilled vegetables. For more Italian goodness, serve with grilled purchased polenta.

INGREDIENTS

- 3 tablespoons slivered almonds
- ¼ cup raisins
- 3 tablespoons red wine vinegar
- 2 tablespoons sugar
- ¼ teaspoon salt
- ⅛ teaspoon black pepper
- 6 uncooked sweet Italian sausage links
- 1 tablespoon olive oil
- 2 green sweet peppers, cut into 1-inch-wide strips
- 2 red sweet peppers, cut into 1-inch-wide strips
- 1 medium red onion, thickly sliced

Prep time: 20 minutes
Grilling time: 10 minutes

DIRECTIONS

1. In a small nonstick skillet cook and stir almonds for 1 to 2 minutes or until golden brown. Stir in raisins. Remove skillet from heat. Let stand for 1 minute. Carefully stir in vinegar, sugar, salt, and pepper. Return to heat; cook and stir just until the sugar dissolves.

2. Prick the sausage links several times with a fork. Drizzle oil over sweet pepper strips and onion slices. Grill sausage and vegetables on the rack of an uncovered grill directly over medium heat for 10 to 15 minutes or until sausage is no longer pink and vegetables are tender, turning once halfway through cooking.

3. In a large bowl toss vegetables with the almond mixture; spoon onto a serving platter. Arrange sausage on top of vegetable mixture. Makes 6 servings.

NUTRITION FACTS PER SERVING:

276 calories
19 g total fat
6 g saturated fat
59 mg cholesterol
604 mg sodium
15 g carbohydrate
1 g fiber
13 g protein

lamb chops with sweet potato chutney

Petite lamb chops make simple but pretty company fare—especially when they're crowned with a richly colored and flavor-packed homemade chutney.

INGREDIENTS

- 8 lamb rib or loin chops, cut 1 inch thick (1½ to 2 pounds total)
- ⅓ cup finely chopped shallots
- ¼ teaspoon crushed red pepper
- ¼ cup packed brown sugar
- ¼ cup vinegar
- 2 tablespoons dried cranberries or currants
- ½ teaspoon grated fresh ginger
- 1 medium sweet potato, peeled and cubed

Prep time: 20 minutes
Cooking time: 10 minutes

DIRECTIONS

1. Trim fat from chops. In a small bowl combine shallots and red pepper. Reserve 2 tablespoons of the shallot mixture for chutney. Rub both sides of chops with remaining shallot mixture. Place chops on the unheated rack of a broiler pan.

2. Meanwhile, for chutney, in a medium saucepan combine the 2 tablespoons shallot mixture, the brown sugar, vinegar, dried cranberries, and ginger. Stir in sweet potato. Bring to boiling; reduce heat. Simmer, covered, for 10 minutes, stirring occasionally.

3. Meanwhile, broil chops 3 to 4 inches from the heat until desired doneness, turning once halfway through cooking. (Allow 7 to 11 minutes for medium.) Serve the chops with the chutney. Makes 4 servings.

NUTRITION FACTS PER SERVING:

317 calories
11 g total fat
4 g saturated fat
97 mg cholesterol
83 mg sodium
24 g carbohydrate
1 g fiber
30 g protein

Whole ginger stays fresh for 2 or 3 weeks in the refrigerator when wrapped loosely in a paper towel and lasts almost indefinitely when frozen. To freeze, place the unpeeled ginger in a freezer bag. You can grate or slice the ginger while it's frozen.

tuscan lamb chop skillet

Tuscans, once disparaged by the rest of Italy as "bean eaters" because of their love of the legume, now wear that mantle with pride. Here, healthful white beans are flavored with rosemary and garlic, then topped with lamb chops.

INGREDIENTS

- 8 lamb rib chops, cut 1 inch thick (about 1½ pounds total)
- 2 teaspoons olive oil
- 3 cloves garlic, minced
- 1 19-ounce can white kidney (cannellini) beans, rinsed and drained
- 1 8-ounce can Italian-style stewed tomatoes
- 1 tablespoon balsamic vinegar
- 2 teaspoons snipped fresh rosemary
   Fresh rosemary sprigs (optional)

Start to finish: 18 minutes

DIRECTIONS

1. Trim fat from chops. In a large skillet cook chops in hot oil over medium heat until desired doneness, turning once halfway through cooking. (Allow 7 to 9 minutes for medium.) Remove chops from skillet; keep warm.

2. Stir garlic into drippings in skillet. Cook and stir for 1 minute. Stir in beans, undrained tomatoes, vinegar, and snipped rosemary. Bring to boiling; reduce heat. Simmer, uncovered, for 3 minutes.

3. Spoon bean mixture onto 4 dinner plates; arrange 2 chops on each serving. If desired, garnish with rosemary sprigs. Makes 4 servings.

NUTRITION FACTS PER SERVING:

272 calories
9 g total fat
3 g saturated fat
67 mg cholesterol
466 mg sodium
24 g carbohydrate
6 g fiber
30 g protein

INGREDIENTS

- 3 tablespoons apple jelly
- 1 green onion, thinly sliced
- 1 tablespoon soy sauce
- 2 teaspoons lemon juice
- ⅛ teaspoon curry powder
- Dash ground cinnamon
- Dash ground red pepper

- 2 small red and/or green apples, cut crosswise into ¼-inch slices
- Lemon juice
- 8 lamb loin chops, cut 1 inch thick (about 2 pounds total)
- Hot cooked couscous (optional)
- 1 tablespoon small fresh mint leaves

apple-glazed lamb chops

Lamb chops make an elegant quick-to-fix dish, and these cinnamon- and apple-spiced chops are the ultimate company fare. Add a side of couscous tossed with fresh mint and finish with a scoop of sorbet for a weekday dinner with friends.

Prep time: 15 minutes
Grilling time: 10 minutes

DIRECTIONS

1. For glaze, in a small saucepan combine apple jelly, green onion, soy sauce, lemon juice, curry powder, cinnamon, and red pepper. Cook and stir over medium heat until bubbly. Remove from heat. Remove seeds from apple slices. Brush apples with lemon juice. Set aside.

2. Trim fat from chops. Grill chops on the rack of an uncovered grill directly over medium heat until desired doneness, turning and brushing once with glaze halfway through cooking.

(Allow 10 to 14 minutes for medium rare or 14 to 16 minutes for medium.) Place apples on grill rack next to chops the last 5 minutes of grilling, turning and brushing once with glaze halfway through cooking.

3. If desired, serve chops and apples with couscous. Sprinkle with mint leaves. Makes 4 servings.

NUTRITION FACTS PER SERVING:

385 calories
14 g total fat
5 g saturated fat
133 mg cholesterol
378 mg sodium
20 g carbohydrate
1 g fiber
43 g protein

tandoori-style lamb chops

You don't need the traditional Indian brick-and-clay oven called a tandoor to make these chops, but the delicious characteristic of tandoori cuisine—quick cooking to seal in juices and flavors—is present in these Indian-spiced lamb chops.

INGREDIENTS

- 8 lamb loin chops, cut 1 inch thick (about 2 pounds total)
- 2 tablespoons cooking oil
- 6 cloves garlic, minced
- 1 tablespoon purchased or homemade garam masala
- 2 teaspoons grated fresh ginger
- ½ teaspoon salt
- 2 medium yellow summer squash and/or zucchini, halved lengthwise
- 4 pita bread rounds
- ½ cup plain low-fat yogurt
- 1 tablespoon snipped fresh mint
- ¼ cup regular chutney or hot chutney

To make your own garam masala, combine 1 teaspoon ground cumin, 1 teaspoon ground coriander, ½ teaspoon pepper, ½ teaspoon ground cardamom, ¼ teaspoon ground cinnamon, and ¼ teaspoon ground cloves.

Prep time: 20 minutes
Grilling time: 10 minutes

DIRECTIONS

1. Trim fat from chops. In a small bowl combine oil, garlic, garam masala, ginger, and salt. Brush onto all sides of the chops and squash.

2. Grill chops on the rack of an uncovered grill directly over medium heat until desired doneness, turning once halfway through cooking. (Allow 10 to 14 minutes for medium rare or 14 to 16 minutes for medium.) While the chops are grilling, add squash to grill. Grill for 7 to 8 minutes or until tender, turning once halfway through cooking. Place pita rounds on grill rack next to chops and squash the last 2 minutes of grilling.

3. Meanwhile, in a small bowl combine yogurt and mint. Transfer squash to a cutting board; cool slightly and cut diagonally into ½-inch slices. Serve squash, pita bread, yogurt mixture, and chutney with chops. Makes 4 servings.

NUTRITION FACTS PER SERVING:

615 calories
22 g total fat
6 g saturated fat
135 mg cholesterol
735 mg sodium
51 g carbohydrate
1 g fiber
51 g protein

INGREDIENTS

1   pound boneless lamb leg or shoulder
¼   cup balsamic vinegar
1   tablespoon snipped fresh savory or 1 teaspoon dried savory, crushed
½   teaspoon pepper

1   8-ounce carton plain low-fat or fat-free yogurt
1   small cucumber, peeled, seeded, and chopped (¾ cup)
2   plum tomatoes, chopped
1   small onion, finely chopped
4   whole wheat pita bread rounds

greek-inspired lamb pockets

Be a dinnertime hero with a meal-in-a-pocket that will win you applause. Meaty lamb leg or shoulder is marinated in balsamic vinegar, pepper, and fresh herbs, quick-grilled to keep it juicy, then tucked into a pita and topped with a creamy yogurt sauce.

Prep time: 20 minutes
Marinating time: 10 minutes
Grilling time: 10 minutes

DIRECTIONS

1. Trim fat from meat. Cut meat into 2×1-inch thin strips. Place meat in a plastic bag set in a shallow dish. For marinade, combine vinegar, savory, and pepper. Pour over meat; close bag. Marinate in the refrigerator at least 10 minutes or up to 4 hours, turning bag once. Meanwhile, for sauce, in a medium bowl combine yogurt, cucumber, tomatoes, and onion. Cover and refrigerate until ready to serve. Wrap pita rounds in foil. Set aside.

2. Drain meat, reserving marinade. On four 12-inch skewers thread meat, accordion-style. Grill kabobs on the rack of an uncovered grill directly over medium heat for 10 to 12 minutes or until meat is slightly pink in center, turning kabobs once and brushing occasionally with marinade up to the last 5 minutes of grilling. Place pita rounds on grill rack next to kabobs the last 5 minutes of grilling.

3. To serve, cut pita rounds in half crosswise. Spoon the sauce into pita halves and fill with meat strips. Makes 4 servings.

NUTRITION FACTS PER SERVING:

361 calories
8 g total fat
3 g saturated fat
61 mg cholesterol
430 mg sodium
46 g carbohydrate
1 g fiber
28 g protein

grilled lambburger roll-ups

Here's perfect alfresco food for friends! Spinach, seasoned lamb, and hummus are rolled up in soft cracker bread and cut into eye-catching spirals. For dessert, offer Red Wine-Marinated Peaches (page 278) with coffee or mint tea.

INGREDIENTS

1 beaten egg

3 tablespoons fine dry bread crumbs

2 tablespoons snipped fresh oregano

1 tablespoon water

2 cloves garlic, minced

¾ teaspoon salt

½ teaspoon freshly ground pepper

1 pound lean ground lamb

2 14- to 15-inch soft cracker bread rounds or four 7- to 8-inch flour tortillas

⅓ cup prepared hummus (garbanzo bean spread)

4 cups torn spinach or red-tipped leaf lettuce

¼ cup crumbled feta cheese

3 tablespoons sliced pitted kalamata or ripe olives

Start to finish: 30 minutes

DIRECTIONS

1. In a large bowl combine egg, bread crumbs, oregano, water, garlic, salt, and pepper. Add ground lamb; mix well. Form mixture into eight 4-inch-long logs.

2. Grill meat on the rack of an uncovered grill directly over medium heat for 14 to 18 minutes or until meat is no longer pink, turning once halfway through cooking. (Or, place in a shallow baking pan. Bake in a 400° oven for 12 to 14 minutes.)

3. Meanwhile, spread the cracker bread or tortillas with hummus. Sprinkle with spinach, feta cheese, and olives. If using cracker bread, place 4 meat pieces, end to end, near an edge of each piece. Starting from edge closest to meat, roll up into a spiral. Slice each roll-up diagonally in fourths. (If using tortillas, place 2 meat pieces, end to end, on each tortilla. Roll up. Slice each roll-up diagonally in half.) Makes 4 servings.

NUTRITION FACTS PER SERVING:

625 calories
26 g total fat
9 g saturated fat
135 mg cholesterol
1,225 mg sodium
64 g carbohydrate
2 g fiber
34 g protein

INGREDIENTS

- ½ cup French-fried onions
- 1 pound boneless beef top sirloin steak, cut 1 inch thick
- 1 tablespoon Cajun seasoning
- 1 tablespoon lime juice
- 1 clove garlic, minced
- 1 10-ounce package European-style salad greens
- 2 carrots, peeled into thin strips or cut into thin bite-size strips
- ½ cup thinly sliced radishes
- ½ cup bottled fat-free ranch salad dressing

spicy steak & ranch salad

Steak and onions as you've never seen them before! Grilled sirloin is perked up by Cajun spices before slicing, then arranged on tossed greens and topped with a scattering of crispy French-fried onions. This new version has the makings of an instant classic.

Start to finish: 25 minutes

DIRECTIONS

1. In a large nonstick skillet cook French-fried onions over medium-high heat about 2 minutes or until browned, stirring occasionally. Set aside.

2. Trim fat from steak. Combine Cajun seasoning, lime juice, and garlic; rub over both sides of steak. In the same skillet cook steak over medium heat until desired doneness, turning once halfway through cooking. (Allow 6 to 8 minutes for medium rare or 9 to 12 minutes for medium.) Remove skillet from heat. Cool slightly and cut steak into thin bite-size slices. If desired, season with salt.

3. On a large serving platter toss together the salad greens, carrots, and radishes. Arrange steak strips on top of greens mixture. Drizzle dressing over salad. Sprinkle with French-fried onions. Makes 4 servings.

NUTRITION FACTS PER SERVING:

310 calories
13 g total fat
4 g saturated fat
76 mg cholesterol
557 mg sodium
16 g carbohydrate
3 g fiber
28 g protein

beef & curry pinwheels on spinach

Pick up roast beef sliced to your liking at the deli, and the work is half done for this protein-rich entrée. Asparagus is a crisp counterpoint to the curry and chutney cream filling that's spread on the beef slices.

INGREDIENTS

- 1 pound asparagus spears, trimmed
- ⅓ of an 8-ounce tub (about ⅓ cup) cream cheese
- 3 tablespoons peach or mango chutney, snipped
- 2 tablespoons finely chopped green onion
- ¼ teaspoon curry powder
- 8 ounces lean cooked beef, thinly sliced (about 8 slices)
- 6 cups torn spinach or mixed salad greens
- 2 tablespoons lemon juice
- 1 tablespoon olive oil
- 2 tablespoons chopped peanuts

A condiment for Indian curries,

sweet-tart chutney (Hindi for "strongly spiced") also sparks simple poultry dishes, salads, and sandwiches. Pick a favorite among these rich jams concocted of chopped fruit (mango is classic), vegetables, and spices enlivened with hot peppers, fresh ginger, or vinegar, and keep a jar on hand for a quick mealtime fix.

Start to finish: 30 minutes

DIRECTIONS

1. In a covered medium skillet cook asparagus spears in a small amount of boiling water for 4 to 6 minutes or until crisp-tender. Drain and set aside.

2. Meanwhile, in a small bowl stir together cream cheese, chutney, green onion, and curry powder. Spread about 1 tablespoon of the cream cheese mixture over each beef slice. Starting from a short side, roll up into a spiral. Cut each beef spiral in half.

3. Divide spinach among 4 dinner plates. Arrange asparagus spears on top of spinach. Stir together the lemon juice and olive oil; drizzle over spinach and asparagus. Arrange the beef spirals on top of salads; sprinkle with peanuts. Makes 4 servings.

NUTRITION FACTS PER SERVING:

317 calories
19 g total fat
6 g saturated fat
71 mg cholesterol
213 mg sodium
16 g carbohydrate
4 g fiber
24 g protein

INGREDIENTS

- ¼ cup apple juice
- ¼ cup salad oil
- 2 tablespoons wine vinegar
  Lettuce leaves
- 2 medium apples or pears, cut into wedges
- 8 ounces lean cooked beef, cut into thin bite-size strips (1½ cups)
- 2 medium carrots, cut into thin bite-size strips
- 1 cup jicama cut into thin bite-size strips
- ¼ cup dried tart cherries or cranberries, snipped

beef & apple salad

Meal appeal comes from taste, aroma, presentation, and texture, an under-appreciated element that adds snap to a dish. This crunchy example includes crisp raw apples, jicama, and carrots, along with slices of beef.

Start to finish: 30 minutes

DIRECTIONS

1. For dressing, in a screw-top jar combine apple juice, salad oil, and vinegar. Cover and shake well.

2. Line 4 dinner plates with lettuce leaves. Arrange the apples, beef, carrots, and jicama on top of lettuce. Top with cherries. Drizzle the dressing over salads. If desired, sprinkle salads with coarsely ground pepper. Makes 4 servings.

NUTRITION FACTS PER SERVING:

327 calories
18 g total fat
4 g saturated fat
33 mg cholesterol
62 mg sodium
25 g carbohydrate
3 g fiber
19 g protein

125

beef & fruit salad

For an exotic presentation, serve the fruit mixture in kiwano (kee-WAH-noh) shells. Also called "horned melon," the kiwano has a jellylike pulp with a tart, yet sweet flavor likened to a combination of banana and cucumber.

INGREDIENTS

12 ounces boneless beef sirloin steak, cut 1 inch thick

⅓ cup reduced-sodium teriyaki sauce or soy sauce

¼ cup lemon juice

¼ cup water

2 teaspoons toasted sesame oil

⅛ teaspoon bottled hot pepper sauce

3 cups shredded napa cabbage

1 cup torn or shredded sorrel or spinach

2 cups fresh fruit (such as cut-up plums, nectarines, or kiwi fruit; halved seedless grapes or strawberries; raspberries; and/or blueberries)

2 kiwanos (optional)

To serve the fruit in kiwano shells, cut
each kiwano in half crosswise. Using a small spoon, scoop out the pulp. Fill the kiwano shells with fruit and set on top of the greens. If desired, spoon the kiwano pulp over the salads.

Prep time: 20 minutes
Marinating time: 30 minutes
Grilling time: 8 minutes

DIRECTIONS

1. Trim fat from steak. Place steak in a plastic bag set in a shallow dish. For marinade, combine teriyaki sauce, lemon juice, water, oil, and hot pepper sauce. Reserve ⅓ cup for dressing. Pour the remaining marinade over steak; close bag. Marinate at room temperature for 30 minutes, turning bag occasionally. (Or, marinate in refrigerator up to 8 hours.)

2. Drain steak, reserving marinade. Grill steak on the rack of an uncovered grill directly over medium heat until desired doneness, turning once and brushing occasionally with marinade up to the last 5 minutes of grilling. (Allow 8 to 12 minutes for medium rare or 12 to 15 minutes for medium.)

3. To serve, divide cabbage and sorrel among 4 dinner plates. Thinly slice steak diagonally. Arrange steak and fruit on top of greens. (Or, if desired, serve fruit in kiwano shells.) Drizzle with the dressing (and, if desired, pulp of kiwano fruit). Makes 4 servings.

NUTRITION FACTS PER SERVING:

248 calories
10 g total fat
3 g saturated fat
57 mg cholesterol
307 mg sodium
19 g carbohydrate
2 g fiber
22 g protein

flank steak with pineapple salsa

The fresh-tasting fruit salsa that enlivens this warm steak salad starts with green picante sauce. Just add pineapple, sweet peppers, and mandarin oranges—and serve.

INGREDIENTS

- 2 cups chopped, peeled, and cored fresh pineapple
- 1 11-ounce can mandarin orange sections, drained
- ½ cup chopped red and/or green sweet pepper
- ⅓ cup mild green picante sauce or green taco sauce
- 12 ounces beef flank steak or boneless sirloin steak, cut ½ inch thick
- ½ teaspoon Mexican seasoning or chili powder
- 1 tablespoon olive oil
- 4 to 6 cups torn mixed salad greens

Start to finish: 20 minutes

DIRECTIONS

1. For pineapple salsa, in a medium bowl gently stir together pineapple, mandarin oranges, sweet pepper, and picante sauce. Set aside.

2. Trim fat from steak. Cut steak across the grain into thin slices. Sprinkle with Mexican seasoning; toss to coat evenly. In a large skillet cook and stir half of seasoned steak in hot oil over medium-high heat for 2 to 3 minutes or until slightly pink in center. Remove from skillet. Repeat with remaining steak.

3. Arrange salad greens on 4 dinner plates. Top with steak slices and pineapple salsa. Makes 4 servings.

NUTRITION FACTS PER SERVING:

245 calories
10 g total fat
3 g saturated fat
40 mg cholesterol
224 mg sodium
23 g carbohydrate
2 g fiber
18 g protein

gingered beef & pasta salad

Become a quick-change artist! When toasted sesame oil, rice vinegar, soy sauce, and ginger replace the usual mayonnaise dressing, a simple beef salad reinvents itself as something altogether new and exotic.

INGREDIENTS

6   ounces dried radiatore or large bow-tie pasta (2 cups)

4   cups mesclun or torn mixed salad greens

6   ounces lean cooked beef, cubed or cut into bite-size strips (1 cup)

1   cup cherry tomatoes, halved, or 1 large tomato, cut into wedges

2   tablespoons soy sauce

1   tablespoon rice vinegar or white wine vinegar

1   tablespoon water

2   teaspoons grated fresh ginger

1   teaspoon sugar

½   teaspoon toasted sesame oil

Rice vinegar, made from rice wine or sake, has a subtle tang and slightly sweet taste. Chinese rice vinegars are stronger than Japanese vinegars, although both are slightly milder than most vinegars. Chinese rice vinegar comes in three types: white, used mainly in hot-and-sour dishes; red, a typical accompaniment for shellfish; and black, used mainly as a condiment.

Start to finish: 30 minutes

DIRECTIONS

1. Cook pasta according to package directions; drain in colander. Rinse with cold water; drain again.

2. In a large salad bowl combine the pasta, mesclun, meat, and tomatoes.

3. Meanwhile, in a small saucepan stir together soy sauce, vinegar, water, ginger, sugar, and sesame oil. Bring to boiling, stirring to dissolve sugar. Remove from heat. Pour over salad; toss gently to coat. Serve immediately. Makes 4 servings.

NUTRITION FACTS PER SERVING:

276 calories
5 g total fat
2 g saturated fat
30 mg cholesterol
550 mg sodium
39 g carbohydrate
2 g fiber
18 g protein

INGREDIENTS

- 3 tablespoons balsamic vinegar
- 2 tablespoons olive oil
- 1 clove garlic, minced
- ½ teaspoon salt
- ½ teaspoon pepper
- 12 ounces boneless beef sirloin steak, cut 1 inch thick
- 1 tablespoon snipped fresh thyme
- 2 teaspoons snipped fresh rosemary
- 4 ¼-inch slices red onion
- 6 cups lightly packed mesclun or torn mixed salad greens
- 8 yellow and/or red pear-shaped tomatoes, halved
- 2 tablespoons crumbled Gorgonzola or other blue cheese

grilled beef, red onion, & blue cheese salad

The natural sweetness of red onion is intensified when the onion slices are brushed with a balsamic vinaigrette and grilled alongside sirloin steak. Aromatic grilled herb bread makes a perfect go-along to this crisp and hearty main-dish salad.

Prep time: 15 minutes
Grilling time: 8 minutes

DIRECTIONS

1. For vinaigrette, in a screw-top jar combine the vinegar, oil, garlic, salt, and pepper; cover and shake well. Trim fat from steak. Remove 1 tablespoon vinaigrette from jar and brush evenly onto both sides of steak. Press thyme and rosemary onto both sides of steak. Brush both sides of the onion slices with some of the remaining vinaigrette, reserving the rest.

2. Grill steak and onion slices on the rack of an uncovered grill directly over medium heat until steak is desired doneness and onion is tender, turning once halfway through cooking. (For steak, allow 8 to 12 minutes for medium rare or 12 to 15 minutes for medium. For onion, allow about 10 minutes.)

3. To serve, divide mesclun among 4 dinner plates. Cut steak across the grain into thin slices. Separate the onion slices into rings. Arrange warm steak and onion rings on top of mesclun. Drizzle with the reserved vinaigrette. Top with tomatoes and cheese. Makes 4 servings.

NUTRITION FACTS PER SERVING:

266 calories
16 g total fat
5 g saturated fat
59 mg cholesterol
373 mg sodium
9 g carbohydrate
2 g fiber
22 g protein

pork salad with cabbage slaw

Apples and pork are a can't-miss combination, so this entrée repeats it twice: chopped apples with sliced pork loin and cider vinegar with crumbled bacon. It's a good change of pace, made easy with a base of packaged coleslaw mix.

INGREDIENTS

- 1 **pound butterflied pork loin chops, cut ¾ inch thick**
- ¼ **teaspoon cracked pepper**
- ⅛ **teaspoon ground nutmeg**
- 5 **cups packaged shredded cabbage with carrot (coleslaw mix)**
- 1 **large apple, coarsely chopped**
- 2 **slices turkey bacon or bacon**
- ⅓ **cup cider vinegar**
- ⅓ **cup apple juice or apple cider**
- 1 **tablespoon honey**
- 2 **teaspoons honey mustard**
- 1 **teaspoon caraway seed**

Start to finish: 25 minutes

DIRECTIONS

1. Trim fat from chops. Sprinkle chops with pepper and nutmeg. Broil chops on the unheated rack of a broiler pan 3 to 4 inches from the heat for 6 to 8 minutes or until chops are slightly pink in center and juices run clear, turning once halfway through cooking.

2. Meanwhile, in a large bowl combine cabbage and apple; set aside. In a medium skillet cook bacon over medium heat until crisp. Drain bacon, reserving the drippings in skillet. Crumble bacon and set aside.

3. Add vinegar, apple juice, honey, honey mustard, and caraway seed to the reserved drippings in skillet. Bring to boiling. Pour over cabbage mixture. Add bacon; toss gently to coat.

4. Divide cabbage mixture among 4 dinner plates. Cut chops into thin slices. Arrange meat slices on top of cabbage mixture. Makes 4 servings.

NUTRITION FACTS PER SERVING:

235 calories
9 g total fat
3 g saturated fat
56 mg cholesterol
171 mg sodium
21 g carbohydrate
3 g fiber
19 g protein

INGREDIENTS

- 1 12-ounce pork tenderloin
- 1 teaspoon coarsely ground pepper
- 1 6-ounce package long grain and wild rice mix
- ½ cup snipped dried apricots
- ¼ cup bottled fat-free Italian salad dressing

- 2 green onions, thinly sliced
- 2 tablespoons frozen orange juice concentrate, thawed
- ½ cup frozen peas
- Fresh apricots, pitted and sliced (optional)

peppered pork & apricot salad

Dazzle guests with a main-dish salad whose vibrant colors—bright green, apricot, black, and cream—make a statement on a serving platter. Use quick-cooking pork tenderloin; then slice it into appealing medallions.

Start to finish: 45 minutes

DIRECTIONS

1. Trim fat from meat. Place meat on a rack in a shallow roasting pan. Sprinkle the pepper evenly over meat. Insert a meat thermometer in center of meat. Roast in a 425° oven for 25 to 30 minutes or until meat thermometer registers 155°. Remove from oven; cover loosely with foil. Let stand for 10 minutes. (The meat's temperature will rise 5° during standing.)

2. Meanwhile, prepare rice mix according to package directions, adding the dried apricots the last 5 minutes of cooking. Spread in a shallow baking pan and cool for 20 minutes.

3. For dressing, in a small bowl combine salad dressing, green onions, and orange juice concentrate. In a large bowl combine rice mixture and peas. Drizzle with the dressing; toss lightly to coat.

4. Spoon rice mixture onto a large serving platter. Cut meat into thin slices; arrange slices on top of rice mixture. If desired, garnish with fresh apricots. Makes 4 servings.

To make the salad ahead, cover and refrigerate the rice mixture and meat slices separately for up to 24 hours. Let stand at room temperature for no more than 30 minutes before serving.

NUTRITION FACTS PER SERVING:

356 calories
6 g total fat
2 g saturated fat
61 mg cholesterol
1,056 mg sodium
50 g carbohydrate
2 g fiber
25 g protein

thai cobb salad

Hit a home run with this refreshing mix of meat, cubed avocado, roasted peanuts, and spicy ginger-soy dressing. Leftover grilled meats work admirably, or deli-sliced meats can pinch hit.

INGREDIENTS

½ cup bottled fat-free Italian salad dressing

1 tablespoon soy sauce

1 to 1½ teaspoons grated fresh ginger

¼ to ½ teaspoon crushed red pepper

8 cups torn mixed salad greens*

1½ cups coarsely chopped cooked pork, beef, or chicken (8 ounces)

1 avocado, seeded, peeled, and cut into ½-inch pieces

1 cup coarsely shredded carrots

¼ cup fresh cilantro leaves

¼ cup thinly sliced green onions

¼ cup honey-roasted peanuts (optional)

Start to finish: 25 minutes

DIRECTIONS

1. For dressing, in a large bowl combine salad dressing, soy sauce, ginger, and crushed red pepper. Add mixed salad greens; toss lightly to coat.

2. Divide salad greens among 4 dinner plates. Top with meat, avocado, carrots, cilantro, green onions, and, if desired, peanuts. Makes 4 servings.

*Note: To carry through with the Asian flavors, include Chinese cabbage as part of the mixed greens.

NUTRITION FACTS PER SERVING:

255 calories
15 g total fat
4 g saturated fat
52 mg cholesterol
743 mg sodium
11 g carbohydrate
4 g fiber
19 g protein

spinach, ham, & melon salad

INGREDIENTS

- ½ of a small cantaloupe
- 7 cups torn spinach
- 1 cup cubed lean cooked ham
- ½ cup pecan halves, toasted (see tip, page 63)
- ½ of a medium red onion, thinly sliced
- ⅓ cup Orange-Poppy Seed Dressing

Dazzle family and friends with a star-studded main dish. Use cookie cutters to give melon slices pretty shapes that stand out next to vibrant green spinach and ruby red slices of onion. The tangy dressing can be made ahead and refrigerated.

Start to finish: 30 minutes

DIRECTIONS

1. Use a melon baller to scoop out the cantaloupe pulp into balls.

2. In a large bowl toss together the cantaloupe balls, spinach, ham, pecans, and red onion slices. Pour Orange-Poppy Seed Dressing over salad; toss gently to coat. Makes 4 servings.

Orange-Poppy Seed Dressing: In a food processor bowl or blender container combine 3 tablespoons sugar, 1½ teaspoons finely shredded orange peel, 2 tablespoons orange juice, 2 tablespoons vinegar, 1 tablespoon finely chopped onion, and dash pepper. Cover and process or blend until combined. With processor or blender running, slowly add ⅓ cup salad oil in a steady stream through hole or opening in top. Process or blend until the mixture is thickened. Stir in 1 teaspoon poppy seed. Cover and refrigerate up to 1 week. Shake well before using. Makes about ¾ cup.

NUTRITION FACTS PER SERVING:

286 calories
20 g total fat
3 g saturated fat
19 mg cholesterol
507 mg sodium
19 g carbohydrate
4 g fiber
12 g protein

red beans & grains

Eliminate the serving dish by using a crusty round of hearth-baked bread for a salad bowl. Inside are red beans, ham, and quinoa—a bead-shape grain that's loaded with protein. Brown rice can substitute for the quinoa.

INGREDIENTS

3 cups diced lean cooked ham (about 1 pound)

2 cups cooked quinoa or brown rice

1 15-ounce can pinto beans, rinsed and drained

1 cup cooked white rice

1 large tomato, chopped

1 yellow or green sweet pepper, chopped

¼ cup thinly sliced green onions

¼ cup snipped fresh parsley

1 fresh jalapeño pepper, finely chopped (see tip, page 158)

1 recipe Peppered Vinaigrette

3 8-inch round loaves crusty bread (country bread)

Red-tipped leaf lettuce

Prep time: 30 minutes
Chilling time: 2 hours

DIRECTIONS

1. In a large bowl combine ham, quinoa, beans, white rice, tomato, sweet pepper, green onions, parsley, and jalapeño pepper. Pour Peppered Vinaigrette over rice mixture; toss gently to coat. Cover and refrigerate for 2 to 24 hours.

2. Just before serving, cut a 1-inch slice from the top of each loaf of bread. Hollow out bread, leaving a ¼- to ½-inch shell. (Save top slice and remaining bread for another use.) Line each bread

bowl with lettuce. Spoon salad into bread bowls. Makes 10 to 12 servings.

Peppered Vinaigrette: In a screw-top jar combine 3 tablespoons olive oil; 3 tablespoons red wine vinegar; 2 teaspoons snipped fresh thyme or ½ teaspoon dried thyme, crushed; 2 cloves garlic, minced; ½ teaspoon black pepper; and ¼ teaspoon ground red pepper. Cover and shake well.

NUTRITION FACTS PER SERVING:

333 calories
9 g total fat
2 g saturated fat
24 mg cholesterol
961 mg sodium
45 g carbohydrate
5 g fiber
18 g protein

INGREDIENTS

- 4 1-inch slices Italian bread
- 2 tablespoons bottled Italian salad dressing or olive oil
- 1 medium red sweet pepper, cut into strips
- ¾ cup bottled Italian salad dressing
- ½ cup sliced celery
- ½ cup sliced pitted green or ripe olives

- 3 tablespoons snipped fresh basil or oregano
- 6 to 8 cups torn romaine
- 8 ounces salami, cut into bite-size strips
- 8 ounces lean cooked ham, cut into bite-size strips
- 8 ounces cubed provolone cheese
- 1½ cups broccoli flowerets
- 1½ cups cherry tomatoes, halved

muffuletta salad

Bring a bit of New Orleans to any gathering with this do-ahead salad that serves a dozen hungry eaters. The salami, ham, cheese, broccoli, and tomatoes are layered and chilled, then topped with toasted bread cubes, recalling the famed muffuletta sandwiches.

Prep time: 30 minutes
Chilling time: 4 hours

DIRECTIONS

1. For croutons, brush Italian bread slices with the 2 tablespoons salad dressing. Cut into 1-inch cubes. Spread in a large shallow baking pan. Bake in a 300° oven about 15 minutes or until crisp, stirring once or twice. Cool. Store in an airtight container.

2. Meanwhile, in a very large bowl combine sweet pepper strips, the ¾ cup salad dressing, celery, olives, and basil. Layer in the following order: romaine, salami, ham, cheese, broccoli, and cherry tomatoes. Cover and refrigerate for 4 to 24 hours.

3. Just before serving, add the croutons to salad; toss gently to combine. Makes 12 servings.

NUTRITION FACTS PER SERVING:

299 calories
22 g total fat
7 g saturated fat
38 mg cholesterol
1,133 mg sodium
11 g carbohydrate
2 g fiber
15 g protein

135

greek lamb salad with yogurt dressing

When menus become ho-hum, bring drama to the table with the elemental Greek trio of lamb, yogurt, and cucumber. Dried tart cherries make the dish sparkle.

INGREDIENTS

- 8 ounces boneless lamb leg sirloin chops, cut ½ inch thick
- 2 teaspoons snipped fresh rosemary or ½ teaspoon dried rosemary, crushed
- 1 clove garlic, minced
- 8 cups torn mixed salad greens or spinach
- 1 15-ounce can garbanzo beans, rinsed and drained
- ¼ cup chopped seeded cucumber
- ½ cup plain low-fat yogurt
- ¼ cup chopped green onions
- 1 clove garlic, minced
- ⅛ to ¼ teaspoon salt
- ⅛ teaspoon pepper
- ¼ cup dried tart cherries or golden raisins

Start to finish: 30 minutes

DIRECTIONS

1. Trim fat from chops. Combine rosemary and 1 clove garlic; rub evenly over both sides of chops. Broil chops on the unheated rack of a broiler pan 3 to 4 inches from the heat for 9 to 11 minutes or until slightly pink in the center, turning once halfway through cooking. (Or, grill on the rack of an uncovered grill directly over medium heat for 9 to 11 minutes, turning once halfway through cooking.) Cut the chops into thin bite-size slices.

2. Meanwhile, in a large bowl toss together salad greens, garbanzo beans, and cucumber. Divide spinach mixture among 4 dinner plates. Arrange meat slices on top of spinach mixture.

3. For dressing, in a small bowl combine yogurt, green onions, 1 clove garlic, salt, and pepper. Drizzle dressing over salads. Sprinkle with cherries. Makes 4 servings.

NUTRITION FACTS PER SERVING:

243 calories
6 g total fat
2 g saturated fat
36 mg cholesterol
569 mg sodium
29 g carbohydrate
8 g fiber
20 g protein

INGREDIENTS

- 1 cup balsamic vinegar
- 8 lamb loin or rib chops, cut 1 inch thick (1½ to 2 pounds total)
- 3 cups sugar snap peas, strings and tips removed
- 6 cups torn mixed salad greens
- ¼ cup hazelnuts or coarsely chopped walnuts, toasted (see tip, page 63)

balsamic-glazed springtime lamb salad

Balsamic vinegar, a less-astringent, sweeter member of the vinegar family, makes a memorable glaze for grilled lamb chops. Add early sugar snap peas and mixed greens, and the dish defines the essence of spring.

Start to finish: 25 minutes

DIRECTIONS

1. For glaze, in a small saucepan bring balsamic vinegar just to boiling. Boil gently, uncovered, about 10 minutes or until vinegar is reduced to ⅓ cup. Set aside.

2. Meanwhile, trim fat from chops. Broil chops on the unheated rack of a broiler pan 3 to 4 inches from the heat for 7 to 11 minutes or until chops are slightly pink in center, turning once halfway through cooking.

3. In a small covered saucepan cook sugar snap peas in a small amount of boiling salted water for 2 to 4 minutes or until crisp-tender. Drain.

4. Divide salad greens among 4 dinner plates. Top each with 2 chops and some of the snap peas. Drizzle with glaze; sprinkle with nuts. Makes 4 servings.

NUTRITION FACTS PER SERVING:

516 calories
21 g total fat
6 g saturated fat
160 mg cholesterol
163 mg sodium
23 g carbohydrate
4 g fiber
55 g protein

beef & vegetable ragout

The earthy, elegant, and traditionally long-simmered French stew called ragout gets an update in taste and reduced preparation time. This version, flavored with port wine and filled with crisp, bright vegetables, can be on the table in 30 minutes.

INGREDIENTS

- 12 ounces beef tenderloin, cut into ¾-inch pieces
- 1 tablespoon olive oil or cooking oil
- 1½ cups sliced fresh shiitake or button mushrooms (4 ounces)
- 1 medium onion, chopped
- 2 cloves garlic, minced
- 3 tablespoons all-purpose flour
- ½ teaspoon salt
- ¼ teaspoon pepper
- 1 14½-ounce can beef broth
- ¼ cup port wine or dry sherry
- 2 cups sugar snap peas, strings and tips removed, or one 10-ounce package frozen sugar snap peas, thawed
- 1 cup cherry tomatoes, halved
  Hot cooked wide noodles or bow-tie pasta (optional)

There's a reason stews and casseroles have remained time-honored traditions at the table. The one-pot meal can stand alone, if necessary. All of the elements of the meal are in one place, so there aren't three pots to watch and wash. For casual entertaining, the one-pot meal is ideal. This hearty and flavorful dish can be made ahead and simply reheated while the noodles are cooking (just add the snap peas right before serving so they stay crisp and green). Serve with some crusty bread or corn bread and a salad, if you like, and your company fare is finished.

Start to finish: 30 minutes

DIRECTIONS

1. In a large nonstick skillet cook and stir meat in hot oil for 2 to 3 minutes or until meat is slightly pink in center. Remove meat; set aside. In the same skillet cook mushrooms, onion, and garlic until tender.

2. Stir in flour, salt, and pepper. Add beef broth and wine. Cook and stir until thickened and bubbly. Stir in sugar snap peas. Cook and stir for 2 to 3 minutes more or until peas are tender. Stir in meat and tomatoes; heat through. If desired, serve meat mixture over noodles. Makes 4 servings.

NUTRITION FACTS PER SERVING:

252 calories
9 g total fat
3 g saturated fat
48 mg cholesterol
647 mg sodium
17 g carbohydrate
3 g fiber
21 g protein

asian beef & noodle bowl

Already quick to toss together, this satisfying Asian noodle supper zooms to conclusion if you stop first at the grocery salad bar and pick up prewashed spinach, shredded carrots, and a jar each of minced garlic and ginger.

INGREDIENTS

- 4 cups water
- 2 3-ounce packages ramen noodles
- 2 teaspoons chili oil or cooking oil*
- 12 ounces beef flank steak or top round steak, cut into bite-size strips
- 2 cloves garlic, minced
- 1 teaspoon grated fresh ginger
- 1 cup beef broth
- 1 tablespoon soy sauce
- 2 cups torn spinach
- 1 cup shredded carrots
- ¼ cup snipped fresh mint or cilantro
- ¼ cup chopped peanuts (optional)

Start to finish: 30 minutes

DIRECTIONS

1. In a large saucepan bring water to boiling. If desired, break up noodles. Drop the noodles into boiling water. (Do not use flavor packets.) Return to boiling; boil for 2 to 3 minutes or until noodles are tender but still firm; stir occasionally. Drain.

2. Pour oil into a wok or large skillet. Preheat over medium-high heat. Stir-fry meat, garlic, and ginger in hot oil for 2 to 3 minutes or until meat is slightly pink in center. Push meat from the center of the wok. Carefully add beef broth and soy sauce. Bring to boiling. Reduce heat and stir meat into broth mixture. Cook and stir for 1 to 2 minutes more or until heated through.

3. Add noodles, spinach, carrots, and mint; toss gently to combine. Ladle into soup bowls. If desired, sprinkle each serving with peanuts. Makes 4 servings.

*Note: If using cooking oil, stir ⅛ to ¼ teaspoon ground red pepper into oil.

NUTRITION FACTS PER SERVING:

211 calories
10 g total fat
3 g saturated fat
47 mg cholesterol
690 mg sodium
11 g carbohydrate
2 g fiber
20 g protein

allspice meatball stew

The exotic flavor of this hearty stew comes from the allspice berry of the pimiento tree. Allspice, which can be purchased whole or ground, gets its name because it tastes like a combination of cinnamon, nutmeg, and cloves.

INGREDIENTS

- 1 16-ounce package frozen prepared Italian-style meatballs
- 3 cups green beans cut into 1-inch pieces or frozen cut green beans
- 2 cups packaged peeled baby carrots
- 1 14½-ounce can beef broth
- 2 teaspoons Worcestershire sauce
- ½ to ¾ teaspoon ground allspice
- ½ teaspoon ground cinnamon
- 2 14½-ounce cans stewed tomatoes

This soup freezes well. Freeze 1-, 2-, or 4-serving portions in sealed freezer containers. To reheat, place frozen soup in a large saucepan. Heat, covered, over medium heat about 30 minutes, stirring occasionally to break apart.

Start to finish: 30 minutes

DIRECTIONS

1. In a Dutch oven combine the meatballs, green beans, carrots, beef broth, Worcestershire sauce, allspice, and cinnamon. Bring to boiling; reduce heat. Simmer, covered, for 10 minutes.

2. Stir in the undrained tomatoes. Return to boiling; reduce heat. Simmer, covered, about 5 minutes more or until vegetables are crisp-tender. Makes 8 servings.

NUTRITION FACTS PER SERVING:

233 calories
13 g total fat
6 g saturated fat
37 mg cholesterol
938 mg sodium
18 g carbohydrate
4 g fiber
12 g protein

pork, corn, & three-pepper soup

INGREDIENTS

- 12 ounces lean boneless pork, cut into bite-size strips
- 1 tablespoon cooking oil
- ½ cup chopped red sweet pepper
- 1 small onion, chopped
- 1 14¾-ounce can cream-style corn
- 1 cup chicken broth
- 1 cup milk
- ½ cup frozen whole kernel corn
- 1 4-ounce can diced green chili peppers
- ¼ cup snipped fresh parsley
- ¼ teaspoon salt
- ¼ teaspoon ground red pepper

Experience a peck of peppers in this soup. There are actually three different types of peppers in this corn-filled soup: red sweet pepper, green chili peppers, and hot ground red pepper. Adjust the heat level by adding more or less ground red pepper.

Start to finish: 30 minutes

DIRECTIONS

1. In a large saucepan cook meat in hot oil for 2 to 3 minutes or until slightly pink in center. Remove from saucepan; cover and keep warm. Add red sweet pepper and onion to saucepan and cook until tender.

2. Stir in the cream-style corn, chicken broth, milk, frozen corn, and undrained chili peppers. Bring to boiling; reduce heat. Simmer, covered, for 5 minutes.

3. Stir in the cooked meat, parsley, salt, and ground red pepper; heat through. Makes 4 servings.

NUTRITION FACTS PER SERVING:

281 calories
12 g total fat
3 g saturated fat
43 mg cholesterol
768 mg sodium
30 g carbohydrate
2 g fiber
19 g protein

caribbean-style pork stew

The flavor of a plantain depends on the ripeness. A ripe, black-skinned plantain tastes like a banana. An almost-ripe, yellow plantain tastes similar to sweet potatoes. Unripe, green plantains taste starchy but lose the starchy flavor upon cooking.

INGREDIENTS

- 1 15-ounce can black beans, rinsed and drained
- 1 14½-ounce can beef broth
- 1¾ cups water
- 12 ounces lean cooked pork, cut into bite-size strips
- 3 plantains, peeled and cubed
- 1 cup chopped tomatoes
- ½ of a 16-ounce package (2 cups) frozen pepper stir-fry vegetables
- 1 tablespoon grated fresh ginger
- 1 teaspoon ground cumin
- ¼ teaspoon salt
- ¼ teaspoon crushed red pepper
- 3 cups hot cooked rice
  Crushed red pepper (optional)
  Fresh pineapple slices (optional)

Start to finish: 30 minutes

DIRECTIONS

1. In a Dutch oven combine the beans, broth, and water. Bring to boiling.

2. Add the meat, plantains, and tomatoes to the bean mixture. Stir in the frozen vegetables, ginger, cumin, salt, and the ¼ teaspoon crushed red pepper. Return to boiling; reduce heat. Simmer, covered, about 10 minutes or until plantains are tender.

3. Serve with hot rice in soup bowls. If desired, sprinkle each serving with additional crushed red pepper and garnish with pineapple. Makes 6 servings.

NUTRITION FACTS PER SERVING:

425 calories
9 g total fat
3 g saturated fat
52 mg cholesterol
547 mg sodium
66 g carbohydrate
6 g fiber
26 g protein

INGREDIENTS

6 cups vegetable broth or chicken broth

8 ounces boneless pork sirloin, cut ½ inch thick

1 large onion, chopped

4 cloves garlic, minced

2 teaspoons grated fresh ginger

1 tablespoon cooking oil

3 small tomatoes, chopped

2 medium carrots, finely chopped

½ cup dried anelli pasta

4 cups thinly sliced Chinese cabbage

¼ cup snipped fresh mint Chinese cabbage leaves (optional)

gingered pork & cabbage soup

Asian cooks have long known that the peppery, slightly sweet taste of ginger perfectly matches mild-flavored pork. Here, the combination is even better joined with a bit of fresh mint.

Start to finish: 40 minutes

DIRECTIONS

1. In a medium saucepan bring vegetable broth to boiling. Meanwhile, trim fat from meat. Cut meat into ½-inch cubes. In a large saucepan cook meat, onion, garlic, and ginger in hot oil until meat is brown.

2. Add hot vegetable broth to meat mixture. Bring to boiling. Stir in tomatoes and carrots. Return to boiling; reduce heat. Simmer, covered, for 15 minutes.

3. Stir in pasta and cook for 6 to 8 minutes or until pasta is tender but still firm. Stir in the sliced Chinese cabbage and mint. Ladle into soup bowls. If desired, garnish each serving with Chinese cabbage leaves. Makes 6 servings.

NUTRITION FACTS PER SERVING:

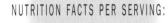

141 calories
6 g total fat
1 g saturated fat
16 mg cholesterol
961 mg sodium
21 g carbohydrate
2 g fiber
8 g protein

When a recipe calls for vegetable broth,

you can use canned broth or bouillon cubes, or prepare a homemade stock. An easy way to make your own vegetable stock is to save the water in which vegetables are boiled and freeze it in a covered container. Keep saving the liquid from the vegetables you prepare, and soon you will have a basic stock that's ready to use.

southern ham chowder

Southern cooks are renowned for pairing ham with vegetables. In this creamy chowder, smoky bits of cooked ham simmer with yellow squash, red sweet pepper, potato, and green onions.

INGREDIENTS

1½ cups thinly sliced yellow summer squash or zucchini

½ cup chopped red or green sweet pepper

½ teaspoon dried thyme, crushed

1 tablespoon margarine or butter

2 cups water

1½ cups chopped potato
Dash black pepper

6 ounces thinly sliced lean cooked ham or turkey ham, chopped

¾ cup finely chopped green onions

½ cup half-and-half or light cream

Do you know the difference between a chowder and a bisque? A chowder typically is a thick, milk- or cream-based soup that contains a variety of seafood and vegetables. It also describes a thick, rich chunky soup. Chowders often are thickened with potatoes or a roux, a flour and fat mixture. A bisque is a thick, rich, and creamy soup made of puréed shellfish or fish and, sometimes, meat or vegetables. Traditionally, it is thickened with rice.

Start to finish: 35 minutes

DIRECTIONS

1. In a large saucepan cook squash, sweet pepper, and thyme in hot margarine over medium heat about 3 minutes or until squash is tender. Add water, potato, and black pepper.

2. Bring to boiling; reduce heat. Simmer, covered, for 12 to 15 minutes or until potato is tender. Remove from heat. Mash slightly with a potato masher. Stir in ham, green onions, and half-and-half; heat through. Makes 3 or 4 servings.

NUTRITION FACTS PER SERVING:

261 calories
12 g total fat
5 g saturated fat
45 mg cholesterol
755 mg sodium
23 g carbohydrate
2 g fiber
16 g protein

INGREDIENTS

- 12 ounces uncooked sweet Italian sausage links
- ¼ cup water
- 1 medium onion, chopped
- 2 cloves garlic, minced
- 1 tablespoon cooking oil
- 2 15-ounce cans white kidney (cannellini) beans, rinsed and drained
- 2 14½-ounce cans reduced-sodium chicken broth
- 1 cup seeded and coarsely chopped plum tomatoes (3 or 4 tomatoes)
- 1½ teaspoons snipped fresh marjoram or ½ teaspoon dried marjoram, crushed
- 7½ cups kale* or spinach, coarsely chopped (10 to 12 ounces)

white bean soup with sausage & kale

Tuscan cuisine influences this earthy soup, with white beans and Italian sausage. Tomatoes and deep green kale add provincial freshness. Serve it with hearty Italian bread and, for dessert, Chocolate Ricotta-Filled Pears (page 280).

Start to finish: 35 minutes

DIRECTIONS

1. Prick the sausage links several times with a fork. In a large skillet combine sausage and water. Bring to boiling; reduce heat. Simmer, covered, about 15 minutes or until sausage is no longer pink. Uncover and cook about 5 minutes more or until sausage is browned, turning frequently. Remove the sausage; cut into ¼- to ⅜-inch slices.

2. Meanwhile, in a large saucepan cook onion and garlic in hot oil about 5 minutes or until onion is tender. Stir in beans, broth, tomatoes, and, if using, dried marjoram. Bring to boiling; reduce heat. Simmer, covered, for 15 minutes.

3. Stir in cooked sausage, kale, and, if using, fresh marjoram. Simmer about 5 minutes more or until kale is tender. Season to taste with pepper. Makes 5 servings.

*Note: Kale has frilly, dark green leaves and a mild cabbagelike flavor, which make it a tasty and striking addition to soups and salads.

NUTRITION FACTS PER SERVING:

282 calories
11 g total fat
5 g saturated fat
39 mg cholesterol
1,202 mg sodium
31 g carbohydrate
10 g fiber
23 g protein

fennel-asparagus soup

Savor the splendor of spring in this garden-fresh soup. Small onions, baby carrots, and tender asparagus partner with baby lima beans for a bowlful of bounty.

INGREDIENTS

6   cups chicken broth
1   10-ounce package frozen baby lima beans
1   cup small red boiling onions, whole pearl onions, or coarsely chopped onion
1   teaspoon fennel seed, crushed
¼   teaspoon pepper
1   cup packaged peeled baby carrots

1   medium fennel bulb
12 ounces asparagus spears, trimmed and cut into 1-inch pieces
4   ounces pancetta (Italian bacon), chopped and crisp-cooked, or 5 slices bacon, crisp-cooked and crumbled

Start to finish: 40 minutes

DIRECTIONS

1. In a Dutch oven combine the chicken broth, lima beans, onions, fennel seed, and pepper. Bring to boiling; reduce heat. Simmer, covered, for 10 minutes. Stir in the carrots and cook for 5 minutes.

2. Meanwhile, cut off and discard the upper stalks of fennel, reserving leaves for garnish. Remove any wilted outer layers from bulb; cut a thin slice from base. Wash and chop fennel.

3. Stir the chopped fennel, asparagus, and pancetta into Dutch oven. Cook about 5 minutes more or until vegetables are tender. Ladle vegetable mixture into soup bowls. Garnish each serving with reserved fennel leaves. Makes 4 servings.

NUTRITION FACTS PER SERVING:

269 calories
7 g total fat
2 g saturated fat
8 mg cholesterol
1,329 mg sodium
34 g carbohydrate
15 g fiber
20 g protein

INGREDIENTS

- 12 ounces lean ground lamb
- 1 large onion, chopped
- 3 cloves garlic, minced
- 2 cups water
- 1 14½-ounce can chicken broth
- ½ cup snipped fresh cilantro
- 1 tablespoon grated fresh ginger
- ¼ teaspoon pepper

- ¼ teaspoon paprika
- ⅛ teaspoon thread saffron, crushed, or dash ground saffron (optional)
- 2 medium apples or pears, cored and thinly sliced
- ¼ cup raisins or snipped pitted dates

moroccan lamb tagine

Lamb's richness pairs well with both spices and fruits, particularly the ginger, apples, and raisins called for here. If you have saffron on hand, add it for extra flavor and a brighter color. Serve this comforting soup with basmati or wild rice.

Start to finish: 35 minutes

DIRECTIONS

1. In a large saucepan cook ground lamb, onion, and garlic until lamb is no longer pink. Drain well. Stir in the water, chicken broth, cilantro, ginger, pepper, paprika, and, if desired, saffron. Bring to boiling; reduce heat. Simmer, covered, for 10 minutes.

2. Stir in the apples and raisins. Return to boiling; reduce heat. Simmer, uncovered, for 1 to 2 minutes more or just until apples are slightly softened. Makes 4 servings.

NUTRITION FACTS PER SERVING:

261 calories
12 g total fat
5 g saturated fat
57 mg cholesterol
381 mg sodium
20 g carbohydrate
2 g fiber
18 g protein

The spice called saffron comes from the stigmas or threadlike filaments of the purple crocus flower. Each flower contains only three stigmas, which are hand-picked and dried. It takes over 14,000 stigmas to provide an ounce of saffron. Because of the labor intensive process of harvesting the stigmas, saffron is very expensive. You only need a small amount to flavor your recipes, though—a little will go a long way. Saffron comes in thin threads. To release the flavor, crush the threads by rubbing them between your fingers.

Poached Orange Roughy with Lemon Sauce
See recipe, page 159

fast and fabulous fish

Shark with Nectarine Salsa 150
Pan-Seared Salmon with Stir-Fried Vegetables 151
Salmon with Cucumber Kabobs 152
Dilly Salmon Fillets 153
Salmon with Fresh Pineapple Salsa 154
Wasabi-Glazed Whitefish with Vegetable Slaw 155
Grilled Tuna with Wilted Spinach 156
Seared Tuna with Grapefruit-Orange Relish 157
Grilled Swordfish with Spicy Tomato Sauce 158
Poached Orange Roughy with Lemon Sauce 159
Blackened Catfish with Roasted Potatoes 160
Grilled Rosemary Trout with Lemon Butter 161
Pan-Seared Scallops 162
Thai-Spiced Scallops 163
Paella-Style Shrimp & Couscous 164
Thai Shrimp & Fresh Vegetable Rice 165
Pepper Shrimp in Peanut Sauce 166
Rosemary-Orange Shrimp Kabobs 167
Asian Grilled Salmon Salad 168
Honey-Glazed Tuna & Greens 169
Fire-&-Ice Rice Salad 170

Scandinavian Shrimp Salad 171
Shrimp & Tropical Fruit 172
Warm Scallop Salad with Toasted Sesame Dressing . . 173
Seared Scallop & Spinach Salad 174
Curried Crab Salad 175
Quick Cioppino 176
Fish Provençale. 177
Lemon & Scallop Soup 178
Paella Soup 179
Bayou Shrimp Soup 180
Shrimp & Greens Soup 181
Chicken & Shrimp Tortilla Soup 182
Spicy Pumpkin & Shrimp Soup 183
Oyster & Corn Chowder 184
Crab Chowder 185
Crab & Pasta Gazpacho 186
Caribbean Clam Chowder 187

shark with nectarine salsa

Shark usually is sold as fillets, but if you can't find it, orange roughy is a fine substitute. Orange roughy, found in the waters near New Zealand and Australia, has firm white flesh with a mild flavor. However, any mild white fish is acceptable.

INGREDIENTS

1 ripe nectarine, cut into ½-inch pieces

1 small cucumber, seeded and cut into ½-inch pieces

1 ripe kiwi fruit, peeled and cut into ½-inch pieces

¼ cup thinly sliced green onions

3 tablespoons orange juice

1 tablespoon white wine vinegar

1 1-pound fresh shark or orange roughy fillet, about 1 inch thick

1 teaspoon olive oil

½ teaspoon freshly ground pepper

Fish is a great candidate for the grill—with a little extra care to prevent it from breaking apart. It helps to place fish fillets on foil (and use a wide spatula if you must turn them) or in a grill basket when grilling. Grill baskets are intended for direct grilling only—most grill-basket handles can't take the heat of indirect cooking on a covered grill. Be sure to grease or brush the foil or basket with cooking oil before adding the fish. Firmer-textured fish steaks can be grilled on a greased grill rack.

Prep time: 30 minutes
Grilling time: 8 minutes

DIRECTIONS

1. For salsa, in a medium bowl combine nectarine, cucumber, kiwi fruit, green onions, orange juice, and vinegar. Cover and refrigerate until ready to serve.

2. Rinse fish; pat dry. Rub oil over both sides of fish and sprinkle with pepper. Place fish in a well-greased wire grill basket, tucking under any thin edges. Grill fish on the rack of an uncovered grill directly over medium heat for 8 to 12 minutes or until fish flakes easily when tested with a fork, turning basket once halfway through cooking. Spoon the salsa over fish. Cut fish into 4 serving-size pieces. Makes 4 servings.

NUTRITION FACTS PER SERVING:

158 calories
3 g total fat
1 g saturated fat
60 mg cholesterol
94 mg sodium
10 g carbohydrate
1 g fiber
22 g protein

pan-seared salmon with stir-fried vegetables

Salmon gets Pan-Asian treatment in this dish with a trio of matchstick-sliced vegetables and a homemade teriyaki sauce fired up with five-spice powder—a mix of star anise, ginger, cinnamon, cloves, and Szechwan peppercorns.

INGREDIENTS

- 1¼ pounds fresh skinless salmon fillets, about ¾ inch thick
- ¼ cup water
- 2 tablespoons dry sherry
- 2 tablespoons soy sauce
- 1 tablespoon toasted sesame oil
- 1 teaspoon cornstarch
- ½ teaspoon five-spice powder
- ¼ teaspoon sugar
- 2 tablespoons cooking oil
- 3 medium carrots, cut into thin bite-size strips
- 3 stalks celery, thinly sliced
- 2 cloves garlic, minced
- 2 teaspoons grated fresh ginger
- 6 medium green onions, cut into 1-inch pieces

Start to finish: 35 minutes

DIRECTIONS

1. Rinse fish; pat dry. Cut fish into 4 serving-size pieces. Set aside. In a small bowl combine 3 tablespoons of the water, 1 tablespoon of the sherry, 1 tablespoon of the soy sauce, the sesame oil, cornstarch, ¼ teaspoon of the five-spice powder, and the sugar. Set aside.

2. In another small bowl combine the remaining 1 tablespoon water, 1 tablespoon sherry, 1 tablespoon soy sauce, and ¼ teaspoon five-spice powder. Brush over both sides of fish. In a large skillet heat oil over medium heat. Add fish; cook for 6 to 9 minutes or until fish flakes easily when tested with a fork, gently turning once halfway through cooking. Remove from skillet; cover and keep warm.

3. In the same skillet stir-fry carrots, celery, garlic, and ginger for 3 minutes. Add green onions; stir-fry about 1 minute more or until vegetables are crisp-tender. Push vegetables from center of the skillet. Stir cornstarch mixture and add to skillet. Cook and stir until thickened and bubbly. Cook and stir for 2 minutes more. Stir the vegetables into sauce to coat.

4. To serve, spoon vegetable mixture onto 4 dinner plates. Top with the fish. Season to taste with salt and pepper. Makes 4 servings.

NUTRITION FACTS PER SERVING:

274 calories
15 g total fat
3 g saturated fat
25 mg cholesterol
677 mg sodium
11 g carbohydrate
3 g fiber
22 g protein

151

salmon with cucumber kabobs

Cooked cucumbers provide a pleasant change of pace on these kabobs. Though their characteristic crispness disappears with cooking, their delicacy does not, making them a perfect companion for light and elegant fish dishes.

INGREDIENTS

4 6- to 8-ounce fresh skinless salmon fillets, ½ to 1 inch thick

⅓ cup lemon juice

1 tablespoon olive oil or cooking oil

2 teaspoons snipped fresh tarragon

1 medium cucumber, halved lengthwise and sliced 1 inch thick

1 medium red onion, cut into wedges

8 cherry tomatoes
    Hot cooked rice (optional)

Prep time: 15 minutes
Marinating time: 10 minutes
Grilling time: 8 minutes

DIRECTIONS

1. Rinse fish; pat dry. Place fish in a plastic bag set in a shallow dish. For marinade, combine lemon juice, oil, and tarragon. Reserve half for basting. Pour the remaining marinade over fish; close bag. Marinate at room temperature for 10 to 20 minutes. Meanwhile, on four 10-inch skewers alternately thread cucumber and onion.

2. Drain fish, discarding marinade. Place fish in a well-greased wire grill basket, tucking under any thin edges. Grill the fish and vegetable kabobs on the rack of an uncovered grill directly over medium heat until fish flakes easily when tested with a fork and vegetables are tender, turning and brushing fish and vegetables once with basting sauce halfway through cooking. (Allow 4 to 6 minutes per ½-inch thickness of fish and 8 to 12 minutes for vegetables.) Add the tomatoes to the ends of kabobs the last 2 minutes of grilling.

3. If desired, serve fish and vegetables with rice. Makes 4 servings.

NUTRITION FACTS PER SERVING:

201 calories
8 g total fat
2 g saturated fat
31 mg cholesterol
106 mg sodium
6 g carbohydrate
1 g fiber
25 g protein

INGREDIENTS

4 6-ounce fresh skinless salmon fillets, ½ to ¾ inch thick

3 tablespoons lemon juice

2 tablespoons snipped fresh dill

2 tablespoons mayonnaise or salad dressing

2 teaspoons Dijon-style mustard
    Dash freshly ground pepper

dilly salmon fillets

A quick, dill-infused, Dijon-flavored mayonnaise caps off these Scandinavian-style salmon fillets. For a built-in salad and extra freshness, serve them on a bed of shredded cucumber.

Prep time: 15 minutes
Marinating time: 10 minutes
Grilling time: 5 minutes

DIRECTIONS

1. Rinse fish; pat dry. Place fish in a shallow dish. For marinade, in a small bowl combine the lemon juice and 1 tablespoon of the dill. Pour over fish. Cover and marinate at room temperature for 10 minutes. Meanwhile, in a small bowl stir together the mayonnaise, the remaining dill, mustard, and pepper; set aside.

2. In a charcoal grill with a cover arrange medium-hot coals around a drip pan. Test for medium heat above the pan. Place fish on a greased grill rack over drip pan. Cover and grill for 3 minutes. Gently turn fish; spread the mayonnaise mixture on top of fish. Cover and grill for 2 to 6 minutes more or until fish flakes easily when tested with a fork. (For a gas grill, adjust for indirect cooking; grill as directed.) Makes 4 servings.

NUTRITION FACTS PER SERVING:

211 calories
11 g total fat
2 g saturated fat
35 mg cholesterol
204 mg sodium
1 g carbohydrate
0 g fiber
25 g protein

salmon with fresh pineapple salsa

You don't need to have a party—just a weeknight dinner will do—to enjoy the sweet-hot fruit salsa that's as pretty as a sprinkling of confetti on top of this grilled salmon fillet. Serve it with hot cooked rice.

INGREDIENTS

2 cups coarsely chopped fresh pineapple

½ cup chopped red sweet pepper

¼ cup finely chopped red onion

3 tablespoons lime juice

1 small fresh jalapeño pepper, seeded and finely chopped (see tip, page 158)

1 tablespoon snipped fresh cilantro or chives

1 tablespoon honey

1 1-pound fresh skinless salmon fillet, about 1 inch thick

¼ teaspoon ground cumin

Start to finish: 30 minutes

DIRECTIONS

1. For salsa, in a medium bowl combine the pineapple, sweet pepper, onion, 2 tablespoons of the lime juice, the jalapeño pepper, cilantro, and honey. Set aside.

2. Rinse fish; pat dry. Brush both sides of fish with the remaining lime juice and sprinkle with cumin. Place fish in a well-greased wire grill basket, tucking under any thin edges. Grill fish on the rack of an uncovered grill directly over medium heat for 8 to 12 minutes or until fish flakes easily when tested with a fork, turning basket once halfway through cooking. Cut fish into 4 serving-size pieces. Serve with the salsa. Makes 4 servings.

NUTRITION FACTS PER SERVING:

170 calories
4 g total fat
1 g saturated fat
20 mg cholesterol
70 mg sodium
17 g carbohydrate
1 g fiber
17 g protein

INGREDIENTS

- 4 4-ounce fresh skinless white-fleshed fish fillets (such as whitefish, sea bass, or orange roughy), about 1 inch thick
- 2 tablespoons light soy sauce
- 1 teaspoon toasted sesame oil
- ½ teaspoon sugar
- ¼ teaspoon wasabi powder or 1 tablespoon prepared horseradish
- 1 medium zucchini, coarsely shredded (about 1⅓ cups)
- 1 cup sliced radishes
- 1 cup fresh pea pods
- 2 tablespoons snipped fresh chives
- 3 tablespoons rice vinegar

wasabi-glazed whitefish with vegetable slaw

Though its presence in this recipe is subtle, fans of fiery wasabi—the bright-green Japanese condiment—will notice its head-clearing heat. Wasabi is found in powdered or paste form in Japanese markets or in larger supermarkets.

Prep time: 15 minutes
Grilling time: 8 minutes

DIRECTIONS

1. Rinse fish; pat dry. In a small bowl combine soy sauce, ½ teaspoon of the sesame oil, ¼ teaspoon of the sugar, and the wasabi powder. Brush soy mixture over fish.

2. Place fish in a well-greased wire grill basket, tucking under any thin edges. Grill fish on the rack of an uncovered grill directly over medium heat for 8 to 12 minutes or until fish flakes easily when tested with a fork, turning basket once halfway through cooking.

3. Meanwhile, for vegetable slaw, in a medium bowl combine zucchini, radishes, pea pods, and chives. Stir together vinegar, the remaining sesame oil, and remaining sugar. Drizzle over the zucchini mixture; toss gently to coat. Serve fish with slaw. Makes 4 servings.

NUTRITION FACTS PER SERVING:

141 calories
3 g total fat
1 g saturated fat
60 mg cholesterol
363 mg sodium
6 g carbohydrate
1 g fiber
24 g protein

155

grilled tuna with wilted spinach

Tuna bears watching as it cooks because it easily can dry out. Here, a beautiful bed of fresh spinach and tiny grape tomatoes is quick-cooked in a skillet on the grill right next to the tuna—so you can keep your fish under a watchful eye.

INGREDIENTS

1¼ pounds fresh skinless tuna fillets, about ¾ inch thick
3 tablespoons balsamic vinegar
1 tablespoon olive oil
¼ teaspoon salt
¼ teaspoon garlic pepper

1 medium red onion, cut into ¼-inch slices
6 cups torn spinach or mixed salad greens
2 cups grape tomatoes or cherry tomatoes, halved
2 tablespoons water

Prep time: 15 minutes
Marinating time: 5 minutes
Grilling time: 6 minutes

DIRECTIONS

1. Rinse fish; pat dry. Cut fish into 4 serving-size pieces. Lightly sprinkle with salt and pepper; place in a shallow dish. For marinade, in a small bowl stir together the vinegar, oil, ¼ teaspoon salt, and garlic pepper. Pour 2 tablespoons of the marinade over fish. Cover and marinate at room temperature for 5 minutes. Drain the fish, reserving the marinade.

2. Place fish in a well-greased wire grill basket, tucking under any thin edges. Grill fish and onion slices on the rack of an uncovered grill directly over medium heat for 6 to 9 minutes or until fish flakes easily when tested with a fork and onion is tender, turning and brushing fish and onion once with reserved marinade halfway through cooking.

3. While the fish and onion are cooking, in a heavy large skillet* toss together the spinach, tomatoes, and water. Place skillet on grill rack next to fish. Cook for 3 to 4 minutes or until spinach begins to wilt, stirring occasionally. Transfer spinach mixture to a serving platter; top with fish and onion slices. Drizzle with remaining vinegar mixture. Makes 4 servings.

*Note: The heat from the grill will blacken the outside of the skillet, so use a cast-iron or old skillet.

NUTRITION FACTS PER SERVING:

299 calories
11 g total fat
2 g saturated fat
59 mg cholesterol
315 mg sodium
10 g carbohydrate
3 g fiber
39 g protein

seared tuna with grapefruit-orange relish

INGREDIENTS

- 2 teaspoons sherry vinegar or white wine vinegar
- 2 teaspoons soy sauce
- ½ teaspoon grated fresh ginger
- 1 tablespoon olive oil
- 1 medium grapefruit, peeled and sectioned
- 1 medium orange, peeled and sectioned
- 2 tablespoons finely chopped red onion
- 2 tablespoons snipped fresh cilantro
- 4 4-ounce fresh tuna steaks, cut ¾ inch thick
- 2 teaspoons olive oil
- Fresh cilantro sprigs (optional)

Tuna steak stays moist and flavorful when cooked as quickly as possible. Pan-searing over high heat is ideal—it seals the juices on the inside and gives the outside an irresistible caramel-colored crust.

Prep time: 20 minutes
Cooking time: 6 minutes

DIRECTIONS

1. For citrus relish, in a small bowl combine vinegar, soy sauce, and ginger. Whisk in the 1 tablespoon olive oil. Cut grapefruit sections into thirds and orange sections in half. Stir fruit pieces, red onion, and the snipped cilantro into vinegar mixture. Set aside.

2. Rinse fish; pat dry. In a large skillet heat the 2 teaspoons olive oil over medium-high heat. Add fish and cook for 6 to 9 minutes or until fish flakes easily when tested with a fork, gently turning once halfway through cooking. Sprinkle with salt and pepper. Serve the fish with citrus relish. If desired, garnish with cilantro sprigs. Makes 4 servings.

NUTRITION FACTS PER SERVING:

256 calories
12 g total fat
2 g saturated fat
47 mg cholesterol
287 mg sodium
7 g carbohydrate
1 g fiber
29 g protein

When shopping for fresh fish,

choose only fish that has a mild smell, not a strong odor. If you're buying fresh fillets or steaks, choose ones that appear moist and recently cut. Fresh fish is very perishable, so it's best to cook it the same day you buy it. If that's not possible, store fish in the coldest part of the refrigerator (usually the bottom shelf) for up to 2 days, or freeze it. Be sure that it is properly wrapped in moisture-and-vaporproof material.

157

grilled swordfish with spicy tomato sauce

This vibrant and fresh example of the best of fusion cooking combines two popular Sicilian foods, swordfish and a spicy, fresh tomato sauce, with couscous, a North African favorite.

INGREDIENTS

- 4 5-ounce fresh swordfish steaks, cut 1 inch thick
- 4 teaspoons cooking oil
- ¼ teaspoon salt
- ¼ teaspoon black pepper
- ¼ cup chopped onion
- 1 small fresh serrano or jalapeño pepper, seeded and finely chopped (see tip)
- ½ teaspoon bottled minced garlic
- ½ teaspoon ground turmeric
- ¼ teaspoon ground coriander
- 1½ cups chopped plum tomatoes
- ¼ teaspoon salt
- 1 tablespoon snipped fresh cilantro
- Hot cooked couscous (optional)

When handling fresh jalapeño peppers or other fresh chili peppers, wear rubber or plastic gloves to prevent skin burns. Disposable plastic gloves are ideal and inexpensive. You can purchase them in pharmacies and paint stores. If skin burns should occur, wash the area well with soapy water. If the juices come in contact with the eyes, flush them with cool water to neutralize the chili pepper oil.

Prep time: 15 minutes
Grilling time: 8 minutes

DIRECTIONS

1. Rinse fish; pat dry. Drizzle 2 teaspoons of the oil over fish. Sprinkle with ¼ teaspoon salt and black pepper. Grill fish on a greased rack of an uncovered grill directly over medium heat for 8 to 12 minutes or until fish flakes easily when tested with a fork, gently turning fish once halfway through cooking.

2. Meanwhile, for the spicy tomato sauce, in a medium skillet heat the remaining oil. Add the onion, serrano pepper, garlic, turmeric, and coriander. Cook about 2 minutes or until onion is tender. Stir in tomatoes and ¼ teaspoon salt. Cook for 2 to 3 minutes more or until tomatoes are heated through. Remove from heat; stir in cilantro. Serve spicy tomato sauce over fish. If desired, serve with couscous. Makes 4 servings.

NUTRITION FACTS PER SERVING:

237 calories
11 g total fat
2 g saturated fat
56 mg cholesterol
402 mg sodium
5 g carbohydrate
1 g fiber
29 g protein

INGREDIENTS

1 **pound fresh orange roughy or red snapper fillets, about ³/₄ inch thick**

1 **14½-ounce can reduced-sodium chicken broth**

2 **teaspoons finely shredded lemon peel**

⅛ **teaspoon black pepper**

1 **pound asparagus spears, trimmed and cut in half**

1 **medium yellow sweet pepper, cut into bite-size strips**

2 **cups hot cooked couscous or rice**

4 **teaspoons cornstarch**

2 **tablespoons snipped fresh chives**

poached orange roughy with lemon sauce

Despite its speed, poaching is an inherently gentle way to cook. It's also one of the lightest and most healthful. Here, poaching in lemon- and pepper-infused broth preserves the delicate flavor and texture of one of the most popular kinds of white fish.

Start to finish: 20 minutes

DIRECTIONS

1. Rinse fish; pat dry. Cut into 4 serving-size pieces.

2. In a 10-inch skillet combine 1 cup of the broth, the lemon peel, and black pepper. Bring to boiling; reduce heat. Carefully add the fish and asparagus. Cook, covered, over medium-low heat for 4 minutes. Add sweet pepper strips. Cook, covered, about 2 minutes more or until fish flakes easily when tested with a fork. Using a slotted spatula, remove the fish and vegetables, reserving liquid in skillet. Spoon the couscous onto a serving platter; arrange the fish and vegetables on top of couscous. Cover and keep warm.

3. For sauce, stir together the remaining broth and cornstarch. Stir into liquid in skillet. Cook and stir until thickened and bubbly. Cook and stir for 2 minutes more. Stir in chives. Spoon sauce over fish, vegetables, and couscous. Makes 4 servings.

NUTRITION FACTS PER SERVING:

249 calories
2 g total fat
0 g saturated fat
60 mg cholesterol
390 mg sodium
29 g carbohydrate
6 g fiber
28 g protein

159

blackened catfish with roasted potatoes

Catch a pan-fried Cajun classic and cook it on your grill! This version of a Southern favorite is served alongside tiny new potatoes, carrots, and onion roasted in olive oil and zippy hot pepper sauce.

INGREDIENTS

- 1 tablespoon olive oil
- ¼ teaspoon salt
  Several dashes bottled hot pepper sauce
- 1½ pounds tiny new potatoes, thinly sliced
- 4 medium carrots, thinly sliced
- 1 medium green sweet pepper, cut into thin strips
- 1 medium onion, sliced
- 4 4- to 5-ounce fresh or frozen catfish or red snapper fillets, ½ to 1 inch thick
- ½ teaspoon Cajun seasoning
  Nonstick cooking spray
- 1 tablespoon snipped fresh chervil or parsley

Prep time: 20 minutes
Grilling time: 35 minutes

DIRECTIONS

1. Fold a 48×18-inch piece of heavy foil in half to make a 24×18-inch rectangle. In a large bowl combine the oil, salt, and pepper sauce. Add the potatoes, carrots, sweet pepper, and onion; toss gently to coat. Place vegetables in center of foil. Bring up 2 opposite edges of foil; seal with a double fold. Fold remaining ends to completely enclose vegetables, leaving space for steam to build.

2. Grill the vegetables on the rack of an uncovered grill directly over medium heat for 35 to 40 minutes or until potatoes and carrots are tender.

3. Meanwhile, thaw fish, if frozen. Rinse fish; pat dry. Sprinkle both sides of fish with Cajun seasoning and coat lightly with cooking spray. Place fish in a well-greased wire grill basket, tucking under any thin edges. While the vegetables are grilling, add fish to grill. Grill until fish flakes easily when tested with a fork (allow 4 to 6 minutes per ½-inch thickness of fish), turning basket once halfway through cooking. To serve, sprinkle fish and vegetables with chervil. Makes 4 servings.

NUTRITION FACTS PER SERVING:

352 calories
6 g total fat
1 g saturated fat
42 mg cholesterol
266 mg sodium
48 g carbohydrate
5 g fiber
28 g protein

grilled rosemary trout with lemon butter

INGREDIENTS

- 4 teaspoons butter, softened
- 1 tablespoon finely chopped shallot or onion
- 1 teaspoon finely shredded lemon peel
- 2 fresh rainbow trout, pan dressed* and boned (8 to 10 ounces each)
- 1 tablespoon snipped fresh rosemary
- 1 tablespoon lemon juice
- 2 teaspoons olive oil
- 2 medium tomatoes, halved crosswise

Taste the delicious reason lemon and butter are the timeless, classic accompaniments to fish! This recipe is so simple you'll want to tote it along on your next fishing trip.

Prep time: 15 minutes
Grilling time: 6 minutes

DIRECTIONS

1. In a small bowl stir together the butter, half of the shallot, and the shredded lemon peel. Sprinkle with salt and coarsely ground pepper. Set aside.

2. Rinse fish; pat dry. Spread each fish open, skin side down. Rub remaining shallot and the rosemary onto fish; sprinkle with additional salt and pepper and drizzle with lemon juice and oil.

3. In a charcoal grill arrange hot coals in bottom of an uncovered grill. Place a greased 12-inch cast-iron skillet directly on coals; preheat skillet. (For a gas grill, place skillet on grill rack; preheat grill and skillet. Reduce heat to medium.) Place fish, skin sides down, in hot skillet. Grill for 6 to 8 minutes or until fish flakes easily when tested with a fork. Meanwhile, place the tomatoes, cut sides up, in skillet next to fish; dot each with ¼ teaspoon of the butter mixture. Grill about 5 minutes or until tomatoes are heated through.

4. Remove skillet from the grill. Cut each fish in half lengthwise. In a small saucepan melt the remaining butter mixture; serve with fish and tomatoes. Makes 4 servings.

*Note: A pan-dressed fish has had the scales and internal organs removed; often the head, fins, and tail also have been removed.

Prefer to avoid using a skillet?

Place the fish, then the tomatoes on a greased rack of an uncovered grill directly over medium heat. Grill as directed.

NUTRITION FACTS PER SERVING:

206 calories
10 g total fat
3 g saturated fat
75 mg cholesterol
109 mg sodium
4 g carbohydrate
1 g fiber
24 g protein

pan-seared scallops

This is a flash in the pan! Sweet scallops are given a Cajun-flavored crust, then tossed with balsamic vinegar-dressed spinach and crisp-cooked bacon. Serve with corn bread and cold beer and you have a meal that's both homey and elegant in no time flat.

INGREDIENTS

1 pound fresh sea scallops
2 tablespoons all-purpose flour
1 to 2 teaspoons blackened steak seasoning or Cajun seasoning
1 tablespoon cooking oil

1 10-ounce package prewashed spinach
1 tablespoon water
2 tablespoons balsamic vinegar
¼ cup cooked bacon pieces

Start to finish: 20 minutes

DIRECTIONS

1. Rinse scallops; pat dry. In a plastic bag combine flour and steak seasoning. Add scallops; toss gently to coat. In a large skillet cook the scallops in hot oil over medium heat for 3 to 5 minutes or until browned and opaque, turning once halfway through cooking. Remove scallops.

2. Add spinach to skillet; sprinkle with water. Cook, covered, over medium-high heat about 2 minutes or until spinach starts to wilt. Add vinegar; toss to coat evenly. Return scallops; heat through. Sprinkle with bacon. Makes 4 servings.

NUTRITION FACTS PER SERVING:

158 calories
6 g total fat
1 g saturated fat
37 mg cholesterol
323 mg sodium
9 g carbohydrate
2 g fiber
18 g protein

thai-spiced scallops

In addition to the salty, sweet, sour, and spicy flavors that spark Thai cooking, this dish features one more: basil, with its peppery, clovelike flavor—and lots of it. These delicious scallops let you sample the whole spectrum of Thai tastes.

INGREDIENTS

- 1 pound fresh or frozen sea scallops
- 2 medium yellow summer squash and/or zucchini, quartered lengthwise and sliced ½ inch thick
- 1½ cups packaged peeled baby carrots
- ⅔ cup bottled sweet and sour sauce
- 2 tablespoons snipped fresh basil
- 1 teaspoon Thai seasoning or five-spice powder
- ½ teaspoon bottled minced garlic

Start to finish: 30 minutes

DIRECTIONS

1. Thaw scallops, if frozen. Fold a 36×18-inch piece of heavy foil in half to make an 18-inch square. Place squash and carrots in center of foil. Sprinkle lightly with salt and pepper. Bring up 2 opposite edges of foil; seal with a double fold. Fold remaining ends to completely enclose vegetables, leaving space for steam to build. Grill the vegetables on the rack of an uncovered grill directly over medium heat for 15 to 20 minutes or until the vegetables are crisp-tender, turning occasionally.

2. Meanwhile, for sauce, in a small bowl combine the sweet and sour sauce, basil, Thai seasoning, and garlic. Transfer ¼ cup of the sauce to another bowl for basting. Reserve remaining sauce until ready to serve.

3. Rinse scallops; pat dry. Halve any large scallops. On four 8- to 10-inch skewers thread scallops. Place kabobs on grill rack next to the vegetables the last 5 to 8 minutes of grilling or until scallops are opaque, turning and brushing once with basting sauce halfway through cooking. Serve the scallops and vegetables with the remaining sauce. Makes 4 servings.

NUTRITION FACTS PER SERVING:

168 calories
1 g total fat
0 g saturated fat
34 mg cholesterol
370 mg sodium
25 g carbohydrate
3 g fiber
16 g protein

163

paella-style shrimp & couscous

Save time-consuming Spanish paella—made with saffron, seafood, and rice—for a weekend cooking adventure. As a quick weeknight dish, consider this curried version, made with colorful vegetables, curry powder, and couscous.

INGREDIENTS

1 14½-ounce can chicken broth

1 teaspoon curry powder

¼ teaspoon bottled hot pepper sauce

1 12-ounce package frozen peeled and deveined shrimp

1 cup quick-cooking couscous

1 6-ounce jar marinated artichoke hearts, drained and coarsely chopped

¾ cup frozen peas

1 cup cherry tomatoes, halved

Start to finish: 20 minutes

DIRECTIONS

1. In a large saucepan bring the broth, curry powder, and pepper sauce to boiling. Add the frozen shrimp. Return just to boiling; reduce heat. Simmer, uncovered, for 1 to 3 minutes or until shrimp turn pink.

2. Stir in the couscous, artichoke hearts, and peas. Cover and remove from heat. Let stand about 5 minutes or until liquid is absorbed. Stir the tomatoes into shrimp mixture. Makes 4 servings.

NUTRITION FACTS PER SERVING:

321 calories
5 g total fat
0 g saturated fat
131 mg cholesterol
639 mg sodium
46 g carbohydrate
9 g fiber
24 g protein

164

thai shrimp & fresh vegetable rice

One great marinade makes an unforgettable meal. If you have time, let the shrimp soak up the lime, soy sauce, and ginger flavors for up to two hours before it's stirred into rice studded with asparagus, sweet red pepper, and peanuts.

INGREDIENTS

- 1 pound fresh or frozen medium shrimp in shells
- 2 tablespoons lime juice
- 4 teaspoons soy sauce
- 1 fresh jalapeño pepper, seeded and finely chopped (see tip, page 158)
- 1 teaspoon grated fresh ginger
- 1 clove garlic, minced
- 1 tablespoon cooking oil
- 1 pound asparagus spears, trimmed and bias-sliced into 1-inch pieces
- 1 small red sweet pepper, cut into thin bite-size strips
- 3 cups hot cooked rice
- ¼ cup chopped peanuts

Start to finish: 35 minutes

DIRECTIONS

1. Thaw shrimp, if frozen. Peel and devein the shrimp, leaving tails intact. Rinse shrimp; pat dry. Place shrimp in a medium bowl. For marinade, combine lime juice, soy sauce, jalapeño pepper, ginger, and garlic. Pour over shrimp; toss to coat. Cover and marinate at room temperature for 15 minutes or in refrigerator up to 2 hours, stirring occasionally. Drain shrimp well, reserving marinade.

2. Pour oil into a wok or large skillet. Preheat over medium-high heat (add more oil if necessary during cooking). Stir-fry shrimp in hot oil for 2 to 3 minutes or until shrimp turn pink. Remove from wok; cover and keep warm. Add asparagus and pepper strips to wok; stir-fry for 2 to 3 minutes or until crisp-tender. Add reserved marinade to wok and bring just to boiling. Stir in cooked rice and peanuts.

3. To serve, transfer rice mixture to 4 bowls or dinner plates. Spoon shrimp on top. Makes 4 servings.

To trim fresh asparagus easily,

snap off and discard the woody bases from the asparagus spears. Wash the asparagus just before using. If you like, you can remove the scales on asparagus stalks. Just use a vegetable peeler when you clean the asparagus.

NUTRITION FACTS PER SERVING:

331 calories
9 g total fat
1 g saturated fat
131 mg cholesterol
571 mg sodium
41 g carbohydrate
2 g fiber
22 g protein

pepper shrimp in peanut sauce

Who could resist this dish? Sweet and spicy peanut sauce dresses up whimsical bow-tie pasta, colorful and crisp sweet peppers, and, best of all, the special treat of grilled shrimp.

INGREDIENTS

- 1 pound fresh or frozen medium shrimp in shells
- 8 ounces dried bow-tie pasta or linguine
- ½ cup water
- ¼ cup orange marmalade
- 2 tablespoons peanut butter
- 2 tablespoons soy sauce
- 2 teaspoons cornstarch
- ¼ teaspoon crushed red pepper
- 2 medium red, yellow, and/or green sweet peppers, cut into 1-inch pieces
- Chopped peanuts (optional)

Start to finish: 35 minutes

DIRECTIONS

1. Thaw shrimp, if frozen. Peel and devein the shrimp, leaving tails intact. Rinse shrimp; pat dry. Set aside. Cook the pasta according to package directions; drain. Return pasta to saucepan and keep warm.

2. Meanwhile, for sauce, in a small saucepan stir together water, orange marmalade, peanut butter, soy sauce, cornstarch, and crushed red pepper. Bring to boiling; reduce heat. Cook and stir for 2 minutes. Remove from heat and keep warm.

3. On eight 12-inch skewers alternately thread shrimp and sweet peppers. Grill kabobs on the rack of an uncovered grill directly over medium heat for 6 to 8 minutes or until shrimp turn pink, turning once halfway through cooking.

4. To serve, add shrimp and peppers to the cooked pasta. Add the sauce; toss gently to coat. If desired, sprinkle each serving with peanuts. Makes 4 servings.

NUTRITION FACTS PER SERVING:

382 calories
7 g total fat
1 g saturated fat
180 mg cholesterol
718 mg sodium
57 g carbohydrate
3 g fiber
24 g protein

INGREDIENTS

- 1 pound fresh large shrimp in shells (about 16 shrimp)
- 8 slices turkey bacon, halved crosswise
- 2 red, yellow, and/or green sweet peppers, cut into 1-inch pieces
- 2 teaspoons finely shredded orange or blood orange peel
- 2 tablespoons orange or blood orange juice
- 2 teaspoons snipped fresh rosemary
- 2 cups hot cooked couscous or rice
- 1 cup cooked or canned black beans, rinsed and drained

rosemary-orange shrimp kabobs

Bacon-wrapped shrimp sounds decadent, but it can be everyday fare when you use light turkey bacon. Here, the bacon gives the shrimp a subtle smokiness, and a brushed-on herbed orange juice adds a pleasing sweetness.

Prep time: 20 minutes
Grilling time: 8 minutes

DIRECTIONS

1. Peel and devein shrimp, leaving tails intact. Rinse shrimp; pat dry. Wrap each shrimp in a half slice of bacon. On long skewers alternately thread shrimp and sweet pepper pieces. In a small bowl combine 1 teaspoon of the orange peel, the orange juice, and rosemary. Brush over kabobs.

2. Grill kabobs on a lightly greased rack of an uncovered grill directly over medium heat for 8 to 10 minutes or until bacon is crisp and shrimp turn pink, turning once halfway through cooking.

3. Meanwhile, in a medium saucepan stir together cooked couscous, beans, and the remaining orange peel; heat through. Serve with the shrimp and peppers. Makes 4 servings.

Blood oranges, also called sanguines or Moro oranges, are becoming increasingly available—and that's a good thing. Sweeter and juicier than most oranges, they get their name from their mottled, deep-red flesh and blushing-red skin. They're wonderful for eating out of hand and, when used in a marinade, impart a rosy hue to foods.

NUTRITION FACTS PER SERVING:

310 calories
7 g total fat
2 g saturated fat
149 mg cholesterol
563 mg sodium
36 g carbohydrate
2 g fiber
26 g protein

asian grilled salmon salad

Fennel, one of the oldest cultivated plants, is used whole to spice sausages, crushed for tomato sauces, and often is added to poaching liquids for fish. Here, it is pressed into salmon steaks before grilling, making a toothsome base for dressed vegetables.

INGREDIENTS

- 4   6- to 8-ounce fresh salmon fillets or steaks, about 1 inch thick
- 1   pound asparagus spears, trimmed
- 1   tablespoon garlic-flavored oil or olive oil
- 1   teaspoon fennel seed, crushed
- 1   head Bibb lettuce, separated into leaves
- 1   medium tomato, cut into thin wedges
- 1   cup fresh enoki mushrooms (2 ounces)
- 1   recipe Asian Dressing

Start to finish: 25 minutes

DIRECTIONS

1. Rinse fish; pat dry. Brush both sides of fish and the asparagus spears lightly with oil. Press fennel seed onto both sides of fish.

2. Place fish on a greased rack of an uncovered grill directly over medium heat. Place asparagus on a piece of heavy foil on grill rack next to fish. Grill for 8 to 12 minutes or until fish flakes easily when tested with a fork and asparagus is tender, gently turning the fish and asparagus once halfway through cooking.

3. Meanwhile, line 4 dinner plates with lettuce leaves. Place fish on top of lettuce. Arrange asparagus, tomato wedges, and enoki mushrooms around fish. Drizzle with Asian Dressing. Makes 4 servings.

Asian Dressing: In a screw-top jar combine 1 tablespoon salad oil, 1 tablespoon rice vinegar, 1 tablespoon soy sauce, 1 teaspoon toasted sesame oil, ¼ teaspoon sugar, and ¼ teaspoon grated fresh ginger or ½ teaspoon chopped pickled ginger. Cover and shake well.

NUTRITION FACTS PER SERVING:

255 calories
13 g total fat
2 g saturated fat
31 mg cholesterol
368 mg sodium
7 g carbohydrate
2 g fiber
28 g protein

INGREDIENTS

- ¼ cup honey
- ¼ cup reduced-sodium soy sauce
- 1 teaspoon toasted sesame oil
- ½ teaspoon crushed red pepper
- 4 5-ounce fresh tuna steaks, cut ½ to 1 inch thick
- 12 cups mesclun or torn mixed bitter salad greens (about 8 ounces)
- 10 to 12 yellow or red pear-shaped tomatoes, halved

honey-glazed tuna & greens

Here's fusion cuisine—a hybrid of Asian and European cooking—made fast. As the tuna is quick-grilled to seal in the juices, a soy-honey sauce with a touch of heat from crushed red pepper caramelizes, creating a beautiful and delicious glaze.

Start to finish: 20 minutes

DIRECTIONS

1. In a small bowl combine the honey, soy sauce, sesame oil, and red pepper. Set aside 2 tablespoons of the mixture to brush on fish and reserve the remaining for dressing.

2. Rinse fish; pat dry. Brush both sides of fish with the 2 tablespoons soy mixture. Grill fish on a greased rack of an uncovered grill directly over medium heat until fish flakes easily when tested with a fork (allow 4 to 6 minutes per ½-inch thickness of fish). Gently turn 1-inch-thick steaks over halfway through cooking. (Or, broil on the greased unheated rack of a broiler pan about 4 inches from the heat (allow 4 to 6 minutes per ½-inch thickness of fish). Gently turn 1-inch-thick steaks over halfway through cooking.)

3. Toss together mesclun and tomatoes; arrange on 4 dinner plates. Cut fish across the grain into ½-inch-wide slices; arrange on greens. Drizzle with the reserved soy mixture. Makes 4 servings.

Toasted sesame oil is a flavoring oil, not a cooking oil, and is used sparingly in recipes because of its strong flavor. Once opened, it should be kept in the refrigerator to prevent it from becoming rancid, and can be stored for up to a year.

NUTRITION FACTS PER SERVING:

279 calories
2 g total fat
0 g saturated fat
24 mg cholesterol
1,015 mg sodium
22 g carbohydrate
1 g fiber
42 g protein

169

fire-&-ice rice salad

Refreshing and bracing, this chilled salad plays both sweet and hot. Papaya and honey work with picante sauce and lime juice to bring a complex set of flavors to a canvas of white rice and shrimp.

INGREDIENTS

- 2 cups cooked white or brown rice, chilled
- 1 cup chopped papaya or nectarines
- 4 ounces cooked, peeled and deveined shrimp, chilled
- ⅓ cup picante sauce
- 2 tablespoons honey
- 2 tablespoons lime juice
- 2 teaspoons olive oil or salad oil
  Lettuce leaves
- 2 teaspoons snipped fresh cilantro or parsley

Start to finish: 15 minutes

DIRECTIONS

1. In a medium bowl combine cooked rice, papaya, and shrimp.

2. For dressing, in a small bowl combine picante sauce, honey, lime juice, and oil; mix well. Pour dressing over rice mixture; toss gently to coat. If desired, cover and refrigerate up to 6 hours.

3. To serve, line 3 dinner plates with lettuce. Top with shrimp mixture. Sprinkle with snipped cilantro. Makes 3 servings.

NUTRITION FACTS PER SERVING:

348 calories
4 g total fat
1 g saturated fat
74 mg cholesterol
286 mg sodium
64 g carbohydrate
1 g fiber
13 g protein

INGREDIENTS

- 12 slices party rye bread or 12 large crackers
- 3 tablespoons reduced-fat cream cheese (Neufchâtel)
- ⅓ cup shredded cucumber
- ⅓ cup thinly sliced red onion
  Fresh dill (optional)
- 6 cups torn mixed salad greens
- 12 ounces cooked, peeled and deveined shrimp
- ¼ cup bottled fat-free white wine vinaigrette salad dressing
- 1 tablespoon snipped fresh dill

scandinavian shrimp salad

Create a Scandinavian smorgasbord all on one plate with vinaigrette-coated shrimp flanked by rye bread topped with cream cheese and cucumber. A critical ingredient is fresh dill, which is sprinkled on top of the bread and snipped into the vinaigrette.

Start to finish: 25 minutes

DIRECTIONS

1. Spread bread slices with cream cheese; top with cucumber and onion. If desired, sprinkle with dill.

2. Divide salad greens among 4 salad bowls or dinner plates; top with shrimp. Stir together salad dressing and the 1 tablespoon dill; drizzle over salads. If desired, garnish with additional fresh dill. Serve with rye bread slices. Makes 4 servings.

NUTRITION FACTS PER SERVING:

218 calories
5 g total fat
2 g saturated fat
174 mg cholesterol
641 mg sodium
20 g carbohydrate
1 g fiber
23 g protein

171

shrimp & tropical fruit

Fruit cocktail goes uptown! With the addition of sweet and savory barbecued shrimp, a fresh-fruit salad of pineapple, papaya, and kiwi fruit becomes a whole meal that hints at the warmth, sun, and fun of a tropical isle.

INGREDIENTS

- 1¼ pounds fresh or frozen jumbo shrimp in shells
- 1 cup bottled barbecue sauce
- ⅔ cup unsweetened pineapple juice
- 2 tablespoons cooking oil
- 4 teaspoons grated fresh ginger or 1½ teaspoons ground ginger
- ¼ of a fresh pineapple, sliced crosswise
- 1 medium papaya, peeled, seeded, and cut up
- 3 medium kiwi fruit, peeled and cut up

Prep time: 25 minutes
Grilling time: 10 minutes

DIRECTIONS

1. Thaw shrimp, if frozen. Peel and devein the shrimp, leaving tails intact. Rinse shrimp; pat dry. On six 10- to 12-inch skewers thread shrimp. For sauce, in a medium bowl stir together barbecue sauce, pineapple juice, oil, and ginger. Brush shrimp with sauce.

2. Grill shrimp on a greased rack of an uncovered grill directly over medium heat for 10 to 12 minutes or until shrimp turn pink, turning once and brushing occasionally with sauce up to the last 5 minutes of cooking. Place pineapple on grill rack next to shrimp the last 5 minutes of grilling, turning once halfway through cooking.

3. Serve shrimp and pineapple with papaya and kiwi fruit. In a small saucepan bring the remaining sauce to boiling. Boil gently, uncovered, for 1 minute; cool slightly. Pass for dipping. Makes 6 servings.

NUTRITION FACTS PER SERVING:

199 calories
6 g total fat
1 g saturated fat
116 mg cholesterol
474 mg sodium
21 g carbohydrate
1 g fiber
14 g protein

INGREDIENTS

- 2½ cups dried gemelli pasta (8 ounces)
- 6 cups shredded Chinese cabbage and/or shredded romaine
- 4 green onions, thinly sliced
- ¼ cup rice vinegar or white wine vinegar
- 3 tablespoons salad oil
- 2 tablespoons soy sauce

- 1 tablespoon honey
- ½ teaspoon crushed red pepper
- 12 ounces fresh sea scallops or peeled and deveined medium shrimp
- 2 tablespoons black or white sesame seed
- 4 romaine leaves (optional)

warm scallop salad with toasted sesame dressing

Sesame seeds turn nutty, crunchy, and golden in minutes in a skillet. If you have access to an Asian market, you can buy them already toasted to save a step.

Start to finish: 30 minutes

DIRECTIONS

1. Cook pasta according to package directions; drain in colander. Rinse with cold water; drain again. In a large bowl toss together the pasta, cabbage, and green onions. Divide mixture among 4 dinner plates.

2. Meanwhile, for dressing, in a small bowl stir together vinegar, 2 tablespoons of the oil, the soy sauce, honey, and crushed red pepper. Set aside.

3. Rinse scallops; pat dry. Set aside. In a skillet cook and stir the sesame seed over medium heat about 5 minutes or until toasted. Remove from skillet.

4. Add the remaining 1 tablespoon oil to skillet; add scallops. Cook and stir for 1 to 3 minutes or until scallops are opaque. If desired, place romaine leaves on top of pasta mixture on plates. Place the scallops in romaine leaves. Drizzle dressing over salads and sprinkle with toasted sesame seed. Makes 4 servings.

Sea scallops are the larger of the two most widely available varieties of this kind of shellfish—bay scallops are the smaller variety. Scallops should be firm, sweet smelling, and free of excess cloudy liquid. Refrigerate shucked scallops covered with their own liquid in a closed container for up to 2 days.

NUTRITION FACTS PER SERVING:

425 calories
14 g total fat
2 g saturated fat
25 mg cholesterol
656 mg sodium
54 g carbohydrate
2 g fiber
21 g protein

seared scallop & spinach salad

Give an old favorite a new lease on life by adding sea scallops to the usual lineup in a bacon-spinach salad. The scallops are dusted with chili powder and red pepper before searing—a guaranteed wake-up call for eaters.

INGREDIENTS

- 8 ounces fresh sea scallops
- 8 cups torn spinach
- 2 cups sliced fresh mushrooms
- 1 cup shredded carrots
- 4 slices bacon, cut into ½-inch pieces
- ½ teaspoon chili powder
- ⅛ to ¼ teaspoon ground red pepper
- ¼ to ⅓ cup chutney, snipped
- ¼ cup water
- 1 to 2 teaspoons Dijon-style mustard

Start to finish: 30 minutes

DIRECTIONS

1. Rinse scallops; pat dry. Set aside. In a large bowl toss together spinach, mushrooms, and carrots; set aside.

2. In a large nonstick skillet cook bacon over medium heat until crisp. Drain the bacon, reserving 1 tablespoon drippings in the skillet.

3. In a medium bowl combine chili powder and ground red pepper. Add the scallops; toss gently to coat.

4. Add scallops to the reserved bacon drippings in

skillet. Cook over medium heat for 1 to 3 minutes or until scallops are opaque. Remove scallops from skillet; set aside. Add chutney, water, and mustard to skillet. Cook over medium-high heat until hot and bubbly. Spoon over spinach mixture, tossing gently to coat.

5. Divide spinach mixture among 4 dinner plates. Top with scallops. Sprinkle with bacon. Makes 4 servings.

NUTRITION FACTS PER SERVING:

160 calories
4 g total fat
1 g saturated fat
22 mg cholesterol
324 mg sodium
19 g carbohydrate
5 g fiber
14 g protein

INGREDIENTS

2 cups cut-up fresh fruit (such as pineapple, cantaloupe, honeydew melon, or strawberries)

1 6-ounce package frozen crabmeat, thawed

¾ cup sliced celery

¼ cup light mayonnaise dressing or salad dressing

¼ cup plain low-fat yogurt

2 tablespoons fat-free milk

½ teaspoon curry powder

4 cups torn mixed salad greens
Fresh raspberries (optional)

curried crab salad

Dispel the myth: Not all curries are hot. Packaged curry powder purchased at a grocery store is generally a sweet mixture of as many as 20 spices. It does magical things when mixed in a sauce and added to crabmeat.

Start to finish: 20 minutes

DIRECTIONS

1. In a large bowl combine the fresh fruit, crabmeat, and celery; set aside.

2. For dressing, in a large bowl stir together the mayonnaise dressing, yogurt, milk, and curry powder.

3. Divide salad greens among 3 dinner plates. Top with crab mixture and drizzle with dressing. If desired, sprinkle with raspberries. Makes 3 servings.

NUTRITION FACTS PER SERVING:

200 calories
9 g total fat
2 g saturated fat
58 mg cholesterol
361 mg sodium
17 g carbohydrate
2 g fiber
14 g protein

175

quick cioppino

San Francisco's Italian immigrants are credited with creating the original cioppino (chuh-PEE-noh). This version of the delicious fish stew is very easy to make.

INGREDIENTS

- 6 ounces fresh cod fillets
- 6 ounces peeled and deveined fresh shrimp
- 1 medium green sweet pepper, cut into thin bite-size strips
- 1 large onion, chopped
- 2 cloves garlic, minced
- 1 tablespoon olive oil or cooking oil
- 2 14½-ounce cans Italian-style stewed tomatoes
- ½ cup water
- 3 tablespoons snipped fresh basil

Start to finish: 20 minutes

DIRECTIONS

1. Rinse fish and shrimp; pat dry. Cut fish into 1-inch pieces; set aside. In a large saucepan cook sweet pepper, onion, and garlic in hot oil until tender. Stir in undrained tomatoes and water. Bring to boiling.

2. Stir in fish and shrimp. Return to boiling; reduce heat. Simmer, covered, for 2 to 3 minutes or until fish flakes easily when tested with a fork and shrimp turn pink. Stir in the basil. Makes 4 servings.

NUTRITION FACTS PER SERVING:

176 calories
4 g total fat
1 g saturated fat
82 mg cholesterol
819 mg sodium
19 g carbohydrate
1 g fiber
17 g protein

fish provençale

The sweet essence of fresh fennel blends nicely with fish, tomatoes, garlic, and onion. This orange-scented soup tastes as good as it smells.

INGREDIENTS

- 8 ounces fresh or frozen skinless haddock, grouper, or halibut fillets
- 1 small fennel bulb
- 3 cups vegetable broth or chicken broth
- 1 large onion, finely chopped
- 1 cup cut-up yellow summer squash and/or zucchini

- 1 cup dry white wine
- 1 teaspoon finely shredded orange or lemon peel
- 3 cloves garlic, minced
- 2 cups chopped tomatoes or one 14½-ounce can diced tomatoes
- 2 tablespoons snipped fresh thyme
  Snipped fresh thyme (optional)

Start to finish: 30 minutes

DIRECTIONS

1. Thaw fish, if frozen. Rinse fish; pat dry. Cut fish into 1-inch pieces; set aside.

2. Cut off and discard the upper stalks of fennel. Remove any wilted outer layers; cut a thin slice from base. Wash fennel; cut in half lengthwise and thinly slice.

3. In a large saucepan combine fennel, vegetable broth, onion, squash, wine, orange peel, and garlic. Bring to boiling; reduce heat. Simmer, covered, for 10 minutes. Stir in fish pieces, tomatoes, and 2 tablespoons thyme. Cook for 2 to 3 minutes more or until fish flakes easily when tested with a fork. If desired, garnish with additional snipped thyme. Makes 4 servings.

Adding wine to soup

often enhances its flavor. Sherry or Madeira blends well with veal or chicken soup. A strongly flavored soup with beef benefits from a tablespoon of dry red table wine. And dry white table wine adds zest to fish soup, crab or lobster bisque, or creamy chowder. Be thrifty with salt in a soup to which wine is added, as the wine intensifies saltiness.

NUTRITION FACTS PER SERVING:

156 calories
3 g total fat
0 g saturated fat
18 mg cholesterol
752 mg sodium
15 g carbohydrate
8 g fiber
14 g protein

lemon & scallop soup

Long-stemmed, tiny-capped, and slightly crunchy, enoki mushrooms play an important role in Asian cooking. These elegant mushrooms have a light, fruity flavor. Toss a few into the soup at the last moment, as they will toughen if heated.

INGREDIENTS

- 12 ounces fresh or frozen bay scallops
- 5 cups reduced-sodium chicken broth
- ½ cup dry white wine or reduced-sodium chicken broth
- 3 tablespoons snipped fresh cilantro
- 2 teaspoons finely shredded lemon peel
- ¼ teaspoon pepper
- 1 pound asparagus spears, trimmed and cut into bite-size pieces
- 1 cup fresh enoki mushrooms or shiitake mushrooms
- ½ cup sliced green onions
- 1 tablespoon lemon juice

Start to finish: 25 minutes

DIRECTIONS

1. Thaw scallops, if frozen. Rinse scallops; pat dry.

2. In a large saucepan combine the chicken broth, wine, cilantro, lemon peel, and pepper. Bring to boiling.

3. Add scallops, asparagus, shiitake mushrooms (if using), and onions. Return just to boiling; reduce heat.

4. Simmer, uncovered, for 3 to 5 minutes or until asparagus is tender and scallops are opaque. Remove saucepan from heat. Stir in the enoki mushrooms (if using) and lemon juice. Serve immediately. Makes 4 servings.

NUTRITION FACTS PER SERVING:

153 calories
2 g total fat
0 g saturated fat
28 mg cholesterol
940 mg sodium
10 g carbohydrate
2 g fiber
20 g protein

INGREDIENTS

- 8 ounces peeled and deveined fresh shrimp
- ½ cup thinly sliced green onions
- ⅓ cup chopped red sweet pepper
- 1 clove garlic, minced
- 1 teaspoon cooking oil
- 1 14½-ounce can reduced-sodium chicken broth
- ½ cup uncooked long grain rice

- 1 bay leaf
- ¼ teaspoon salt
- ⅛ teaspoon ground red pepper
- ⅛ teaspoon ground turmeric
- 8 ounces lean cooked pork, cut into ¾-inch cubes
- 1 cup frozen peas
- 2 teaspoons snipped fresh oregano

paella soup

Brighten the menu when you serve this colorful soup. From the root of a tropical plant, turmeric gives this rice, shrimp, and pork mixture an inviting yellow glow. Once applied as a perfume many years ago, turmeric is now used to flavor foods.

Start to finish: 35 minutes

DIRECTIONS

1. Rinse shrimp; pat dry. Set aside. In a large saucepan cook green onions, sweet pepper, and garlic in hot oil for 2 minutes.

2. Stir in chicken broth, rice, bay leaf, salt, red pepper, and turmeric. Bring to boiling; reduce heat. Simmer, covered, for 15 minutes. Stir in shrimp, cooked pork, and peas. Simmer, covered, for 2 to 3 minutes more or until shrimp turn pink. Remove bay leaf. Stir in fresh oregano. Makes 4 servings.

NUTRITION FACTS PER SERVING:

324 calories
10 g total fat
3 g saturated fat
139 mg cholesterol
879 mg sodium
25 g carbohydrate
2 g fiber
31 g protein

bayou shrimp soup

Enjoy the flavor of gumbo without all the fuss. This stew incorporates familiar gumbo ingredients—rice, tomatoes, sausage, and shrimp—minus the long cooking time.

INGREDIENTS

- 8 ounces cooked andouille or other smoked sausage links, thinly sliced
- 1 medium green sweet pepper, chopped
- 1 medium onion, chopped
- 1 14½-ounce can reduced-sodium chicken broth
- 2 tablespoons snipped fresh thyme or 1½ teaspoons dried thyme, crushed
- 1 tablespoon steak sauce
- ¼ teaspoon crushed red pepper (optional)
- 8 ounces frozen peeled, cooked shrimp
- 2 cups chopped tomatoes
- 1½ cups cooked rice

When buying shrimp, follow these pointers:

Since most shrimp available today has been previously frozen, always check to see if defrosted shrimp is firm and shiny. If purchasing frozen shrimp, make sure it is frozen solidly and has little or no odor, no brown spots, and no signs of freezer burn, indicated by a white, dry appearance around the edges.

Start to finish: 35 minutes

DIRECTIONS

1. In a large saucepan cook the sausage, sweet pepper, and onion over medium-high heat for 6 to 7 minutes or until vegetables are tender, stirring frequently. Add chicken broth, dried thyme (if using), and steak sauce. If not using andouille sausage, add the crushed red pepper.

2. Bring to boiling; reduce heat. Simmer, covered, for 10 minutes.

3. Add shrimp, tomatoes, cooked rice, and, if using, fresh thyme. Cook and stir until heated through. Makes 4 servings.

NUTRITION FACTS PER SERVING:

404 calories
20 g total fat
7 g saturated fat
149 mg cholesterol
1,345 mg sodium
27 g carbohydrate
2 g fiber
28 g protein

shrimp & greens soup

INGREDIENTS

12 ounces peeled and deveined fresh or frozen shrimp

1 large leek, sliced

2 cloves garlic, minced

1 tablespoon olive oil

3 14½-ounce cans reduced-sodium chicken broth or vegetable broth

1 tablespoon snipped fresh Italian flat-leaf parsley or regular parsley

1 tablespoon snipped fresh marjoram or thyme

¼ teaspoon lemon-pepper seasoning

2 cups shredded bok choy or spinach leaves

Although great any time of year, this fresh-tasting seafood soup is light enough to serve during the summer. The savory combination of shrimp, shredded bok choy, and leek is embellished with an accent of lemon pepper.

Start to finish: 30 minutes

DIRECTIONS

1. Thaw shrimp, if frozen. Rinse shrimp; pat dry. Set aside. In a large saucepan cook leek and garlic in hot oil over medium-high heat about 2 minutes or until leek is tender.

2. Carefully add the chicken broth, parsley, marjoram, and lemon-pepper seasoning. Bring to boiling; add shrimp. Return to boiling; reduce heat.

3. Simmer, uncovered, for 2 minutes. Stir in the bok choy. Cook about 1 minute more or until shrimp turn pink. Makes 4 servings.

NUTRITION FACTS PER SERVING:

147 calories
6 g total fat
1 g saturated fat
131 mg cholesterol
1,093 mg sodium
5 g carbohydrate
2 g fiber
18 g protein

chicken & shrimp tortilla soup

Your family will be intrigued when you sprinkle shreds of crisp-baked corn tortillas over the top of this eye-catching Southwestern soup. Make the tortilla shreds ahead of time and store them in an airtight container.

INGREDIENTS

- 6 ounces peeled and deveined fresh or frozen medium shrimp
- 1 recipe Crisp Tortilla Shreds
- 1 large onion, chopped
- 1 teaspoon cumin seed
- 1 tablespoon cooking oil
- 4½ cups reduced-sodium chicken broth
- 1 14½-ounce can Mexican-style stewed tomatoes
- 3 tablespoons snipped fresh cilantro
- 2 tablespoons lime juice
- 1⅔ cups shredded cooked chicken breast

Start to finish: 30 minutes

DIRECTIONS

1. Thaw shrimp, if frozen. Rinse shrimp; pat dry. Prepare Crisp Tortilla Shreds; set aside.

2. In a large saucepan cook onion and cumin seed in hot oil about 5 minutes or until onion is tender. Carefully add broth, undrained tomatoes, cilantro, and lime juice.

3. Bring to boiling; reduce heat. Simmer, covered, for 8 minutes. Stir in shrimp and chicken. Cook for 2 to 3 minutes more or until shrimp turn pink, stirring occasionally. Ladle into soup bowls. Top each serving with tortilla shreds. Makes 6 servings.

Crisp Tortilla Shreds:
Brush four 5½-inch corn tortillas with 1 tablespoon cooking oil. In a small bowl combine ½ teaspoon salt and ⅛ teaspoon pepper; sprinkle over tortillas. Cut tortillas into thin shreds. Arrange in a single layer on a baking sheet. Bake in a 350° oven about 8 minutes or until tortillas are crisp.

NUTRITION FACTS PER SERVING:

160 calories
5 g total fat
1 g saturated fat
80 mg cholesterol
794 mg sodium
8 g carbohydrate
0 g fiber
21 g protein

INGREDIENTS

- 2 medium onions, sliced
- 2 medium carrots, thinly sliced
- 1 tablespoon snipped fresh cilantro
- 2 teaspoons grated fresh ginger
- 2 cloves garlic, minced
- ½ teaspoon ground allspice
- 2 tablespoons margarine or butter
- 1 14½-ounce can chicken broth
- 1 15-ounce can pumpkin
- 1 cup milk
- 1 8-ounce package frozen, peeled cooked shrimp, thawed
- Fresh shrimp in shells, peeled, deveined, and cooked (optional)
- Plain low-fat yogurt or dairy sour cream (optional)
- Snipped fresh chives (optional)

spicy pumpkin & shrimp soup

During the week, convenience is key. Here's a way to turn a can of pumpkin into an exciting soup. Just the right blend of ginger, cilantro, allspice, and garlic complements the pumpkin for a terrific flavor.

It is unsafe to thaw fish, seafood, or any type of meat at room temperature. Thaw them in one of two ways:
- The best way to thaw is to place the unopened original container in the refrigerator overnight.
- Place wrapped package under cold running water until thawed.

Start to finish: 30 minutes

DIRECTIONS

1. In a covered large saucepan cook the onions, carrots, cilantro, ginger, garlic, and allspice in hot margarine for 10 to 12 minutes or until the vegetables are tender, stirring once or twice.

2. Transfer the mixture to a blender container or food processor bowl. Add ½ cup of the chicken broth. Cover and blend or process until nearly smooth.

3. In the same saucepan combine pumpkin, milk, and remaining broth. Stir in the blended vegetable mixture and the 8 ounces shrimp; heat through. If desired, on small skewers thread additional cooked shrimp. Ladle soup into soup bowls. If desired, top each serving with a spoonful of yogurt, a sprinkling of chives, and a shrimp skewer. Makes 4 servings.

NUTRITION FACTS PER SERVING:

222 calories
9 g total fat
2 g saturated fat
116 mg cholesterol
579 mg sodium
19 g carbohydrate
5 g fiber
18 g protein

oyster & corn chowder

If you think an oyster chowder will take too long to make, this soup will surprise you. Buy oysters already shucked from the seafood section of the supermarket. They cook in just 5 minutes to create a creamy jalapeño-spiced chowder.

INGREDIENTS

1 large onion, chopped
½ cup chopped red sweet pepper
1 garlic clove, minced
1 tablespoon olive oil
1 14½-ounce can chicken broth
1½ cups chopped potato or ¼ cup uncooked long grain rice
1 or 2 fresh jalapeño peppers, seeded and finely chopped (see tip, page 158)

Dash salt
Dash black pepper
8 ounces shucked fresh oysters with their liquid
1 cup fresh or frozen whole kernel corn
1 tablespoon snipped fresh oregano
½ cup half-and-half or light cream

Start to finish: 40 minutes

DIRECTIONS

1. In a medium saucepan cook onion, sweet pepper, and garlic in hot oil over medium heat until vegetables are tender. Carefully stir in chicken broth, potato, jalapeño peppers, salt, and black pepper.

2. Bring to boiling; reduce heat. Simmer, covered, about 10 minutes or until potato is nearly tender. Stir in the undrained oysters, fresh or frozen corn, and oregano.

3. Return to boiling; reduce heat. Simmer, covered, about 5 minutes more or until the oysters are plump and opaque. Stir in half-and-half; heat through. Makes 3 servings.

NUTRITION FACTS PER SERVING:

312 calories
13 g total fat
4 g saturated fat
57 mg cholesterol
596 mg sodium
39 g carbohydrate
4 g fiber
13 g protein

INGREDIENTS

- 1 6-ounce package frozen crabmeat or one 6-ounce can crabmeat, drained, flaked, and cartilage removed
- 1 medium zucchini, cut into 2-inch strips
- 1 medium red or green sweet pepper, chopped
- 2 tablespoons margarine or butter
- 2 tablespoons all-purpose flour
- 4 cups milk

- 2 tablespoons sliced green onion
- ½ teaspoon bouquet garni seasoning
- ¼ teaspoon salt
- ⅛ teaspoon black pepper
- 1 3-ounce package cream cheese, cut up
- 1 teaspoon snipped fresh thyme
  Fresh thyme sprigs (optional)

crab chowder

This winning chowder features the prize of all seafood—crabmeat. It's even more enticing with bouquet garni seasoning—a mixture of several herbs—and a small amount of cream cheese.

Start to finish: 25 minutes

DIRECTIONS

1. Thaw crabmeat, if frozen. In a medium saucepan cook zucchini and sweet pepper in hot margarine until crisp-tender. Stir in the flour. Add the milk, green onion, bouquet garni seasoning, salt, and black pepper.

2. Cook and stir over medium-high heat until thickened and bubbly. Add the cream cheese; cook and stir until cream cheese melts. Stir in the crabmeat and snipped thyme; heat through. Ladle into soup bowls. If desired, garnish each serving with fresh thyme sprigs. Makes 4 servings.

NUTRITION FACTS PER SERVING:

314 calories
19 g total fat
9 g saturated fat
64 mg cholesterol
844 mg sodium
18 g carbohydrate
1 g fiber
19 g protein

crab & pasta gazpacho

Gazpacho—the chilled tomato-and-vegetable soup—was born in Spain but reinvented in California, where it's a summer menu favorite. This fast, fresh version full of sweet crab, juicy nectarines, and fragrant basil couldn't be from anywhere else.

INGREDIENTS

- 1 cup dried small shell macaroni or bow-tie pasta (4 ounces)
- 4 cups hot-style vegetable juice, chilled
- 1 tablespoon lime juice or lemon juice
- 6 ounces cooked lump crabmeat, flaked, or chopped cooked chicken (about 1¼ cups)
- 2 medium nectarines, chopped (1⅓ cups)
- 2 plum tomatoes, chopped
- ¼ cup chopped seeded cucumber
- 2 tablespoons snipped fresh basil
  Lime wedges (optional)

Start to finish: 25 minutes

DIRECTIONS

1. Cook pasta according to package directions; drain in colander. Rinse with cold water; drain again.

2. Meanwhile, in a large bowl stir together vegetable juice and lime juice. Stir in pasta, crabmeat, nectarines, tomatoes, cucumber, and basil. Ladle into soup bowls. If desired, serve with lime wedges. Makes 6 servings.

NUTRITION FACTS PER SERVING:

162 calories
1 g total fat
0 g saturated fat
28 mg cholesterol
947 mg sodium
28 g carbohydrate
2 g fiber
11 g protein

caribbean clam chowder

Clams combine with sweet potatoes, tomatoes, chili peppers, and a hint of lime and rum to make a soup full of exuberant flavor.

INGREDIENTS

- ½ pint shucked fresh clams or one 6½-ounce can minced clams
- 2 cups peeled and cubed sweet potatoes (1 to 2 medium)
- 1 medium onion, chopped
- 1 stalk celery, chopped
- ¼ cup chopped red sweet pepper
- 2 cloves garlic, minced
- 1½ teaspoons snipped fresh thyme or ½ teaspoon dried thyme, crushed
- 1 10-ounce can chopped tomatoes and green chili peppers
- 1 tablespoon lime juice
- 1 tablespoon dark rum (optional)

Start to finish: 35 minutes

DIRECTIONS

1. Drain clams, reserving juice. Add enough water to clam juice to make 2½ cups liquid. If using fresh clams, chop clams; set aside.

2. In a large saucepan bring the clam liquid to boiling. Stir in the sweet potatoes, onion, celery, sweet pepper, garlic, and, if using, dried thyme. Return to boiling; reduce heat. Simmer, covered, about 10 minutes or until sweet potatoes are tender.

3. Mash mixture slightly with a potato masher. Stir in clams, undrained tomatoes, lime juice, rum (if desired), and, if using, fresh thyme. Return to boiling; reduce heat. Cook for 1 to 2 minutes more or until heated through. Makes 4 servings.

NUTRITION FACTS PER SERVING:

128 calories
1 g total fat
0 g saturated fat
19 mg cholesterol
337 mg sodium
22 g carbohydrate
3 g fiber
9 g protein

Fresh herbs impart an undeniably superior flavor and aroma to foods—so try to use them whenever possible. When purchasing fresh herbs, look for perky leaves with no brown spots. Fresh herbs are highly perishable, so buy them as you need them. For short-term storage, immerse freshly cut stems in water about 2 inches deep. Cover the leaves loosely with a plastic bag or plastic wrap and refrigerate for several days.

Middle Eastern Bulgur-Spinach Salad
See recipe, page 230

vegetarian dinners

Corn Waffles with Tomato Salsa 190
Christmas Limas with Pesto Bulgur 191
Tangy Bean Salad Wraps .192
Spaghetti Squash with Balsamic Beans 193
Southwestern Black Bean Cakes with Guacamole . . . 194
Moo Shu Vegetable & Egg Crepes 195
Cheese Frittata with Mushrooms & Dill 196
Corn & Tomato Bread Pudding 197
Egg & Apple Bruschetta 198
Southwest Skillet 199
Egg Ragout 200
Sweet & Spicy Spring Rolls 201
Grilled Gazpacho Medley Open-Faced Sandwich 202
Grilled Eggplant & Sweet Pepper Sandwiches 203
Peppery Artichoke Pitas 204
Open-Face Portobello Sandwiches 205
Sautéed Onion & Tomato Sandwiches 206
Grilled Sicilian-Style Pizza 207
Roasted Vegetables Parmesan 208
Indian-Spiced Squash 209
Peppers Stuffed with Cinnamon Bulgur 210
Spinach Risotto with Acorn Squash 211
Wild Rice Quesadillas 212
Saffron Pilaf with Grilled Vegetables 213
Lentil & Veggie Tostadas .214
Couscous Burritos 215
Garlic Pilaf with Cajun Eggplant 216
Broccoli Rabe over Polenta 217
Polenta with Mushrooms & Asparagus 218
Polenta with Fresh Tomato Sauce 219
Italian Mozzarella Salad 220
Warm Beet Salad with Roasted Garlic Dressing 221
Mexican Fiesta Salad 222

Grilled Vegetable Salad with Garlic Dressing 223
Pasta Coleslaw 224
Three-Cheese Orzo Salad .225
Penne Salad with Italian Beans & Gorgonzola 226
Fontina & Melon Salad 227
Mediterranean Couscous Salad 228
Tomato, Mozzarella, & Polenta Platter 229
Middle Eastern Bulgur-Spinach Salad 230
Papaya & Olives with Brown Rice 231
Chunky Ratatouille Stew 232
Spring Vegetable Soup 233
Tomato & Wild Mushroom Soup 234
Tomato-Basil Soup 235
Mushroom, Noodle, & Tofu Soup 236
Spring Green Pasta Soup .237
Asparagus & Cheese Potato Soup 238
Jalapeño Corn Chowder 239
Vegetable Cheese Chowder 240
Creamy Carrot & Pasta Soup 241
Italian Greens & Cheese Tortellini 242
Mushroom Tortelloni in Curry Cream 243
Black & White Bean Chili .244
Greek Minestrone 245
Garbanzo Bean Stew 246
Mixed Bean & Portobello Ragout 247
Curried Lentil Soup 248
Pesto-Vegetable Soup 249
Wild Rice, Barley, & Mushroom Soup 250
Squash & Papaya Soup 251

corn waffles with tomato salsa

Morning to night, waffles have timeless appeal. For a simple supper, try this twist on tacos—stud waffles with kernels of corn and top them with a lively black bean salsa. A cornmeal mix streamlines preparation.

INGREDIENTS

- 6 plum tomatoes, halved
- 2 teaspoons olive oil
- 1 15-ounce can black beans or small white beans, rinsed and drained
- ⅓ cup sliced green onions
- 2 tablespoons snipped fresh cilantro or parsley
- 2 tablespoons lime juice
- 1 to 2 fresh serrano peppers, chopped (see tip, page 158)
- ¼ teaspoon salt
- 1 8½-ounce package corn muffin mix
- ½ cup fresh or frozen whole kernel corn
- ¼ cup plain fat-free yogurt
  Fresh cilantro sprigs (optional)

Start to finish: 30 minutes

DIRECTIONS

1. For salsa, brush tomato halves with 1 teaspoon of the olive oil; place on unheated rack of a broiler pan. Broil 4 to 5 inches from the heat for 8 to 10 minutes or until the tomatoes begin to char, turning once halfway through cooking. Remove from the broiler pan and cool slightly; coarsely chop.

2. Meanwhile, in a medium bowl combine beans, green onions, snipped cilantro, lime juice, serrano peppers, the remaining 1 teaspoon olive oil, and salt. Stir in tomatoes and any juices. Set aside.

3. For waffles, prepare corn muffin mix according to package directions, except stir the corn into batter. (If necessary, add 1 to 2 additional tablespoons milk to thin batter.)

4. Pour about half of the batter onto the grid of a preheated, lightly greased waffle baker. Close the lid quickly; do not open until done. Bake according to manufacturer's directions. When done, use a fork to lift waffle off grid; keep warm. Repeat with remaining batter.

5. To serve, cut waffles in half. Divide warm waffles among 4 dinner plates. Top with salsa and yogurt. If desired, garnish with cilantro sprigs. Makes 4 servings.

NUTRITION FACTS PER SERVING:

417 calories
12 g total fat
3 g saturated fat
55 mg cholesterol
841 mg sodium
70 g carbohydrate
8 g fiber
15 g protein

INGREDIENTS

- 1⅓ cups vegetable broth or chicken broth
- ⅔ cup bulgur
- 2 cups cooked Christmas lima beans, pinto beans, or cranberry beans or one 15-ounce can pinto beans, rinsed and drained
- 1 medium red sweet pepper, chopped
- ⅓ cup pesto
- ¼ cup thinly sliced green onions
  Toasted bread slices

christmas limas with pesto bulgur

Dappled red over pale green, Christmas limas are aptly named and easy to spot, but it's their nutty flavor that makes them a standout in this Italian-inspired meal. Cook the beans ahead or use canned beans when dinner is really last minute.

Start to finish: 20 minutes

DIRECTIONS

1. In a medium saucepan bring broth to boiling; stir in bulgur. Return to boiling; reduce heat. Simmer, covered, for 10 minutes. Remove from heat.

2. Stir in the beans, sweet pepper, pesto, and green onions. Season to taste with freshly ground black pepper. Serve with toasted bread slices. Makes 6 servings.

NUTRITION FACTS PER SERVING:

288 calories
11 g total fat
0 g saturated fat
2 mg cholesterol
542 mg sodium
41 g carbohydrate
5 g fiber
9 g protein

To cook beans,

rinse ¾ cup dried beans and combine with 5 cups water in a large Dutch oven. Bring to boiling; reduce heat. Simmer, uncovered, for 2 minutes. Remove from heat. Cover and let stand for 1 hour. Rinse and drain beans. Return beans to pan. Add 5 cups fresh water. Bring to boiling; reduce heat. Simmer, covered, for 1¼ to 1½ hours or until tender; drain. (Or, place beans in 5 cups cold water in a Dutch oven. Cover and let soak in a cool place overnight.)

tangy bean salad wraps

Using a variety of tortillas flavored with tomato-basil, pesto, fresh herb, or whole wheat makes this rapid wrap, stuffed with favorite Mexican ingredients, new every time you serve it.

INGREDIENTS

4 8-inch flavored or plain flour tortillas

1 15-ounce can black beans, rinsed, drained, and slightly mashed

½ cup chopped green sweet pepper or 1 fresh jalapeño pepper, seeded and finely chopped (see tip, page 158)

2 tablespoons snipped fresh cilantro

⅓ cup light mayonnaise dressing or salad dressing

1 tablespoon lime juice
   Leaf lettuce

Fiber- and protein-rich

dried beans now come in a dazzling array of colors and sizes, from the once-rare heirloom varieties to intriguing exotics. Homecooked beans are as convenient as canned and better for you, as they are free of preservatives and sodium. When time permits, freeze cooked beans in 2-cup portions to substitute for a 15-ounce can of beans.

Start to finish: 15 minutes

DIRECTIONS

1. Wrap the tortillas in foil. Heat in a 350° oven for 10 minutes to soften. (Or, wrap tortillas in microwave-safe paper towels. Microwave on 100% power (high) for 30 seconds.)

2. Meanwhile, in a medium bowl combine black beans, sweet pepper, and cilantro. Stir in mayonnaise dressing and lime juice. To serve, spread mixture evenly over tortillas. Top with lettuce leaves. Roll up the tortillas. Makes 4 servings.

NUTRITION FACTS PER SERVING:

230 calories
9 g total fat
2 g saturated fat
0 mg cholesterol
531 mg sodium
32 g carbohydrate
6 g fiber
9 g protein

spaghetti squash with balsamic beans

INGREDIENTS

- 1 medium spaghetti squash (2½ to 3 pounds), halved and seeded
- 1 10-ounce package frozen baby lima beans
- 1 15-ounce can red kidney beans, rinsed and drained
- ½ of a 7-ounce jar (½ cup) roasted red sweet peppers, rinsed, drained, and cut into short strips
- ½ teaspoon salt
- ¼ cup balsamic vinegar
- 3 tablespoons olive oil
- 1 tablespoon honey mustard
- 2 cloves garlic, minced

It's not magic, just Mother Nature. When cooked, the golden flesh of spaghetti squash separates into strands that look like the ever popular pasta. Top the squash strands with this sassy sauce of sweet-tart beans.

Start to finish: 30 minutes

DIRECTIONS

1. Place the squash halves in a large Dutch oven with about 1 inch of water. Bring to boiling. Cook, covered, for 15 to 20 minutes or until squash is tender.

2. Meanwhile, in a medium saucepan cook the lima beans according to package directions, adding kidney beans the last 3 minutes of cooking; drain. Return the beans to saucepan. Stir in roasted red peppers and salt; heat through.

3. Meanwhile, for the vinaigrette,* in a screw-top jar combine vinegar, oil, honey mustard, and garlic. Cover and shake well. Pour over warm bean mixture; toss to coat.

4. Use a fork to scrape the squash pulp from the shells in strands; return strands to each shell. Spoon warm bean mixture over squash strands in shells, drizzling any excess vinaigrette on top. Season to taste with freshly ground black pepper. To serve, cut each squash shell in half.

Makes 4 servings.

*Note: The vinaigrette may be prepared ahead and refrigerated for up to 2 days. Allow it to sit at room temperature while preparing squash and beans.

NUTRITION FACTS PER SERVING:

421 calories
11 g total fat
2 g saturated fat
0 mg cholesterol
466 mg sodium
65 g carbohydrate
13 g fiber
21 g protein

southwestern black bean cakes with guacamole

These spicy bean cakes are finger foods that are filling enough to make a meal. They're flavored with a chipotle—a dried, smoked jalapeño pepper—that comes in adobo sauce, a Mexican mélange of ground chili peppers, herbs, and vinegar.

INGREDIENTS

- 2 slices whole wheat bread, torn
- 3 tablespoons fresh cilantro leaves
- 2 cloves garlic
- 1 15-ounce can black beans, rinsed and drained
- 1 7-ounce can chipotle peppers in adobo sauce
- 1 teaspoon ground cumin
- 1 egg
- ½ of a medium avocado, seeded and peeled
- 1 tablespoon lime juice
- 1 small plum tomato, chopped

Prep time: 20 minutes
Grilling time: 8 minutes

DIRECTIONS

1. Place torn bread in a food processor bowl or blender container. Cover and process or blend until bread resembles coarse crumbs; transfer to a large bowl and set aside.

2. Place cilantro and garlic in the food processor bowl or blender container; cover and process or blend until finely chopped. Add the beans, 1 of the chipotle peppers, 1 to 2 teaspoons of the adobo sauce (reserve the remaining peppers and sauce for another use), and cumin. Process or blend using on/off pulses until beans are coarsely chopped and mixture begins to pull away from side. Add mixture to bread crumbs in bowl. Add egg; mix well. Shape mixture into four ½-inch-thick patties.

3. Grill patties on a lightly greased rack of an uncovered grill directly over medium heat for 8 to 10 minutes or until patties are heated through, turning once halfway through cooking.

4. Meanwhile, for the guacamole, in a small bowl mash avocado. Stir in lime juice; season to taste with salt and black pepper. Serve patties with guacamole and tomato. Makes 4 servings.

NUTRITION FACTS PER SERVING:

178 calories
7 g total fat
1 g saturated fat
53 mg cholesterol
487 mg sodium
25 g carbohydrate
9 g fiber
11 g protein

moo shu vegetable & egg crepes

If there's ever a Chinese take-out Hall of Fame, this menu all-star would surely be in it. A speedy home-cooked rendition, expedited by a sweet and sour sauce that starts in a bottle and finishes in a second, delivers dinner in short order.

INGREDIENTS

- 12 asparagus spears, trimmed and cut into 3-inch pieces
- 2 medium carrots, cut into thin 3-inch strips
- 2 green onions, cut into 2-inch pieces
- 3 tablespoons bottled sweet and sour sauce
- 1 tablespoon orange juice or unsweetened pineapple juice
- 1 teaspoon grated fresh ginger
- 5 eggs
- ¼ cup water
- 1 tablespoon cooking oil

Start to finish: 30 minutes

DIRECTIONS

1. In a large saucepan cook the asparagus, carrots, and green onions in a small amount of boiling, lightly salted water for 7 to 9 minutes or until vegetables are crisp-tender; drain.

2. Meanwhile, for sauce, in a small bowl stir together sweet and sour sauce, orange juice, and ginger; set aside.

3. For egg crepes, beat the eggs and water until combined but not frothy. In an 8- or 10-inch nonstick skillet with flared sides, heat 1 teaspoon of the oil until a drop of water sizzles. Lift and tilt skillet to coat sides with oil. Add about ½ cup of the egg mixture to skillet. Cook over medium heat, without stirring, until mixture begins to set on bottom and around edge. Using a spatula, lift and fold the partially cooked egg mixture so the uncooked portion flows underneath. When mixture is set, but still shiny and moist, remove from heat. Repeat to make 2 more crepes.

4. To assemble, spread about 2 teaspoons sauce onto center of each crepe. Arrange one-third of the vegetables on one-quarter of the crepe. Fold crepe in half over the vegetables; fold in half again. Serve with remaining sauce. Makes 3 servings.

NUTRITION FACTS PER SERVING:

223 calories
13 g total fat
3 g saturated fat
355 mg cholesterol
188 mg sodium
13 g carbohydrate
2 g fiber
12 g protein

195

cheese frittata with mushrooms & dill

The fuss-free Italian frittata is far easier to make than its French cousin, the omelet. This spur-of-the-moment skillet supper is terrific with Mexicali Stuffed Zucchini (page 260) and a loaf of crusty peasant-style bread.

INGREDIENTS

- 6 beaten eggs
- $\frac{1}{3}$ cup shredded Gruyère or Swiss cheese
- $\frac{1}{4}$ cup water
- $\frac{1}{4}$ teaspoon salt
- $\frac{1}{8}$ teaspoon freshly ground pepper
- 2 tablespoons margarine or butter
- $1\frac{1}{2}$ cups thinly sliced fresh mushrooms (such as shiitake, chanterelle, cremini, or button) (4 ounces)
- $\frac{1}{4}$ cup sliced green onions
- 1 tablespoon snipped fresh Italian flat-leaf parsley
- 1 tablespoon snipped fresh dill

Start to finish: 25 minutes

DIRECTIONS

1. In a medium bowl beat together eggs, cheese, water, salt, and pepper.

2. In a 10-inch nonstick skillet melt margarine over medium-high heat. Add mushrooms and cook for 4 to 5 minutes or until liquid evaporates. Stir in green onions, parsley, and dill.

3. Pour egg mixture over mushroom mixture. Cook, uncovered, over medium heat. As the egg mixture begins to set, run a spatula around edge of skillet, lifting egg mixture so uncooked portion flows underneath. Continue cooking and lifting edge until egg mixture is almost set (surface will be moist). Remove from heat.

4. Cover and let stand for 3 to 4 minutes or until top is set. Cut into wedges. Makes 4 servings.

NUTRITION FACTS PER SERVING:

216 calories
17 g total fat
5 g saturated fat
331 mg cholesterol
332 mg sodium
3 g carbohydrate
0 g fiber
13 g protein

INGREDIENTS

- 3 tablespoons snipped dried tomatoes (not oil-packed)
- 4 beaten eggs
- 1½ cups milk, half-and-half, or light cream
- 1 tablespoon snipped fresh basil or 1 teaspoon dried basil, crushed
- 4 cups torn English muffins or dry French bread
- 1½ cups fresh or frozen whole kernel corn
- 1 cup shredded reduced-fat cheddar cheese or hot pepper cheese (4 ounces)
- 1 tomato, cut into thin wedges (optional)

corn & tomato bread pudding

The proof of a delicious dinner is in this pudding, a classic baked custard dessert reinvented as a savory main course. Cut cubes from only firm, day-old (or older) bread, as fresh bread is too soft to soak up all the milk and eggs and hold its shape.

Prep time: 20 minutes
Baking time: 30 minutes

DIRECTIONS

1. Soak dried tomatoes in enough hot water to cover for 15 minutes; drain.

2. Meanwhile, in a medium bowl beat together eggs, milk, and basil; set aside. In an ungreased 2-quart square baking dish toss together the torn English muffins, corn, cheese, and dried tomatoes. Carefully pour egg mixture evenly over corn mixture in baking dish.

3. Bake in a 375° oven about 30 minutes or until a knife inserted near the center comes out clean. Cool slightly. To serve, if desired, spoon bread pudding on top of tomato wedges. Makes 6 servings.

To make this dish ahead, prepare the egg mixture and the corn mixture, but keep them separate. Cover and refrigerate each for up to 24 hours. Combine and bake as directed.

NUTRITION FACTS PER SERVING:

275 calories
9 g total fat
4 g saturated fat
160 mg cholesterol
486 mg sodium
32 g carbohydrate
3 g fiber
16 g protein

197

egg & apple bruschetta

To create special Italian-style garlic toast—better known as bruschetta (broo-SKEH-tah)—start with a country loaf of bread that has a crispy crust. Then pile on eggs, apple, and nuts tossed with tangy blue cheese dressing.

INGREDIENTS

- 2 teaspoons olive oil
- 1 clove garlic, minced
- 4 1-inch-thick slices crusty white bread or twelve ½-inch-thick slices baguette-style French bread
- 3 hard-cooked eggs, chopped
- ¾ cup shredded tart apple
- 2 tablespoons chopped walnuts, toasted (see tip, page 63)
- 2 tablespoons bottled blue cheese salad dressing

To hard-cook eggs, place them in a medium saucepan. Add enough cold water to come 1 inch above the eggs. Bring to boiling; reduce heat. Simmer, covered, for 15 minutes; drain. Run cold water over the eggs or place eggs in ice water until cool enough to handle; drain. Peel eggs. If desired, cover and refrigerate for up to 2 days.

Start to finish: 25 minutes

DIRECTIONS

1. Stir together the oil and garlic. Using a pastry brush, brush some of the oil mixture over one side of each bread slice. Place bread slices on a baking sheet. Bake in a 450° oven about 10 minutes or until tops of bread slices are golden brown.

2. Meanwhile, in a medium bowl gently toss together the eggs, apple, walnuts, and salad dressing. Top each toasted bread slice with some of the egg mixture. Serve the bruschetta immediately. Makes 4 servings.

NUTRITION FACTS PER SERVING:

213 calories
12 g total fat
2 g saturated fat
162 mg cholesterol
288 mg sodium
19 g carbohydrate
1 g fiber
8 g protein

198

INGREDIENTS

- 2 tablespoons sliced almonds
- 1 yellow sweet pepper, coarsely chopped
- 1 fresh jalapeño pepper, seeded and chopped (see tip, page 158)
- 1 tablespoon olive oil or cooking oil
- 4 medium tomatoes (about 1¼ pounds), peeled and coarsely chopped
- 1½ to 2 teaspoons Mexican Seasoning or 1 to 1½ teaspoons chili powder and ½ teaspoon ground cumin
- ¼ teaspoon salt
- 4 eggs
- 1 medium ripe avocado, seeded, peeled, and sliced (optional)
- Fresh chili peppers (optional)

southwest skillet

It's home on the range with a stove-top main course built on classic Southwestern flavors. Round up everything you need in the aisles of most supermarkets.

Start to finish: 25 minutes

DIRECTIONS

1. Spread the almonds in a large skillet. Cook over medium heat for 4 to 5 minutes or until lightly browned, stirring occasionally. Remove toasted almonds from skillet; set aside. In the same skillet cook the sweet pepper and chopped jalapeño pepper in hot oil about 2 minutes or until tender. Stir in the tomatoes, Mexican seasoning, and salt. Bring to boiling; reduce heat. Simmer, covered, for 5 minutes.

2. Break one of the eggs into a measuring cup. Carefully slide the egg into simmering tomato mixture. Repeat with remaining eggs. Sprinkle the eggs lightly with salt and black pepper.

3. Cover and cook eggs over medium-low heat for 3 to 5 minutes or until the whites are completely set and yolks begin to thicken but are not firm. To serve, using a slotted spoon, transfer eggs to 4 dinner plates. Stir mixture in skillet; spoon around eggs on plates. Sprinkle with the toasted almonds. If desired, serve with avocado slices and garnish with fresh chili peppers. Makes 4 servings.

NUTRITION FACTS PER SERVING:

166 calories
11 g total fat
2 g saturated fat
213 mg cholesterol
216 mg sodium
10 g carbohydrate
2 g fiber
9 g protein

egg ragout

This simple supper is the perfect conclusion to any weekend recreation, from a hike in the woods to a snooze on the couch. It's a scrumptious, creamy, egg-and-vegetable mélange that makes the most of pantry staples.

INGREDIENTS

1½ cups sugar snap peas, strings and tips removed

1 cup baby sunburst squash, cut in quarters

4 green onions, thinly bias-sliced

4 teaspoons margarine or butter

2 tablespoons all-purpose flour

1¼ cups milk

2 tablespoons grated Parmesan cheese

1 teaspoon sweet-hot mustard or Dijon-style mustard

4 hard-cooked eggs (see tip, page 198), coarsely chopped

4 bagels, split and toasted, or 4 slices whole wheat bread, toasted

Start to finish: 25 minutes

DIRECTIONS

1. In a covered medium saucepan cook sugar snap peas and sunburst squash in a small amount of boiling salted water for 2 to 4 minutes or until vegetables are crisp-tender; drain.

2. For sauce, in a large saucepan cook green onions in hot margarine over medium heat until tender. Stir in flour. Add milk all at once. Cook and stir until thickened and bubbly. Stir in Parmesan cheese and mustard; add cooked vegetables. Cook and stir about 1 minute more or until heated through. Gently stir in eggs. Serve over bagels. Makes 4 servings.

NUTRITION FACTS PER SERVING:

392 calories
13 g total fat
4 g saturated fat
221 mg cholesterol
600 mg sodium
49 g carbohydrate
1 g fiber
19 g protein

sweet & spicy spring rolls

With coconut for sweet and fiery Japanese wasabi for spicy, these vegetable-packed rolls are a sense sensation. Wasabi, a sushi condiment, tastes like horseradish.

INGREDIENTS

- 6 8-inch round rice papers
- 2 teaspoons grated fresh ginger
- 1 to 2 teaspoons wasabi paste
- 1 teaspoon lime juice
- 1/3 cup light mayonnaise dressing or salad dressing
- 2 cups packaged shredded broccoli (broccoli slaw mix)
- 1/2 of a 10½-ounce package extra-firm tofu (fresh bean curd), drained and finely chopped (1 cup)
- 1/4 cup flaked coconut
- 6 romaine leaves
- 1 recipe Dipping Sauce

Start to finish: 25 minutes

DIRECTIONS

1. Carefully dip each rice paper quickly in water and place between paper towels or clean cotton dish towels. Let stand for 10 minutes.

2. Meanwhile, in a small bowl combine the ginger, wasabi paste, and lime juice. Stir in mayonnaise dressing.

3. In a large bowl toss together shredded broccoli, tofu, and coconut. Add the mayonnaise mixture; toss gently to coat.

4. Line each rice paper with a romaine leaf. Spoon broccoli mixture over romaine. Wrap rice paper around broccoli mixture. Serve with Dipping Sauce. Makes 6 servings.

Dipping Sauce: In a small bowl combine 1 tablespoon soy sauce, 1 tablespoon lime juice, and 1/4 teaspoon crushed red pepper.

NUTRITION FACTS PER SERVING:

123 calories
5 g total fat
1 g saturated fat
0 mg cholesterol
318 mg sodium
16 g carbohydrate
1 g fiber
3 g protein

201

grilled gazpacho medley open-faced sandwich

Stay as cool as a cucumber with this hearty sandwich featuring the flavors of the cold soup, gazpacho. Tomatoes, garlic, cucumber, and a pickled jalapeño get mixed with black beans, then scooped into grilled French bread "bowls" and topped with cheese.

INGREDIENTS

- 1 medium cucumber, seeded and chopped
- 1 cup cooked or canned black beans, rinsed and drained
- ¼ cup snipped fresh cilantro
- 2 tablespoons cider vinegar
- 1 tablespoon olive oil
- 1 pickled jalapeño pepper, finely chopped
- 1 clove garlic, minced
- ½ to 1 teaspoon chili powder
- 3 large tomatoes, halved
- 1 large sweet onion (such as Vidalia or Walla Walla), sliced ½ inch thick
- 1 loaf French bread
- 1 cup shredded cheddar cheese (4 ounces)

Prep time: 20 minutes
Grilling time: 14 minutes

DIRECTIONS

1. In a medium bowl combine the cucumber, beans, cilantro, vinegar, oil, jalapeño pepper, garlic, and chili powder. Season to taste with salt and black pepper. Set aside.

2. In a grill with a cover place the tomatoes and onion slices on a lightly greased rack directly over medium heat. Grill, uncovered, for 12 to 15 minutes or until lightly charred, turning onion slices once halfway through cooking. Transfer vegetables to a cutting board; cool slightly and coarsely chop. Add chopped vegetables to the cucumber mixture; toss gently to combine.

3. Meanwhile, halve the French bread lengthwise. Cut each bread half crosswise into 3 pieces. Using a fork, hollow out the bread pieces slightly. Place the bread pieces, cut sides down, on the grill rack. Grill, uncovered, about 1 minute or until toasted. Remove from grill.

4. Spoon the bean mixture into the bread pieces; sprinkle sandwiches with cheddar cheese. Place the sandwiches, filled sides up, on the grill rack. Cover and grill for 1 to 2 minutes or until cheese is melted. Makes 6 servings.

NUTRITION FACTS PER SERVING:

329 calories
11 g total fat
5 g saturated fat
20 mg cholesterol
634 mg sodium
46 g carbohydrate
3 g fiber
14 g protein

INGREDIENTS

- 2 medium red, yellow, and/or green sweet peppers
- 1 small eggplant (about 12 ounces), cut into 12 slices
- 1 tablespoon olive oil
- 8 ½-inch-thick slices French bread
- 4 ounces soft goat cheese (chèvre)
- ¼ cup Dijon-style mustard

grilled eggplant & sweet pepper sandwiches

Grills fire up when hot summer days shut down kitchens, and simple feasts—such as this Mediterranean stack of smoky eggplant and sweet peppers anchored with a smear of tangy goat cheese—are the rule.

Start to finish: 25 minutes

DIRECTIONS

1. Quarter sweet peppers lengthwise; remove and discard the stems, seeds, and membranes.

2. Brush eggplant slices with oil. Grill eggplant slices and sweet pepper quarters on the rack of an uncovered grill directly over medium-hot heat for 7 to 9 minutes or until eggplant is tender and sweet peppers are slightly charred, turning once halfway through cooking. Toast French bread slices on grill rack next to vegetables the last 1 minute of grilling. Remove vegetables and bread from grill.

3. Spread 1 side of each bread slice with goat cheese and Dijon mustard. Layer 3 eggplant slices and 2 sweet pepper quarters on 4 of the bread slices. Top with the remaining bread slices. Serve warm. Makes 4 servings.

NUTRITION FACTS PER SERVING:

240 calories
13 g total fat
5 g saturated fat
25 mg cholesterol
698 mg sodium
21 g carbohydrate
2 g fiber
9 g protein

203

peppery artichoke pitas

Stuck in traffic? No time to shop? These pitas, filled with ingredients pulled mostly from the pantry—tender artichokes, cooked beans, and bottled garlic dressing—put a premium on convenience and a great dinner on the table.

INGREDIENTS

1 15-ounce can Great Northern beans, rinsed and drained

1 13¾- to 14-ounce can artichoke hearts, drained and coarsely chopped

½ cup torn arugula or spinach

¼ cup bottled creamy garlic salad dressing

¼ teaspoon cracked pepper

3 pita bread rounds, halved crosswise

Arugula is a peppery salad green sometimes mistaken for dandelion. Mature leaves are large and very pungent—tasty accents to milder greens in a mixed salad. Less assertive young leaves can be used alone. Rinse leaves well in cold water, pat dry, and refrigerate in a plastic bag for up to 2 days.

Start to finish: 20 minutes

DIRECTIONS

1. In a medium bowl combine the beans, artichoke hearts, arugula, garlic salad dressing, and pepper.

2. To serve, spoon the bean mixture into pita bread halves. Makes 6 servings.

NUTRITION FACTS PER SERVING:

227 calories
5 g total fat
1 g saturated fat
3 mg cholesterol
269 mg sodium
38 g carbohydrate
6 g fiber
10 g protein

INGREDIENTS

- 1 medium tomato, chopped
- 2 teaspoons snipped fresh basil, thyme, and/or oregano
- ⅛ teaspoon salt
- 2 medium fresh portobello mushrooms (about 4 inches in diameter)
- 1 teaspoon balsamic vinegar or red wine vinegar
- ½ teaspoon olive oil
- ½ of a 12-inch Italian flat bread (focaccia), quartered, or ½ of a 12-inch thin-crust Italian bread shell (Boboli)
- Finely shredded Parmesan cheese (optional)

open-face portobello sandwiches

Turn a familiar hors d'oeuvre—bread-stuffed mushrooms—upside down for a new lease on life as a stunning open-face sandwich. Now it's bread on the bottom, mushrooms on top.

Start to finish: 25 minutes

DIRECTIONS

1. In a small bowl combine the tomato, basil, and salt; set aside. Clean the mushrooms; cut off stems even with caps. Discard stems.

2. Combine vinegar and oil; gently brush over the mushroom caps. Broil the mushrooms on the unheated rack of a broiler pan 4 to 5 inches from the heat for 6 to 8 minutes or just until tender, turning once halfway through cooking. (Or, grill on the rack of an uncovered grill directly over medium heat for 6 to 8 minutes, turning once halfway through cooking.) Drain mushrooms on paper towels. Thinly slice the mushrooms.

3. Place bread on a baking sheet. Broil 4 to 5 inches from the heat for 2 to 3 minutes or until heated through. (Or, grill on grill rack for 2 to 3 minutes.)

4. To serve, top bread with mushroom slices and tomato mixture. If desired, sprinkle with Parmesan cheese. Makes 4 servings.

NUTRITION FACTS PER SERVING:

161 calories
3 g total fat
1 g saturated fat
2 mg cholesterol
71 mg sodium
29 g carbohydrate
3 g fiber
7 g protein

205

sautéed onion & tomato sandwiches

When laps double as the dining table, the best TV dinner is something easy and out-of-hand. This hearty whole-grain sandwich serves perfectly. Pass around beer, brownies, and your biggest napkins.

INGREDIENTS

- 2 medium onions, sliced
- 1 teaspoon olive oil
- 8 slices hearty whole grain bread (toasted, if desired)
  Honey mustard
- 3 small red and/or yellow tomatoes, thinly sliced
- 4 lettuce leaves, shredded
  Small fresh basil leaves
- 4 ounces spreadable Brie cheese or soft-style cream cheese

Start to finish: 20 minutes

DIRECTIONS

1. In a large skillet cook onion slices in hot oil over medium-high heat for 5 to 7 minutes or until tender and just starting to brown. Remove the skillet from heat; cool onions slightly.

2. To assemble sandwiches, lightly spread one side of 4 bread slices with honey mustard. Top with the onion slices, tomato slices, and lettuce. Sprinkle with basil.

Spread one side of each of the 4 remaining bread slices with Brie cheese; place on top of sandwiches. Makes 4 servings.

NUTRITION FACTS PER SERVING:

287 calories
12 g total fat
6 g saturated fat
28 mg cholesterol
490 mg sodium
35 g carbohydrate
1 g fiber
12 g protein

grilled sicilian-style pizza

Sicilians like their escarole—a mild, leafy kind of endive—sautéed with lots of olive oil and served with chewy bread to sop up the juices. For maximum flavor in this grilled adaptation of that idea, use the tangy Italian cheese Pecorino Romano.

INGREDIENTS

- 1 12-inch Italian bread shell (Boboli)
- 2 plum tomatoes, thinly sliced
- 1 large yellow or red tomato, thinly sliced
- 4 ounces fresh mozzarella or buffalo mozzarella cheese, thinly sliced
- ⅓ cup halved pitted kalamata olives
- 1 tablespoon olive oil
- 1 cup coarsely chopped escarole or curly endive
- ¼ cup shaved or shredded Pecorino Romano or Parmesan cheese (1 ounce)

Prep time: 20 minutes
Grilling time: 8 minutes

DIRECTIONS

1. Top the bread shell with tomatoes, mozzarella cheese, and olives. Drizzle oil over all. Fold a 24×18-inch piece of heavy foil in half lengthwise to make a 12×9-inch rectangle. Place the bread shell on foil, turning edges of foil up to edge of pizza.

2. In a charcoal grill with a cover arrange medium-hot coals around a drip pan. Test for medium heat above the pan. Place pizza on the grill rack over drip pan. Cover and grill about 8 minutes or until pizza is heated through, topping with escarole the last 2 minutes of grilling. (For a gas grill, adjust for indirect cooking; grill as directed.)

3. To serve, sprinkle the pizza with Romano cheese and freshly ground pepper. Makes 4 servings.

NUTRITION FACTS PER SERVING:

459 calories
19 g total fat
4 g saturated fat
26 mg cholesterol
893 mg sodium
54 g carbohydrate
3 g fiber
24 g protein

They may have the same last name, but the similarity ends there. Fresh mozzarella—made from whole milk—has a much softer texture and sweeter, more delicate flavor than regular mozzarella, which is made in low-fat and fat-free versions and is aged to give it a longer shelf life. Fresh mozzarella, usually packaged in whey or water and shaped into irregular balls, must be eaten within a few days of purchase. It's available in Italian markets and cheese shops and, increasingly, in many supermarkets.

207

roasted vegetables parmesan

These simply seasoned vegetables are hot! They're a delectable toss of zucchini, onion, sweet pepper, mushrooms, and carrots; tomatoes and garbanzo beans are stirred in during the final minutes in the oven. Shred your own Parmesan cheese for the most flavor.

INGREDIENTS

- 2 medium zucchini, cut into 1-inch chunks
- 1 medium onion, cut into 8 wedges
- 1 medium red or green sweet pepper, cut into 1-inch chunks
- 8 ounces fresh mushrooms, stems removed
- 1 cup packaged peeled baby carrots

- 1 tablespoon olive oil
- ½ teaspoon salt
- 1 15-ounce can garbanzo beans, rinsed and drained
- 1 14½-ounce can diced tomatoes with garlic and Italian herbs
- ½ cup shredded Parmesan cheese (2 ounces)

Prep time: 15 minutes
Roasting time: 22 minutes

DIRECTIONS

1. In a large roasting pan combine zucchini, onion, sweet pepper, mushrooms, and carrots. Drizzle with oil; toss to coat. Spread the vegetables evenly in roasting pan. Sprinkle with salt.

2. Roast vegetables in a 500° oven for 12 minutes. Remove from oven; stir in the beans and undrained tomatoes. Reduce the temperature to 375°. Roast, uncovered, about 10 minutes more or until heated through. To serve, sprinkle with cheese. Makes 6 servings.

NUTRITION FACTS PER SERVING:

160 calories
6 g total fat
0 g saturated fat
7 mg cholesterol
867 mg sodium
20 g carbohydrate
5 g fiber
8 g protein

INGREDIENTS

- ¼ cup shelled raw pumpkin seeds (pepitas)
- 1 tablespoon grated fresh ginger
- 2 tablespoons olive oil
- 2 pounds winter squash, peeled, seeded, and cut into ½-inch pieces (about 4 cups)
- ½ cup dried cranberries or raisins
- 1 teaspoon ground cinnamon
- 1 teaspoon ground coriander
- ½ teaspoon ground cumin
- ½ teaspoon curry powder
- 1 14½-ounce can vegetable broth or chicken broth
- 4 cups hot cooked brown rice
  Condiments (such as sliced bananas, pineapple chunks, sliced green onions, and/or chutney) (optional)

indian-spiced squash

Everyone's a cook when it comes to a curry, and this vegetarian version proves why. Its array of traditional condiments lets diners season to taste at the table, so no two mouthfuls are ever the same.

Start to finish: 30 minutes

DIRECTIONS

1. In a large skillet cook pumpkin seeds over medium heat for 4 to 5 minutes or until puffed and lightly browned, stirring occasionally. (Watch carefully as pumpkin seeds may pop in skillet.) Remove from skillet; set pumpkin seeds aside.

2. In the same skillet cook and stir ginger in hot oil over medium heat for 1 minute. Add squash and cook over medium-high heat for 3 to 5 minutes or until squash starts to brown. Stir in the cranberries, cinnamon, coriander, cumin, and curry powder. Cook for 1 minute.

3. Carefully add broth to squash mixture. Bring to boiling; reduce heat. Cook, covered, for 10 to 15 minutes or until squash is tender, but not mushy. To serve, spoon squash mixture over rice and sprinkle with pumpkin seeds. If desired, pass condiments. Makes 4 servings.

NUTRITION FACTS PER SERVING:

450 calories
13 g total fat
2 g saturated fat
0 mg cholesterol
441 mg sodium
81 g carbohydrate
9 g fiber
9 g protein

peppers stuffed with cinnamon bulgur

This easy stove-top supper—full of Middle Eastern flavors—can appear on your table in half the time of most stuffed-pepper entrées, so it's a good choice on even the busiest of days.

INGREDIENTS

1¾ cups water
½ cup shredded carrot
¼ cup chopped onion
1 teaspoon instant vegetable or chicken bouillon granules
3 inches stick cinnamon or dash ground cinnamon
⅛ teaspoon salt
¾ cup bulgur

⅓ cup dried cranberries or raisins
4 small or 2 large sweet peppers,* any color
¾ cup shredded Muenster, brick, or mozzarella cheese (3 ounces)
½ cup water
2 tablespoons sliced almonds or chopped pecans, toasted (see tip, page 63)

Start to finish: 30 minutes

DIRECTIONS

1. In a large skillet combine the 1¾ cups water, the carrot, onion, bouillon granules, cinnamon, and salt. Bring to boiling; reduce heat. Simmer, covered, for 5 minutes. Stir in the bulgur and cranberries. Remove from heat. Cover and let stand for 5 minutes. If using stick cinnamon, remove from the bulgur mixture. Drain off excess liquid.

2. Meanwhile, halve the sweet peppers lengthwise; remove and discard the seeds and membranes.

3. Stir shredded cheese into bulgur mixture; spoon into sweet pepper halves. Place the sweet pepper halves in skillet. Add the ½ cup water. Bring to boiling; reduce heat. Simmer, covered, for 5 to 10 minutes or until sweet peppers are crisp-tender and bulgur mixture is heated through. Sprinkle with nuts. Makes 4 servings.

*Note: Four large poblano peppers may be substituted for sweet peppers. Prepare as directed.

NUTRITION FACTS PER SERVING:

250 calories
9 g total fat
4 g saturated fat
20 mg cholesterol
432 mg sodium
35 g carbohydrate
8 g fiber
10 g protein

spinach risotto with acorn squash

Stubby Italian Arborio rice creates a luscious dish. During cooking, the grains not only soften, but their special starch transforms the broth into a creamy, unforgettable sauce.

INGREDIENTS

- 1 1½- to 2-pound acorn or butternut squash, halved lengthwise and seeded
- 1 cup chopped red onion
- 4 cloves garlic, minced
- 1 tablespoon olive oil
- 1 cup uncooked Arborio rice or short grain rice
- 3 cups vegetable broth or chicken broth
- 3 cups packed chopped spinach
- 2 tablespoons shredded Parmesan cheese

Start to finish: 30 minutes

DIRECTIONS

1. Cut each squash half crosswise into 1-inch slices. In a covered large saucepan cook squash in a small amount of boiling water for 10 to 15 minutes or until tender. Drain and keep warm.

2. Meanwhile, in another large saucepan cook onion and garlic in hot oil over medium heat about 4 minutes or until onion is tender. Add the rice; cook and stir for 1 minute more.

3. In a medium saucepan bring broth to boiling. Reduce heat and simmer. Slowly add 1 cup of the broth to the rice mixture, stirring constantly. Continue to cook and stir until the liquid is absorbed. Add another ½ cup of the broth; continue to cook and stir until the liquid is absorbed. Add another 1 cup broth, stirring constantly until liquid is absorbed. (This should take about 15 minutes.)

4. Stir in remaining ½ cup broth. Cook and stir until rice is slightly creamy and just tender. Stir in spinach and Parmesan cheese. Serve risotto with squash slices. Makes 4 servings.

NUTRITION FACTS PER SERVING:

296 calories
6 g total fat
1 g saturated fat
2 mg cholesterol
778 mg sodium
60 g carbohydrate
5 g fiber
8 g protein

wild rice quesadillas

Adding earthy flavor to a favorite fast food, wild rice shrugs off its black-tie reputation and goes casual. When minutes matter, use any variety of leftover cooked rice or plan to cook the rice ahead of time.

INGREDIENTS

1½ cups cooked wild rice

1 cup shredded asadero, queso quesadilla, or Monterey Jack cheese (4 ounces)

2 to 3 tablespoons salsa

1 to 2 tablespoons snipped fresh cilantro

4 7- or 8-inch flour tortillas

1 cup chopped assorted fresh vegetables (such as sweet pepper, carrots, zucchini, onion, and/or broccoli)

Salsa

To cook the wild rice, rinse and drain ½ cup wild rice. In a small saucepan bring 1½ cups water and ⅛ teaspoon salt to boiling. Stir in rice; reduce heat. Simmer, covered, about 40 minutes or until rice is tender and most of the water is absorbed. Drain, if necessary. If desired, cover and refrigerate for up to 3 days.

Start to finish: 20 minutes

DIRECTIONS

1. In a medium bowl stir together cooked wild rice, cheese, the 2 to 3 tablespoons salsa, and cilantro.

2. Place a tortilla in a large nonstick skillet or on a griddle. Top with half of the rice mixture and half of the vegetables. Top with another tortilla. Cook over medium heat about 2 minutes or until cheese is almost melted. Carefully turn tortilla over and cook for 1 to 2 minutes more or until rice mixture is heated through. Remove quesadilla from skillet; repeat with remaining ingredients.

3. To serve, cut each quesadilla into 6 triangles. Serve with additional salsa. Makes 3 servings.

NUTRITION FACTS PER SERVING:

360 calories
15 g total fat
8 g saturated fat
34 mg cholesterol
410 mg sodium
41 g carbohydrate
3 g fiber
16 g protein

INGREDIENTS

- 1 14½-ounce can vegetable broth
- 1 cup uncooked jasmine, basmati, or wild-pecan long grain rice
- ¼ cup water
- ⅛ teaspoon thread saffron, crushed, or dash ground saffron*
- 2 tablespoons olive oil
- ½ teaspoon bottled minced garlic

- 1 red sweet pepper, quartered
- 1 large zucchini, halved lengthwise
- 1 eggplant, cut into ½-inch slices
- ¼ cup crumbled herbed semisoft goat cheese (chèvre)
- 2 tablespoons coarsely chopped hazelnuts or pecans, toasted (see tip, page 63)

saffron pilaf with grilled vegetables

Similar to paella—Spain's national dish—this sunny-colored saffron rice dish is bursting with flavor, but from a rainbow of grilled vegetables instead of the standard shrimp and meat. Serve it with a hearty red wine.

Prep time: 20 minutes
Grilling time: 10 minutes

DIRECTIONS

1. In a large saucepan combine the vegetable broth, rice, water, and saffron. Bring to boiling; reduce heat. Simmer, covered, about 15 minutes or until rice is tender and liquid is absorbed. Remove from heat; keep warm.

2. Meanwhile, in a small bowl combine oil and garlic; brush over the sweet pepper, zucchini, and eggplant. Grill vegetables on a lightly greased rack of an uncovered grill directly over medium heat about 10 minutes or until tender, turning once halfway through cooking. Season vegetables to taste with salt and black pepper.

3. Transfer vegetables to a cutting board; cool slightly. Cut vegetables into bite-size pieces; stir into cooked rice. Top with goat cheese and nuts. Makes 4 servings.

*__Note:__ You may substitute ¼ teaspoon ground turmeric for the saffron.

NUTRITION FACTS PER SERVING:

333 calories
12 g total fat
2 g saturated fat
7 mg cholesterol
443 mg sodium
48 g carbohydrate
5 g fiber
9 g protein

lentil & veggie tostadas

Sign up here for Dinner 101! This hearty, healthful entrée is ideal weeknight family fare and so easy that even rookie chefs can help prepare it.

INGREDIENTS

1¾ cups water

¾ cup red lentils, rinsed and drained

¼ cup chopped onion

1 to 2 tablespoons snipped fresh cilantro

1 clove garlic, minced

½ teaspoon salt

½ teaspoon ground cumin

4 tostada shells

2 cups chopped assorted fresh vegetables (such as broccoli, tomato, zucchini, and/or yellow summer squash)

¾ cup shredded Monterey Jack cheese (3 ounces)

Start to finish: 25 minutes

DIRECTIONS

1. In a medium saucepan stir together water, lentils, onion, cilantro, garlic, salt, and cumin. Bring to boiling; reduce heat. Simmer, covered, for 12 to 15 minutes or until lentils are tender and most of the liquid is absorbed. Use a fork to mash the cooked lentils.

2. Spread the lentil mixture on tostada shells; top with vegetables and cheese. Place on a large baking sheet. Broil 3 to 4 inches from the heat about 2 minutes or until cheese is melted. Serve the tostadas immediately. Makes 4 servings.

NUTRITION FACTS PER SERVING:

288 calories
11 g total fat
5 g saturated fat
20 mg cholesterol
497 mg sodium
34 g carbohydrate
7 g fiber
16 g protein

INGREDIENTS

- 8 8-inch flavored or plain flour tortillas
- 1 cup vegetable broth or chicken broth
- 1 4-ounce can diced green chili peppers, drained
- ¼ teaspoon ground turmeric
     Dash black pepper

- ⅔ cup quick-cooking couscous
- ¼ cup sliced green onions
- 1 cup chopped tomatoes
- ¾ cup chopped green sweet pepper
- ½ cup finely shredded reduced-fat Mexican-blend cheese
     Salsa (optional)

couscous burritos

Moroccan pasta in a Mexican burrito? Why not! Let this speedy international wrap rocket your taste buds in an entirely new direction.

Start to finish: 20 minutes

DIRECTIONS

1. Wrap the tortillas in foil. Heat in a 350° oven for 10 minutes to soften. (Or, wrap tortillas in microwave-safe paper towels. Microwave on 100% power (high) for 30 seconds.)

2. Meanwhile, in a small saucepan combine the broth, green chili peppers, turmeric, and black pepper. Bring to boiling. Remove from heat and stir in couscous and green onions. Let stand, covered, for 5 minutes. Fluff couscous with a fork. Stir in tomatoes and sweet pepper.

3. To assemble each burrito, spoon about ⅓ cup of the couscous mixture onto a tortilla just below center. Top with 2 tablespoons of the cheese. Roll up the tortilla. If desired, serve with salsa. Makes 4 servings.

NUTRITION FACTS PER SERVING:

359 calories
8 g total fat
3 g saturated fat
5 mg cholesterol
661 mg sodium
60 g carbohydrate
7 g fiber
13 g protein

215

garlic pilaf with cajun eggplant

Native to the Americas, protein-packed quinoa (KEEN-wah) is an ancient grain but a recent arrival on American tables. It cooks like rice and has a mild flavor and slightly chewy texture. You'll find it at natural food stores and larger supermarkets.

INGREDIENTS

- ½ cup chopped onion
- 1 teaspoon olive oil
- 6 cloves garlic, minced
- 2 cups water
- 1 cup quinoa, rinsed and drained, or uncooked long grain rice
- 1 cup coarsely shredded carrot
- 1 teaspoon Cajun seasoning
- ½ teaspoon salt
- 1 15-ounce can hominy, rinsed and drained
- 1 tablespoon snipped fresh basil, rosemary, chives, thyme, or oregano
- 1 medium eggplant, cut into ½-inch slices
- 2 teaspoons olive oil
  Cajun seasoning

Start to finish: 30 minutes

DIRECTIONS

1. In a medium saucepan cook onion in the 1 teaspoon hot oil over medium heat for 3 minutes. Add garlic; cook for 1 minute more. Stir in the water, quinoa, carrot, the 1 teaspoon Cajun seasoning, and the salt.

2. Bring to boiling; reduce heat. Simmer, covered, about 15 minutes or until quinoa is tender and liquid is absorbed.

Stir in hominy and desired herb. Cover and let stand for 1 minute.

3. Meanwhile, lightly brush the eggplant slices with the 2 teaspoons oil; sprinkle with additional Cajun seasoning. Broil on the unheated rack of a broiler pan 4 to 5 inches from the heat for 5 to 6 minutes or just until tender, turning once halfway through cooking.

4. To serve, divide eggplant slices among 4 dinner plates. Top with the quinoa mixture. Makes 4 servings.

NUTRITION FACTS PER SERVING:

296 calories
7 g total fat
1 g saturated fat
0 mg cholesterol
499 mg sodium
52 g carbohydrate
7 g fiber
8 g protein

INGREDIENTS

- 1 cup quick-cooking polenta mix
- 1 cup vegetable broth or chicken broth
- 1 tablespoon cornstarch
- 1 cup chopped sweet onion (such as Vidalia or Walla Walla)
- 4 teaspoons olive oil
- 3 cloves garlic, minced
- 1 pound broccoli rabe, coarsely chopped (about 7 cups), or 3 cups coarsely chopped broccoli flowerets
- ½ of a 7-ounce jar (½ cup) roasted red sweet peppers, rinsed, drained, and chopped
- ¼ cup pine nuts or slivered almonds, toasted (see tip, page 63)

broccoli rabe over polenta

Italians adore chubby broccoli's more slender cruciferous cousin, broccoli rabe (also called rapini). Here its pleasantly bitter flavor and crunchy texture contrast with the more subtle and creamy polenta.

Start to finish: 30 minutes

DIRECTIONS

1. Prepare the polenta according to the package directions. Cover and keep warm. In a small bowl stir together broth and cornstarch. Set aside.

2. In a large skillet cook onion in hot oil over medium heat for 4 to 5 minutes or until tender. Add garlic; cook for 30 seconds more. Stir in broccoli rabe; cover and cook about 3 minutes or just until tender. (If using broccoli flowerets, cook and stir for 3 to 4 minutes or until crisp-tender.) Stir in the roasted sweet peppers.

3. Stir cornstarch mixture; add to vegetable mixture. Cook and stir until thickened and bubbly. Cook and stir for 2 minutes more.

4. To serve, divide polenta among 4 dinner plates. Spoon the vegetable mixture over cooked polenta. Sprinkle each serving with nuts. Makes 4 servings.

NUTRITION FACTS PER SERVING:

394 calories
11 g total fat
1 g saturated fat
0 mg cholesterol
256 mg sodium
67 g carbohydrate
11 g fiber
12 g protein

217

polenta with mushrooms & asparagus

Something green always beats the winter blues. This rustic polenta, starring spring's first asparagus, may bring just the lift you need. A little chocolate for dessert will prolong the good mood.

INGREDIENTS

- 1 cup quick-cooking polenta mix
- 1 small onion, chopped
- 1 tablespoon olive oil
- 3 cups sliced fresh mushrooms (such as cremini, shiitake, or oyster) (8 ounces)
- 1 pound asparagus spears, trimmed and cut into 1-inch pieces (2¼ cups)
- 3 cloves garlic, minced
- ⅓ cup dry white wine, Marsala wine, vegetable broth, or chicken broth
- ¼ teaspoon salt
- ⅓ cup chopped walnuts or pecans, or pine nuts, toasted (see tip, page 63)
- ¼ cup finely shredded Parmesan cheese

Start to finish: 30 minutes

DIRECTIONS

1. Prepare the polenta according to package directions. Cover and keep polenta warm.

2. Meanwhile, in a large skillet cook onion in hot oil over medium heat until tender. Stir in mushrooms, asparagus, and garlic. Cook, uncovered, about 4 minutes or until almost tender. Stir in wine and salt. Cook, uncovered, over medium-high heat for 1 minute.

3. To serve, divide polenta among 4 bowls. Spoon the mushroom mixture over polenta. Sprinkle each serving with nuts and Parmesan cheese. Makes 4 servings.

NUTRITION FACTS PER SERVING:

426 calories
12 g total fat
1 g saturated fat
5 mg cholesterol
220 mg sodium
64 g carbohydrate
10 g fiber
14 g protein

polenta with fresh tomato sauce

Making polenta the traditional way takes a strong stirring hand and time for cooking, chilling, and slicing. This expeditious version serves up medallions of polenta that are crisp on the outside and creamy on the inside, on top of a rosemary-olive tomato sauce.

INGREDIENTS

- ½ teaspoon bottled minced garlic
- 4 teaspoons olive oil
- 6 plum tomatoes, coarsely chopped (about 2 cups)
- ¼ cup pitted halved kalamata olives or sliced pitted ripe olives
- 2 teaspoons snipped fresh rosemary or 2 tablespoons snipped fresh thyme
- 1 16-ounce package prepared polenta
- ½ cup shredded smoked Gouda or Swiss cheese (2 ounces)

Start to finish: 18 minutes

DIRECTIONS

1. For sauce, in a medium saucepan cook garlic in 2 teaspoons of the hot oil over medium heat for 30 seconds. Add tomatoes; cook for 2 minutes. Stir in olives and rosemary. Bring to boiling; reduce heat. Simmer, uncovered, for 8 minutes, stirring occasionally. Season to taste with salt and pepper.

2. Meanwhile, cut polenta into 8 slices. In a large nonstick skillet or on a griddle heat the remaining 2 teaspoons oil over medium heat. Add polenta; cook about 6 minutes or until golden brown, turning once halfway through cooking. Sprinkle with cheese. Serve polenta on top of tomato sauce. Makes 4 servings.

NUTRITION FACTS PER SERVING:

226 calories
10 g total fat
3 g saturated fat
16 mg cholesterol
608 mg sodium
27 g carbohydrate
5 g fiber
8 g protein

Fresh herbs turn ordinary dishes

into extraordinary ones. Some herbs—typically those with a sturdier constitution such as rosemary, bay leaf, and sage—are good for long-simmering or roasting. More delicate fresh herbs—such as basil, coriander, dill, and oregano—are best added right at the end of cooking. To substitute dry herbs for fresh, generally use one-third the amount of fresh herb called for in a recipe. (If a recipe uses 1 tablespoon fresh herb, add 1 teaspoon dry.)

italian mozzarella salad

Fresh mozzarella is a softer, more delicately flavored cousin of the cheese slathered on pizza. Celebrate its incomparable flavor tossed in a salad of mixed beans, given spark by a garlicky basil dressing.

INGREDIENTS

- 1 15-ounce can black beans or garbanzo beans, rinsed and drained
- 1 15-ounce can butter beans or Great Northern beans, rinsed and drained
- 2 red and/or yellow tomatoes, cut into thin wedges
- 1 small cucumber, quartered lengthwise and sliced (1 cup)
- ¼ cup thinly sliced green onions
- 1 recipe Basil Dressing or ½ cup bottled oil and vinegar salad dressing
- 8 ounces round- or log-shaped fresh mozzarella or part-skim Scamorza cheese

Scamorza, an Italian cheese

that's similar to mozzarella, is often aged and smoked. But when young, it's eaten fresh, like mozzarella.

Start to finish: 20 minutes

DIRECTIONS

1. In a large bowl combine beans, tomatoes, cucumber, and green onions.

2. Add the Basil Dressing; toss gently to coat.

3. Cut the cheese into thin slices. Add to bean mixture; toss gently to combine. Makes 4 servings.

Basil Dressing: In a screw-top jar combine ¼ cup red wine vinegar; ¼ cup olive oil or salad oil; 1 tablespoon snipped fresh basil or 1 teaspoon dried basil, crushed; 1 teaspoon Dijon-style mustard; 1 clove garlic, minced; and ¼ teaspoon crushed red pepper. Cover and shake well. If desired, refrigerate up to 2 days. Makes about ½ cup.

NUTRITION FACTS PER SERVING:

434 calories
23 g total fat
8 g saturated fat
32 mg cholesterol
919 mg sodium
37 g carbohydrate
6 g fiber
27 g protein

warm beet salad with roasted garlic dressing

INGREDIENTS

- 1 pound green beans
- 1 16-ounce can sliced beets, drained
- 2 tablespoons orange juice
- 2 tablespoons olive oil
- 1 tablespoon balsamic vinegar
- 2 teaspoons bottled roasted minced garlic
- ⅛ teaspoon salt
- ¼ cup soft-style herbed cream cheese or ¼ cup spreadable Brie cheese
- 8 slices French bread, lightly toasted
- Mixed salad greens

Garlic groupies, this stellar salad has your name on it, spelled out in a garlic-spiked dressing for succulent beets and crunchy green beans. Serve the vegetables warm so they absorb the sauce to the fullest.

Start to finish: 30 minutes

DIRECTIONS

1. In a covered large saucepan cook green beans in a small amount of boiling, lightly salted water about 15 minutes or until almost tender. Add beets and cook, covered, for 2 to 3 minutes more or until the beets are heated through. Drain and keep warm.

2. Meanwhile, for dressing, in a screw-top jar combine orange juice, oil, vinegar, garlic, and salt. Cover and shake well. Pour dressing over warm beans and beets. Spread cream cheese over French bread slices.

3. To serve, divide salad greens among 4 salad bowls or dinner plates. Top with the warm or room temperature beet mixture. If desired, sprinkle salads with coarsely ground pepper. Serve with French bread slices. Makes 4 servings.

In place of the homemade dressing, you can substitute a bottled garlic salad dressing or stir the bottled roasted minced garlic into a bottled Italian salad dressing.

NUTRITION FACTS PER SERVING:

320 calories
13 g total fat
4 g saturated fat
12 mg cholesterol
632 mg sodium
43 g carbohydrate
4 g fiber
8 g protein

mexican fiesta salad

Prepare this creamy salad in the morning and look forward all day to a hearty, corn-and-bean-studded treat. Lime and cilantro infuse the sour cream dressing.

INGREDIENTS

- 2 cups dried penne or rotini pasta
- ½ cup frozen whole kernel corn
- ½ cup light dairy sour cream
- ⅓ cup mild or medium chunky salsa
- 1 tablespoon snipped fresh cilantro
- 1 tablespoon lime juice
- 1 15-ounce can black beans, rinsed and drained
- 3 medium plum tomatoes, chopped (1 cup)
- 1 medium zucchini, chopped (1 cup)
- ½ cup shredded sharp cheddar cheese (2 ounces)

Start to finish: 30 minutes

DIRECTIONS

1. Cook pasta according to package directions, adding corn to the water with pasta the last 5 minutes of cooking; drain in colander. Rinse with cold water; drain again.

2. Meanwhile, for dressing, in a small bowl stir together sour cream, salsa, cilantro, and lime juice. Set aside.

3. In a large bowl combine pasta mixture, black beans, tomatoes, zucchini, and cheese. Pour dressing over pasta mixture; toss gently to coat. Serve immediately. (Or, if desired, cover and refrigerate up to 24 hours. Before serving, if necessary, stir in enough milk to make of desired consistency.) Makes 4 servings.

NUTRITION FACTS PER SERVING:

373 calories
9 g total fat
4 g saturated fat
19 mg cholesterol
470 mg sodium
61 g carbohydrate
7 g fiber
20 g protein

grilled vegetable salad with garlic dressing

INGREDIENTS

- 2 red and/or yellow sweet peppers
- 2 Japanese eggplants, halved lengthwise
- 2 medium zucchini or yellow summer squash, halved lengthwise, or 8 to 10 yellow sunburst or pattypan squash*
- 1 tablespoon olive oil
- 2 cups dried rigatoni pasta
- 1 recipe Roasted Garlic Dressing

- ¾ cup cubed fontina cheese (3 ounces)
- 1 to 2 tablespoons snipped fresh Italian flat-leaf parsley or regular parsley
- Fresh Italian flat-leaf parsley or regular parsley sprigs (optional)

Vegetables, sweet and smoky from the grill, give pasta and cheese a jolt of flavor and color. By doing the grilling ahead, and storing the savory dressing in the refrigerator, this maximum-impact dish is done in the time it takes to simmer pasta.

Start to finish: 25 minutes

DIRECTIONS

1. Halve the sweet peppers lengthwise; remove and discard the stems, seeds, and membranes. Brush the sweet peppers, eggplants, and zucchini with oil. Grill the vegetables on the rack of an uncovered grill directly over medium-hot heat for 8 to 12 minutes or until tender, turning occasionally. Remove vegetables from grill; cool slightly. Cut vegetables into 1-inch pieces.

2. Meanwhile, cook pasta according to package directions; drain in colander. Rinse with cold water; drain again. In a large bowl combine pasta and grilled vegetables. Pour Roasted Garlic Dressing over pasta mixture; toss gently to coat. Stir in cheese; sprinkle with snipped parsley. If desired, garnish with parsley sprigs. Makes 4 servings.

Roasted Garlic Dressing: In a screw-top jar combine 3 tablespoons balsamic vinegar or red wine vinegar, 2 tablespoons olive oil, 1 tablespoon water, 1 teaspoon bottled roasted minced garlic, ¼ teaspoon salt, and ¼ teaspoon black pepper. Cover and shake well.

*Note: If using sunburst or pattypan squash, precook in a small amount of boiling water for 3 minutes before grilling.

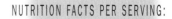

NUTRITION FACTS PER SERVING:

369 calories
19 g total fat
6 g saturated fat
61 mg cholesterol
317 mg sodium
40 g carbohydrate
5 g fiber
12 g protein

223

pasta coleslaw

Coleslaw, our legacy from the early Dutch settlers (who called it kool sla), tastes newly minted with pasta, sweet mandarin oranges, and healthy shredded broccoli, available prepackaged as broccoli slaw.

INGREDIENTS

- 4 ounces dried tiny bow-tie pasta (about 1½ cups)
- ⅔ cup light mayonnaise dressing or salad dressing
- 2 tablespoons white balsamic vinegar
- 1 tablespoon coarse-grain brown mustard
- ½ teaspoon sugar
- ½ teaspoon celery seed
- 3 cups packaged shredded broccoli (broccoli slaw mix)
- 1 15½-ounce can red kidney beans, rinsed and drained
- ¼ cup sliced green onions
- 1 11-ounce can mandarin orange sections, drained

Start to finish: 25 minutes

DIRECTIONS

1. Cook pasta according to package directions; drain in colander. Rinse with cold water; drain again.

2. Meanwhile, for dressing, stir together the mayonnaise dressing, vinegar, mustard, sugar, and celery seed. Set dressing aside.

3. In a large bowl combine pasta, broccoli, kidney beans, and green onions. Pour the dressing over pasta mixture; toss gently to coat. Stir in the orange sections. Serve immediately or cover and refrigerate for several hours. Makes 4 servings.

NUTRITION FACTS PER SERVING:

395 calories
15 g total fat
3 g saturated fat
0 mg cholesterol
563 mg sodium
58 g carbohydrate
8 g fiber
12 g protein

INGREDIENTS

- 2 cups sugar snap peas, strings and tips removed
- 1¼ cups dried orzo pasta (rosamarina)
- 1 6-ounce jar marinated artichoke hearts
- 2 cups red or yellow cherry tomatoes and/or baby pear-shaped tomatoes, halved
- 1 cup cubed mozzarella cheese (4 ounces)

- 1 4-ounce package crumbled feta or peppercorn feta cheese (1 cup)
- ¼ cup shredded Parmesan cheese
- ¼ cup white wine vinegar
- ¼ cup water
- 1 tablespoon snipped fresh dill or 1 teaspoon dried dillweed
- 2 teaspoons sugar

three-cheese orzo salad

Orzo is pasta shaped like rice that cooks in less than 10 minutes. It's a useful base for vegetables, and, like all pastas, was born to be served with cheese. Make it a triple indulgence with feta, mozzarella, and Parmesan.

Prep time: 30 minutes
Chilling time: 4 hours

DIRECTIONS

1. In a large saucepan cook the sugar snap peas in boiling, lightly salted water for 1 minute. Using a slotted spoon, transfer peas to a colander. Rinse with cold water; drain and set aside.

2. Add pasta to the same saucepan. Boil gently for 8 to 10 minutes or until pasta is tender but still firm; drain in colander. Rinse with cold water; drain again.

3. Meanwhile, drain the artichoke hearts, reserving marinade. Cut artichokes into bite-size pieces. In a large bowl toss together the sugar snap peas, pasta, artichokes, tomatoes, and cheeses.

4. For dressing, in a screw-top jar combine the reserved artichoke marinade, vinegar, water, dill, and sugar. Cover and shake well. Pour dressing over salad; toss gently to coat. Cover and refrigerate for 4 to 24 hours. Makes 8 servings.

NUTRITION FACTS PER SERVING:

233 calories
8 g total fat
4 g saturated fat
23 mg cholesterol
336 mg sodium
28 g carbohydrate
1 g fiber
12 g protein

225

penne salad with italian beans & gorgonzola

Assertive blue-veined Gorgonzola, tart sorrel, and bitter radicchio lose some attitude, but not their tasty sass, paired with meaty green beans, pasta, and a mellow herb dressing.

INGREDIENTS

- 6 ounces dried penne or cut ziti pasta, or elbow macaroni
- 8 ounces Italian green beans, bias-sliced into 2-inch pieces
- ⅓ cup bottled fat-free Italian salad dressing
- 1 tablespoon snipped fresh tarragon or ½ teaspoon dried tarragon, crushed
- ½ teaspoon freshly ground pepper
- 2 cups torn radicchio or 1 cup finely shredded red cabbage
- 4 cups sorrel or spinach leaves
- ½ cup crumbled Gorgonzola or other blue cheese (2 ounces)

If you can't find fresh Italian green beans, substitute one 9-ounce package frozen Italian green beans, thawed. Add the thawed frozen beans to the water with pasta the last 3 to 4 minutes of cooking.

Start to finish: 25 minutes

DIRECTIONS

1. Cook pasta according to package directions, adding green beans to the water with pasta the last 5 to 7 minutes of cooking; drain pasta mixture in colander. Rinse with cold water; drain again.

2. In a large bowl combine the Italian salad dressing, tarragon, and pepper. Add pasta mixture and radicchio; toss gently to coat.

3. To serve, divide sorrel leaves among 4 dinner plates. Top with pasta mixture. Sprinkle each serving with Gorgonzola cheese. Makes 4 servings.

NUTRITION FACTS PER SERVING:

269 calories
6 g total fat
3 g saturated fat
13 mg cholesterol
566 mg sodium
42 g carbohydrate
3 g fiber
12 g protein

INGREDIENTS

- 1½ cups dried large bow-tie pasta (about 6 ounces)
- 2 cups cantaloupe and/or honeydew melon chunks
- 1 cup cubed fontina or Swiss cheese (4 ounces)
- ⅓ cup bottled fat-free poppy seed salad dressing
- 1 to 2 tablespoons snipped fresh mint
- 2 cups watercress, stems removed
  Cantaloupe and/or honeydew melon shells (optional)

fontina & melon salad

Put the "lazy" back in Sundays. Organize brunch around a new take on the fruit-and-cheese course, made in a flash with bottled poppy seed dressing. Accompany with mimosas, the Sunday paper, and a cushiony chair.

Start to finish: 25 minutes

DIRECTIONS

1. Cook pasta according to package directions; drain in colander. Rinse with cold water; drain again.

2. In a large bowl toss together the pasta, cantaloupe chunks, and cheese. Combine salad dressing and mint. Pour over pasta mixture; toss gently to coat. Serve salad immediately or cover and refrigerate up to 24 hours.

3. To serve, stir watercress into pasta mixture. If desired, serve the salad in melon shells. Makes 4 servings.

NUTRITION FACTS PER SERVING:

319 calories
11 g total fat
6 g saturated fat
73 mg cholesterol
309 mg sodium
41 g carbohydrate
1 g fiber
14 g protein

227

mediterranean couscous salad

This Mediterranean meal is fast, flavorful, and healthy. A lemon and oregano dressing enlivens feta cheese and vegetables on a bed of quick-cooking couscous.

INGREDIENTS

- 1¾ cups water
- 1 cup quick-cooking couscous
- 1 recipe Lemon-Oregano Vinaigrette
- 1 medium red sweet pepper, chopped
- ½ cup chopped seeded cucumber
- ¼ cup sliced or chopped pitted kalamata olives or ripe olives
- ¼ cup crumbled feta cheese (1 ounce)
- 1 recipe Pita Chips or crisp crackers

Start to finish: 25 minutes

DIRECTIONS

1. In a small saucepan bring the water to boiling. Remove from heat; stir in the couscous. Let stand, covered, for 5 minutes. Fluff couscous with a fork.

2. Place couscous in a large bowl. Drizzle Lemon-Oregano Vinaigrette over couscous. Cool couscous for 10 minutes. Add the sweet pepper, cucumber, and olives; toss to combine. Sprinkle with cheese. Serve with Pita Chips. Makes 4 servings.

Lemon-Oregano Vinaigrette: In a screw-top jar combine 3 tablespoons lemon juice; 2 tablespoons olive oil; 1 tablespoon snipped fresh oregano or ¾ teaspoon dried oregano, crushed; and 1 tablespoon snipped fresh mint or ¼ teaspoon dried mint, crushed. Cover; shake well.

Pita Chips: Cut 2 pita bread rounds in half horizontally; cut each half into 6 wedges. Arrange wedges in a single layer on a baking sheet. Brush lightly with 1 tablespoon olive oil or coat with nonstick cooking spray. Sprinkle with ¼ to ½ teaspoon garlic salt. Bake in a 400° oven for 6 to 8 minutes or until crisp and lightly browned.

NUTRITION FACTS PER SERVING:

392 calories
14 g total fat
3 g saturated fat
6 mg cholesterol
287 mg sodium
57 g carbohydrate
8 g fiber
10 g protein

tomato, mozzarella, & polenta platter

Let your imagination run a little wild when it comes to tonight's salad supper. Instead of bread, try toasty polenta croutons. Use lettuce as the bowl and indulge in slices of delicate and creamy fresh mozzarella, garden tomatoes, and tangy kalamata olives.

INGREDIENTS

- 1 large head Boston or Bibb lettuce
- 8 ounces fresh mozzarella cheese, sliced
- 2 medium red tomatoes, cut into wedges
- 2 medium yellow tomatoes, sliced
- ¼ cup fresh basil leaves
- 1 16-ounce package prepared polenta, cut into ¾-inch slices
- 2 teaspoons olive oil
- ⅓ cup kalamata olives
- ¼ cup bottled red wine vinegar and oil salad dressing

Start to finish: 18 minutes

DIRECTIONS

1. Line a platter with lettuce leaves. Arrange the mozzarella cheese, tomatoes, and basil leaves on top of lettuce leaves, leaving room for polenta.

2. In a large nonstick skillet cook polenta slices in hot oil over medium heat for 4 to 6 minutes or until warm and lightly browned, turning once halfway through cooking. Add polenta and olives to platter. Serve with dressing. Makes 4 servings.

For a handsome presentation, make a basket out of the head of Boston or Bibb lettuce by removing the center leaves. Arrange the salad ingredients in the lettuce basket.

NUTRITION FACTS PER SERVING:

395 calories
25 g total fat
9 g saturated fat
44 mg cholesterol
928 mg sodium
30 g carbohydrate
5 g fiber
16 g protein

middle eastern bulgur-spinach salad

Bulgur or cracked wheat is a Middle Eastern staple. It's often cooked with lamb, but this vegetarian mélange of grain, fruits, and vegetables is equally satisfying and boasts a preparation that's simplicity itself.

INGREDIENTS

- 1 cup bulgur
- 1 cup boiling water
- ½ cup plain yogurt
- ¼ cup bottled red wine vinaigrette salad dressing
- 2 tablespoons snipped fresh parsley
- ½ teaspoon ground cumin
- 6 cups torn spinach
- 1 15-ounce can garbanzo beans, rinsed and drained
- 1 cup coarsely chopped apple
- ½ of a medium red onion, thinly sliced and separated into rings
- 3 tablespoons raisins (optional)

Start to finish: 30 minutes

DIRECTIONS

1. In a medium bowl combine bulgur and boiling water. Let stand about 10 minutes or until bulgur has absorbed all of the water. Cool for 15 minutes.

2. Meanwhile, for dressing, in a small bowl stir together yogurt, vinaigrette salad dressing, parsley, and cumin.

3. In a large bowl combine bulgur, spinach, garbanzo beans, apple, onion, and, if desired, raisins. Pour dressing over salad; toss gently to coat. Makes 4 servings.

NUTRITION FACTS PER SERVING:

340 calories
11 g total fat
2 g saturated fat
2 mg cholesterol
673 mg sodium
53 g carbohydrate
16 g fiber
13 g protein

papaya & olives with brown rice

As payback for the extra minutes it takes to cook, brown rice rewards with the full dietary benefits of the whole grain—including the nutritious bran that white rice sheds when polished.

INGREDIENTS

- 3 cups cooked brown rice
- ¼ cup chopped papaya or mango
- 3 tablespoons pitted ripe olives, coarsely chopped
- 2 tablespoons snipped fresh chives
- 2 tablespoons balsamic vinegar
- 1 tablespoon olive oil
- 3 tablespoons slivered almonds, toasted (see tip, page 63)

  Lettuce leaves
- 1 to 2 papayas, seeded and cut into wedges

Start to finish: 15 minutes

DIRECTIONS

1. In a large bowl combine cooked rice, papaya, olives, chives, vinegar, and oil; toss gently to combine.

2. Serve immediately or cover and refrigerate up to 6 hours.

3. Just before serving, stir in almonds. Serve the rice mixture on 3 lettuce-lined dinner plates with papaya wedges. Makes 3 servings.

To cook the brown rice, in a
medium saucepan bring 2 cups water and ¼ teaspoon salt to boiling. Stir in 1 cup rice. Return to boiling; reduce heat. Simmer, covered, for 45 minutes. Let stand for 5 minutes. If desired, cover and refrigerate for up to 3 days.

NUTRITION FACTS PER SERVING:

357 calories
12 g total fat
2 g saturated fat
0 mg cholesterol
55 mg sodium
57 g carbohydrate
5 g fiber
8 g protein

231

chunky ratatouille stew

Simmer the pleasures of a summer garden into this stew. Like typical ratatouille, it combines eggplant, tomatoes, onion, green sweet pepper, and green beans or zucchini. For a fun presentation, serve in hollowed eggplant halves.

INGREDIENTS

- 1 large onion, chopped
- 1 cup chopped green sweet pepper
- 1 tablespoon olive oil
- 2 cups small whole fresh mushrooms (about 6 ounces), stems removed
- 2 cups peeled and chopped eggplant (about 6 ounces)
- 4 ounces green beans, cut into 1-inch pieces, or 1 small zucchini, thinly sliced (about 1 cup)
- 2 cups beef broth
- 2 tablespoons dry red wine
- 1 14½-ounce can diced tomatoes with roasted garlic and red pepper
- 1 tablespoon snipped fresh basil
- ½ cup shredded provolone cheese (2 ounces)

Start to finish: 35 minutes

DIRECTIONS

1. In a Dutch oven cook the onion and green pepper in hot oil until tender. Stir in the mushrooms, eggplant, and green beans. Add beef broth and wine.

2. Bring to boiling; reduce heat. Simmer, covered, for 8 to 10 minutes or until vegetables are tender. Stir in undrained tomatoes and basil; heat through. Ladle into soup bowls. Sprinkle each serving with provolone cheese. Makes 4 servings.

NUTRITION FACTS PER SERVING:

163 calories
8 g total fat
3 g saturated fat
10 mg cholesterol
955 mg sodium
16 g carbohydrate
3 g fiber
8 g protein

INGREDIENTS

- 2 14½-ounce cans (3½ cups) vegetable broth or chicken broth
- 1 8-ounce can water chestnuts, drained and coarsely chopped
- 2 ounces dried angel hair pasta, broken (about 1 cup)
- ½ teaspoon snipped fresh savory or thyme

- 2 tablespoons cornstarch
- 8 ounces asparagus spears, trimmed and cut into 1-inch pieces
- ½ cup frozen peas
- 2 tablespoons snipped fresh mint
- 4 5-inch bread bowls or sliced French bread

spring vegetable soup

This is one super meal-in-a-bowl. Served in hollowed loaves of bread, this elegant potage scores high points for presentation—just the ticket for a casual dinner get-together or family celebration.

Start to finish: 25 minutes

DIRECTIONS

1. In a medium saucepan combine 3 cups of the broth, the water chestnuts, pasta, and savory. Bring to boiling; reduce heat. Simmer, covered, for 5 minutes.

2. Meanwhile, in a small bowl stir together remaining ½ cup broth and the cornstarch; add to saucepan. Stir in asparagus and peas. Cook and stir until thickened and bubbly. Cook and stir about 2 minutes more or until vegetables are tender and pasta is tender but still firm. Stir in the mint.

3. To serve, ladle soup into bread bowls. Or, ladle into soup bowls and serve with French bread slices. Makes 4 servings.

For bread bowls, hollow out small round loaves, leaving ½-inch-thick shells. If desired, brush the insides with 2 tablespoons melted margarine or butter. Bake in a 350° oven about 10 minutes or until the bread is lightly toasted.

NUTRITION FACTS PER SERVING:

268 calories
3 g total fat
0 g saturated fat
0 mg cholesterol
1,203 mg sodium
56 g carbohydrate
2 g fiber
9 g protein

tomato & wild mushroom soup

When foraging for the wild mushrooms that give this soup its woodsy depth of flavor, look no further than the produce section of your local supermarket. There you'll find a bounty of exotic types ready to be gathered.

INGREDIENTS

- 1 medium onion, chopped
- 2 cloves garlic, minced
- 1 tablespoon olive oil
- 8 ounces fresh mushrooms (such as porcini, chanterelle, portobello, or button), coarsely chopped (3 cups)
- 1 pound plum tomatoes, chopped (about 3 cups)
- 3 cups vegetable broth or chicken broth
- ¼ cup finely shredded Romano or Parmesan cheese
- ¼ cup shredded fresh basil or 2 tablespoons snipped fresh thyme or marjoram

If the common button or other

cultivated mushrooms bore you, take a walk on the wild side with fresh exotics such as fragrant Italian porcini, trumpetlike chanterelles, or meaty morels. Intensely flavored dried porcini and morel mushrooms are another option. To rehydrate, soak them in warm water for 30 minutes; rinse and drain well.

Start to finish: 30 minutes

DIRECTIONS

1. In a large saucepan cook onion and garlic in hot oil over medium heat until onion is tender. Stir in mushrooms. Cook for 5 to 7 minutes more or until mushrooms are tender, stirring occasionally.

2. Add the tomatoes and broth to mushroom mixture. Bring to boiling; reduce heat. Simmer, covered, for 10 minutes.

3. Ladle into soup bowls. Sprinkle each serving with cheese and basil or other herb. Season to taste with freshly ground pepper. Makes 3 servings.

NUTRITION FACTS PER SERVING:

140 calories
9 g total fat
1 g saturated fat
7 mg cholesterol
1,049 mg sodium
17 g carbohydrate
3 g fiber
7 g protein

INGREDIENTS

2   medium carrots, finely chopped
2   stalks celery, finely chopped
1   large onion, finely chopped
6   cloves garlic, minced
1   tablespoon olive oil
1   cup water
2   pounds tomatoes, chopped
       (about 6 cups)

½   cup snipped fresh basil or
       2 tablespoons dried basil,
       crushed, and ½ cup snipped
       fresh parsley
1   teaspoon salt
1   tablespoon balsamic vinegar

tomato-basil soup

This soup is inspired by the cuisine of Northern Italy, where tomatoes and basil are popular ingredients. Try it during the summer months when you can use vegetables and herbs fresh from the garden or farmers' market.

Start to finish: 40 minutes

DIRECTIONS

1. In a covered large saucepan cook carrots, celery, onion, and garlic in hot oil over medium-low heat for 10 minutes, stirring occasionally. Transfer to a blender container or food processor bowl; add the water. Cover and blend or process until smooth. Return to saucepan.

2. Stir in half of the tomatoes, half of the fresh basil or all of the dried basil, and the salt. Bring to boiling; reduce heat. Simmer, covered, for 15 minutes. Remove from heat.

3. Stir in the remaining tomatoes, the remaining fresh basil or all of the parsley, and the balsamic vinegar; heat through. Makes 4 servings.

NUTRITION FACTS PER SERVING:

145 calories
5 g total fat
1 g saturated fat
0 mg cholesterol
618 mg sodium
26 g carbohydrate
6 g fiber
4 g protein

235

mushroom, noodle, & tofu soup

Japanese udon (oo-DOHN) noodles are similar to spaghetti. Look for them in Asian markets or in the Oriental section of your supermarket.

INGREDIENTS

- 1 49-ounce can (about 6 cups) reduced-sodium chicken broth
- 1 10- to 12-ounce package extra-firm tofu (fresh bean curd), drained and cut into ½-inch cubes
- 1 tablespoon soy sauce
- 1 tablespoon toasted sesame oil
- 6 ounces sliced fresh shiitake or button mushrooms (about 2¼ cups)
- 1 tablespoon grated fresh ginger
- 1 clove garlic, minced
- 1 tablespoon cooking oil
- 1 16-ounce package frozen sugar snap pea stir-fry vegetables
- 2 ounces dried udon noodles or spaghetti, broken
- 1 tablespoon snipped fresh cilantro

Store fresh mushrooms

in the refrigerator. Instead of an airtight container, use a brown paper sack or a cotton bag that will let them breathe. Avoid soaking or washing mushrooms prior to storage; they will absorb water and deteriorate more quickly. Just before using the mushrooms, clean them by wiping with a damp cloth or paper towel.

Start to finish: 30 minutes

DIRECTIONS

1. In a large saucepan bring the broth to boiling. Meanwhile, in a medium bowl gently stir together tofu, soy sauce, and sesame oil; set aside.

2. In a medium saucepan cook the sliced mushrooms, ginger, and garlic in hot cooking oil for 4 minutes. Add to the hot broth. Stir in the frozen vegetables and udon noodles.

3. Bring to boiling; reduce heat. Simmer, covered, for 10 to 12 minutes or until vegetables and noodles are tender, stirring once or twice. Gently stir in the tofu mixture and the cilantro; heat through. Makes 6 servings.

NUTRITION FACTS PER SERVING:

162 calories
7 g total fat
1 g saturated fat
0 mg cholesterol
868 mg sodium
17 g carbohydrate
1 g fiber
9 g protein

spring green pasta soup

Thin strips of cooked egg, exquisite spring vegetables, and wispy threads of angel hair pasta compose a delicate soup with the airy lightness of a heavenly omelet.

INGREDIENTS

4   cups reduced-sodium chicken broth

2   cups water

2   slightly beaten eggs

2   teaspoons cooking oil

4   ounces dried angel hair pasta, broken into 2-inch pieces

2   medium leeks, sliced, or ⅔ cup sliced green onions

2   cloves garlic, minced

4   ounces sugar snap peas, strings and tips removed and halved crosswise

8   ounces asparagus, trimmed and cut into 1-inch pieces (about 1 cup)

2   tablespoons snipped fresh dill

2   teaspoons finely shredded lemon peel

Medium asparagus spears, trimmed (optional)

Start to finish: 30 minutes

DIRECTIONS

1. In a large saucepan bring the chicken broth and water to boiling.

2. Meanwhile, in a medium skillet cook eggs in hot oil over medium heat, without stirring, for 2 to 3 minutes or until eggs are set. To remove cooked eggs, loosen edge and invert skillet over a cutting board; cut eggs into thin, bite-size strips. Set aside.

3. Add pasta, leeks, and garlic to chicken broth. Boil gently, uncovered, about 3 minutes or until pasta is almost tender. Add sugar snap peas, asparagus pieces, dill, and lemon peel. Return to boiling. Boil gently about 2 minutes more or until vegetables are crisp-tender. Stir in egg strips. Ladle into soup bowls. If desired, garnish with asparagus spears. Makes 4 servings.

NUTRITION FACTS PER SERVING:

235 calories
7 g total fat
1 g saturated fat
107 mg cholesterol
684 mg sodium
33 g carbohydrate
4 g fiber
12 g protein

asparagus & cheese potato soup

A treasure of spring—tender, purple-tinged asparagus—is featured in this soup. Sour cream lends a tangy flavor to this creamy delight.

INGREDIENTS

- 1 large onion, chopped
- 4 teaspoons cooking oil
- 3 tablespoons all-purpose flour
- 2 cups 1-inch pieces asparagus spears or broccoli flowerets
- 2 cups milk
- 1 14½-ounce can chicken broth
- 8 ounces red potatoes, cubed (about 1½ cups)
- ¼ teaspoon salt
- ⅛ teaspoon ground red pepper
- 1 cup shredded sharp cheddar cheese (4 ounces)
- 1 small tomato, seeded and chopped
- ⅓ cup dairy sour cream

Start to finish: 35 minutes

DIRECTIONS

1. In a large saucepan cook onion in hot oil over medium heat until tender. Sprinkle flour over onion and stir to coat. Add the asparagus, milk, chicken broth, potatoes, salt, and red pepper.

2. Cook and stir until thickened and bubbly; reduce heat. Simmer, covered, for 10 to 12 minutes or just until vegetables are tender, stirring occasionally. Add cheddar cheese, tomato, and sour cream; stir until cheese is melted. Makes 4 servings.

NUTRITION FACTS PER SERVING:

383 calories
21 g total fat
11 g saturated fat
48 mg cholesterol
730 mg sodium
31 g carbohydrate
3 g fiber
18 g protein

jalapeño corn chowder

Spectacular and rich, this chowder features the popular Southwestern flavors of corn, jalapeño peppers, and red sweet peppers. Although not a must, crumbled feta cheese sprinkled over each serving adds a salty tang to the soup.

INGREDIENTS

- 3 cups frozen whole kernel corn or 3 cups fresh corn kernels (cut from 6 to 7 ears of corn)
- 1 14½-ounce can chicken broth
- 1¼ cups cooked small pasta (such as ditalini or tiny shell macaroni)
- 1 cup milk, half-and-half, or light cream
- ¼ of a 7-ounce jar roasted red sweet peppers, drained and chopped (¼ cup)
- 1 or 2 fresh jalapeño peppers, seeded and finely chopped (see tip, page 158)
- ½ cup crumbled feta cheese (optional)

Start to finish: 20 minutes

DIRECTIONS

1. In a blender container or food processor bowl combine half of the corn and the chicken broth. Cover and blend or process until almost smooth.

2. In a large saucepan combine the broth mixture and the remaining corn. If using fresh corn, bring to boiling; reduce heat. Simmer, covered, for 2 to 3 minutes or until corn is crisp-tender.

3. Stir in cooked pasta, milk, roasted peppers, and jalapeño peppers; heat through. Ladle into soup bowls. If desired, top each serving with feta cheese. Makes 4 servings.

NUTRITION FACTS PER SERVING:

247 calories
3 g total fat
1 g saturated fat
5 mg cholesterol
363 mg sodium
47 g carbohydrate
1 g fiber
11 g protein

239

vegetable cheese chowder

Frozen vegetables are the secret to this quick chowder. A little smoked Gouda cheese produces the robust flavor.

INGREDIENTS

- 1 16-ounce package loose-pack frozen broccoli, cauliflower, and carrots
- ½ cup water
- 2 cups milk
- ⅓ cup all-purpose flour
- ⅛ teaspoon pepper
- 1 14½-ounce can chicken broth
- 1 cup shredded smoked or regular Gouda cheese (4 ounces)

When a recipe calls for chicken, beef, or vegetable broth, you can use a homemade stock recipe or substitute commercially canned broth. Just remember that the canned varieties usually are saltier than homemade stocks, so hold off on adding extra salt until the end of cooking. Then, season to taste. Another option is to try a canned reduced-sodium broth. Bouillon cubes and granules diluted according to package directions may be used, but they are also saltier than homemade stocks.

Start to finish: 20 minutes

DIRECTIONS

1. In a large saucepan combine frozen vegetables and water. Bring to boiling; reduce heat. Simmer, covered, about 4 minutes or until vegetables are just tender. Do not drain.

2. Meanwhile, in a screw-top jar combine ⅔ cup of the milk, the flour, and pepper; cover and shake well. Add to saucepan; add the remaining milk and chicken broth. Cook and stir until thickened and bubbly. Cook and stir for 1 minute more. Add the Gouda cheese; cook and stir over low heat until cheese is almost melted. Makes 4 servings.

NUTRITION FACTS PER SERVING:

370 calories
20 g total fat
13 g saturated fat
81 mg cholesterol
942 mg sodium
22 g carbohydrate
3 g fiber
25 g protein

INGREDIENTS

2 14½-ounce cans (3½ cups) chicken broth

2 cups sliced carrots

1 large potato, peeled and chopped

1 cup chopped onion

1 tablespoon grated fresh ginger

½ to 1 teaspoon purchased or homemade Jamaican jerk seasoning (see tip, page 106)

8 ounces dried tricolor radiatore or rotini pasta

1½ cups milk or one 12-ounce can evaporated fat-free milk

Fresh chives (optional)

creamy carrot & pasta soup

Do you hear the reggae rhythms? Or is it just the hot Jamaican spices in this creamy pasta soup that dance in your mouth? It's a tropical trip via a dash of jerk seasoning—a unique island blend of spices, herbs, and fiery chilies that is Jamaica's own.

Start to finish: 30 minutes

DIRECTIONS

1. In a large saucepan combine the chicken broth, carrots, potato, onion, ginger, and Jamaican jerk seasoning. Bring to boiling; reduce heat. Simmer, covered, for 15 to 20 minutes or until the vegetables are very tender. Cool slightly.

2. Meanwhile, cook the pasta according to package directions; drain.

3. Place one-fourth of the vegetable mixture in a food processor bowl. Cover and process until smooth. Process remaining vegetable mixture one-fourth at a time. Return all to saucepan. Stir in pasta and milk; heat through. Ladle into soup bowls. If desired, sprinkle each serving with chives. Makes 4 servings.

NUTRITION FACTS PER SERVING:

363 calories
4 g total fat
2 g saturated fat
8 mg cholesterol
750 mg sodium
65 g carbohydrate
3 g fiber
16 g protein

italian greens & cheese tortellini

Tender spinach and sugar snap peas team with cheese tortellini in this lemon-scented soup. Sprinkle each serving with fresh Parmesan cheese for a sharp flavor accent.

INGREDIENTS

1½ cups finely chopped onion

5 cloves garlic, minced

1 teaspoon dried Italian seasoning, crushed

1 tablespoon olive oil

2 14½-ounce cans (3½ cups) reduced-sodium chicken broth

1½ cups water

1 9-ounce package refrigerated cheese-filled tortellini

2 cups sugar snap peas, strings and tips removed and halved crosswise

2 cups shredded spinach

2 teaspoons lemon juice

2 tablespoons finely shredded Parmesan cheese

Start to finish: 35 minutes

DIRECTIONS

1. In a Dutch oven cook the onion, garlic, and Italian seasoning in hot oil over medium heat until onion is tender. Add chicken broth and water. Bring to boiling; add tortellini. Return to boiling; reduce heat. Simmer, uncovered, for 4 minutes.

2. Stir in sugar snap peas, spinach, and lemon juice. Return to boiling; reduce heat. Simmer, uncovered, for 2 minutes more. Ladle into soup bowls. Top each serving with Parmesan cheese. Makes 4 servings.

NUTRITION FACTS PER SERVING:

320 calories
10 g total fat
2 g saturated fat
33 mg cholesterol
881 mg sodium
42 g carbohydrate
3 g fiber
17 g protein

INGREDIENTS

- 1 shallot, finely chopped
- 1 fresh jalapeño pepper, seeded and finely chopped (see tip, page 158)
- 2 teaspoons curry powder
- 1 clove garlic, minced
- 1 tablespoon cooking oil
- 1 14½-ounce can chicken broth
- 1 14-ounce can unsweetened coconut milk
- 1 9-ounce package refrigerated mushroom-filled tortelloni
- 1 tablespoon snipped fresh basil
- 1 medium tomato, chopped
  Chopped peanuts (optional)

mushroom tortelloni in curry cream

Indonesian in flavor, this quick-cooking soup captures your attention with its wonderful aroma. Curry, coconut, and basil all add to the allure. If you're unable to find tortelloni, a larger version of tortellini, use tortellini instead.

Start to finish: 30 minutes

DIRECTIONS

1. In a medium saucepan cook shallot, jalapeño pepper, curry powder, and garlic in hot oil about 1 minute or until shallot is tender. Stir in chicken broth. Bring to boiling; reduce heat. Simmer, covered, for 5 minutes.

2. Stir in the coconut milk, tortelloni, and basil. Cook and stir about 5 minutes more or until pasta is tender but still firm. Stir in the tomato. Cook and stir until heated through, but do not boil.

3. Ladle into soup bowls. If desired, sprinkle each serving with chopped peanuts. Makes 4 servings.

NUTRITION FACTS PER SERVING:

306 calories
14 g total fat
7 g saturated fat
24 mg cholesterol
649 mg sodium
35 g carbohydrate
3 g fiber
10 g protein

black & white bean chili

Calling all hearty appetites! This satisfying blend of black beans, white kidney beans, jicama, and chili peppers boasts a pronounced south-of-the-border flavor.

INGREDIENTS

1 medium onion, chopped

1 clove garlic, minced

1 tablespoon cooking oil

1 15-ounce can white kidney (cannellini) beans, rinsed and drained

1 15-ounce can black beans, rinsed and drained

1 14½-ounce can chicken broth

1 cup chopped peeled jicama or potato

1 4-ounce can diced green chili peppers

1 teaspoon ground cumin

2 tablespoons snipped fresh cilantro

1 tablespoon lime juice

¼ cup crumbled queso fresco or feta cheese (1 ounce)

Jicama is often referred to as the Mexican potato. This large, bulbous root vegetable has a thin brown skin and white crunchy flesh. Unlike regular potatoes, jicama has a sweet, nutty flavor and is good both raw and cooked. It is available from November through May and can be purchased in Mexican markets and most large supermarkets. Jicama will last up to 5 days stored in the refrigerator. The thin skin should be peeled just before using. When cooked, jicama retains its crisp, water chestnut-type texture.

Start to finish: 35 minutes

DIRECTIONS

1. In a large saucepan cook onion and garlic in hot oil until tender. Stir in the white kidney beans, black beans, chicken broth, jicama or potato, green chili peppers, and cumin.

2. Bring to boiling; reduce heat. Simmer, covered, about 10 minutes or until jicama is crisp-tender or potato is tender. Stir in cilantro and lime juice; heat through. Ladle into soup bowls. Top each serving with cheese. Makes 4 servings.

NUTRITION FACTS PER SERVING:

254 calories
9 g total fat
3 g saturated fat
15 mg cholesterol
1,012 mg sodium
37 g carbohydrate
10 g fiber
19 g protein

INGREDIENTS

- 2 stalks celery, finely chopped
- 1 large onion, finely chopped
- 2 cloves garlic, minced
- 1 tablespoon olive oil
- 5 cups beef broth
- 1 cup water
- ½ cup uncooked Arborio rice or short grain rice
- 6 cups torn spinach
- 1 15-ounce can Great Northern beans, rinsed and drained
- 3 medium tomatoes, chopped (about 2 cups)
- 1 medium zucchini, coarsely chopped (about 1½ cups)
- ¼ cup snipped fresh thyme
- ¼ teaspoon cracked pepper
- ½ cup crumbled feta cheese (2 ounces)
- Spinach leaves (optional)

greek minestrone

Arborio rice is an Italian-grown grain that is shorter and plumper than any other short-grain rice. Traditionally used to make creamy risotto, it adds a similar texture to this bean and vegetable soup.

Start to finish: 40 minutes

DIRECTIONS

1. In a Dutch oven cook the celery, onion, and garlic in hot oil until tender. Add the beef broth, water, and rice. Bring to boiling; reduce heat. Simmer, covered, for 15 minutes.

2. Add the torn spinach, beans, tomatoes, zucchini, thyme, and pepper. Cook and stir until heated through. Ladle into soup bowls. Top each serving with cheese. If desired, garnish with spinach leaves. Makes 6 servings.

NUTRITION FACTS PER SERVING:

252 calories
6 g total fat
2 g saturated fat
8 mg cholesterol
834 mg sodium
39 g carbohydrate
8 g fiber
13 g protein

garbanzo bean stew

No need to wait for cooler weather to serve this colorful stew. It is a satisfying meal any time of year. The feta cheese—an optional addition—lends a tangy, fresh flavor.

INGREDIENTS

- 1 large onion, chopped
- 1 medium green sweet pepper, chopped
- 3 cloves garlic, minced
- 2 teaspoons cooking oil
- 1½ teaspoons ground cumin
- ½ teaspoon paprika
- ⅛ to ¼ teaspoon ground red pepper
- 2 cups reduced-sodium chicken broth
- 1½ cups water
- 1 10-ounce package frozen whole kernel corn
- 2 tablespoons snipped fresh oregano
- 1 15-ounce can garbanzo beans, rinsed and drained
- 1 medium tomato, chopped
- 2 tablespoons lemon juice
- ¼ cup crumbled feta cheese (optional)
- 2 tablespoons thinly sliced green onion

Start to finish: 20 minutes

DIRECTIONS

1. In a covered large saucepan cook onion, sweet pepper, and garlic in hot oil until onion is tender, stirring occasionally. Stir in cumin, paprika, and ground red pepper; cook for 1 minute.

2. Carefully add the broth, water, frozen corn, and oregano. Bring to boiling; reduce heat. Simmer, covered, for 5 to 10 minutes or until corn is tender. Stir in beans, tomato, and lemon juice. Heat through.

3. Ladle into soup bowls. Sprinkle each serving with feta cheese (if desired) and sliced green onion. Makes 4 servings.

NUTRITION FACTS PER SERVING:

217 calories
6 g total fat
1 g saturated fat
0 mg cholesterol
672 mg sodium
38 g carbohydrate
5 g fiber
9 g protein

INGREDIENTS

- 1   10-ounce package frozen baby lima beans
- 1   cup green beans cut into 1-inch pieces
- 1½ cups sliced and halved fresh portobello mushrooms or sliced button mushrooms (about 4 ounces)
- 1   tablespoon olive oil
- 1   tablespoon cold water

- 2   teaspoons cornstarch
- 1   14½-ounce can Cajun- or Italian-style stewed tomatoes
- 1   cup canned garbanzo beans, rinsed and drained

mixed bean & portobello ragout

Ragout is simply a thick, savory stew of French origin. This healthy, meatless ragout features a host of legumes and meaty portobellos, which are oversize brown mushrooms with an Italian-sounding name. Serve it with crusty bread.

Start to finish: 20 minutes

DIRECTIONS

1. In a covered medium saucepan cook lima beans and green beans in a small amount of boiling, lightly salted water according to the lima bean package directions; drain.

2. Meanwhile, in a large skillet cook the mushrooms in hot oil over medium heat for 5 minutes, stirring occasionally. Combine water and cornstarch; stir into mushrooms. Stir in undrained tomatoes and garbanzo beans. Cook and stir until thickened and bubbly. Cook and stir for 2 minutes more. Stir the cooked lima and green beans into tomato mixture; heat through. Makes 4 servings.

NUTRITION FACTS PER SERVING:

214 calories
5 g total fat
1 g saturated fat
0 mg cholesterol
528 mg sodium
36 g carbohydrate
10 g fiber
10 g protein

curried lentil soup

Humble lentils step out in spicy style with a flavor kick of ginger, curry powder, cumin, and cilantro. If you like, a spoonful of sour cream swirled into the soup adds a complementary richness.

INGREDIENTS

6 cups reduced-sodium chicken broth
1½ cups thinly sliced green onions
2 medium carrots, chopped
1 cup brown lentils, rinsed and drained
1 tablespoon grated fresh ginger
1 teaspoon curry powder
1 teaspoon ground cumin
⅛ to ¼ teaspoon ground red pepper
¼ cup snipped fresh cilantro
½ cup dairy sour cream (optional)
Green onions and/or fresh cilantro sprigs (optional)

Start to finish: 40 minutes

DIRECTIONS

1. In a large saucepan combine the chicken broth, sliced green onions, carrots, lentils, ginger, curry powder, cumin, and red pepper. Bring to boiling; reduce heat. Simmer, covered, for 25 to 30 minutes or until the lentils are tender.

2. Stir in snipped cilantro; cook for 1 minute more. Ladle into soup bowls. If desired, top each serving with sour cream and garnish with green onions and/or cilantro sprigs. Makes 4 servings.

NUTRITION FACTS PER SERVING:

201 calories
3 g total fat
0 g saturated fat
0 mg cholesterol
986 mg sodium
32 g carbohydrate
3 g fiber
15 g protein

pesto-vegetable soup

A swirl of basil pesto provides the perfect flavor accent for this vegetable and pasta soup. Pesto can be purchased already prepared at your supermarket or deli.

INGREDIENTS

- **2** cloves garlic, minced
- **1** tablespoon olive oil
- **2** 14½-ounce cans (3½ cups) vegetable broth
- **½** cup dried ditalini pasta or small shell macaroni
- **1** cup packaged frozen stir-fry vegetables
- **3** cups torn arugula or Swiss chard, or shredded Chinese cabbage
- **2** cups torn spinach
- **3** tablespoons pesto

Start to finish: 25 minutes

DIRECTIONS

1. In a large saucepan cook the garlic in hot oil for 30 seconds. Add vegetable broth. Bring to boiling; add the pasta. Return to boiling; reduce heat. Boil gently, uncovered, for 6 minutes, stirring occasionally.

2. Stir in the stir-fry vegetables; return to boiling. Stir in arugula and spinach; cook and stir for 2 minutes more. Ladle into soup bowls. Swirl pesto into each serving. Makes 3 servings.

NUTRITION FACTS PER SERVING:

261 calories
17 g total fat
1 g saturated fat
2 mg cholesterol
1,281 mg sodium
29 g carbohydrate
1 g fiber
7 g protein

wild rice, barley, & mushroom soup

It's hard to resist this enticing soup. The nutty flavor and chewy texture of wild rice and barley make pleasant contrasts to the earthy flavor and soft texture of the mushrooms. Add a splash of Madeira for a sophisticated accent.

INGREDIENTS

- 1 cup water
- ¼ cup quick-cooking barley
- 3 medium leeks, thinly sliced
- 1 medium carrot, sliced
- 1 small parsnip, finely chopped
- 1 clove garlic, minced
- 1 tablespoon margarine or butter
- 3 cups sliced fresh mushrooms (about 8 ounces)
- 1 tablespoon snipped fresh sage or 1 teaspoon dried sage, crushed
- 2½ cups vegetable broth
- ¾ cup cooked wild rice
- 2 tablespoons Madeira wine or dry sherry (optional)

Start to finish: 25 minutes

DIRECTIONS

1. In a small saucepan combine the water and barley. Bring to boiling; reduce heat. Simmer, covered, for 10 minutes.

2. Meanwhile, in a large saucepan cook leeks, carrot, parsnip, and garlic in hot margarine for 5 minutes. Stir in the mushrooms and, if using, dried sage. Cook for 5 to 10 minutes more or just until mushrooms are tender. Stir in the vegetable broth, cooked wild rice, and, if desired, Madeira. If using, stir in fresh sage. Cook and stir until heated through. Season to taste with salt and pepper. Makes 3 servings.

NUTRITION FACTS PER SERVING:

223 calories
6 g total fat
1 g saturated fat
0 mg cholesterol
854 mg sodium
45 g carbohydrate
9 g fiber
7 g protein

squash & papaya soup

Despite a demure demeanor, this golden fruit-and-vegetable soup is hot stuff. Giving it bold personality are nuances of Indian curry mixed with hints of garlic, ginger, and red pepper. Pour the soup over wheat berries for a satisfying meal.

INGREDIENTS

2 cloves garlic, minced
1 tablespoon olive oil
1 teaspoon curry powder
½ teaspoon ground ginger
⅛ teaspoon ground red pepper (optional)
2 14½-ounce cans (3½ cups) vegetable broth or chicken broth

3 cups chopped, peeled and seeded butternut squash
1 cup finely chopped papaya, peaches, or nectarines
2⅔ cups cooked wheat berries
2 tablespoons snipped fresh cilantro (optional)

Prep time: 25 minutes
Cooking time: 20 minutes

DIRECTIONS

1. In a large saucepan cook garlic in hot oil over medium heat for 30 seconds. Add curry powder, ginger, and, if desired, red pepper. Cook and stir for 1 minute more. Stir in broth, squash, and papaya.

2. Bring to boiling; reduce heat. Simmer, covered, about 20 minutes or until squash is tender. Cool slightly.

3. Place half of the squash mixture in a food processor bowl or blender container. Cover and process or blend until smooth. Repeat with the remaining squash mixture. Return all to saucepan and heat through.

4. To serve, divide wheat berries among 4 soup bowls. Ladle soup over wheat berries. If desired, sprinkle each serving with cilantro. Makes 4 servings.

NUTRITION FACTS PER SERVING:

248 calories
5 g total fat
1 g saturated fat
0 mg cholesterol
823 mg sodium
53 g carbohydrate
4 g fiber
7 g protein

To cook the wheat berries,

bring 3 cups water to boiling. Add 1 cup wheat berries. Return to boiling; reduce heat. Simmer, covered, about 1 hour or until tender. Drain well. If desired, cover and refrigerate for up to 3 days. Reheat before serving.

Fruited Cheese Spirals
See recipe, page 256

appetizers, sides, and desserts

Asparagus with Raspberry-Dijon Dipping Sauce 254
White Bean Dip with Toasted Pita Chips 255
Fruited Cheese Spirals 256
Grilled Antipasto Skewers 257
Antipasto on a Stick 258
Baked Kasseri Cheese Spread 259
Mexicali Stuffed Zucchini 260
Roasted Vegetables with Balsamic Vinegar 261
Eggplant with Gorgonzola 262
Piquant Grilled Broccoli & Olives 263
Vegetable Kabobs 264
Grilled Tomatoes with Pesto 265
Orange & New Potato Salad 266
Warm Tarragon Potato Salad 267
Fried Green Tomatoes on a Bed of Greens 268
Warm Asparagus, Fennel, & Spinach Salad 269

Pear & Endive Salad with Honey Vinaigrette 270
Potato-Leek Pancakes 271
Corn Cakes with Fresh Corn & Chives 272
Sweet & Spicy Pepper-Pineapple Salsa 273
Grilled Corn Relish 274
Gingered Shortcake with Spiced Fruit 275
Espresso-Orange Sauce 276
Bananas Suzette over Grilled Pound Cake 277
Red Wine-Marinated Peaches 278
Almond Cookie Cups with Sorbet 279
Chocolate Ricotta-Filled Pears 280
Nectarine-Raspberry Crisp 281

asparagus with raspberry-dijon dipping sauce

INGREDIENTS

- 8 ounces sugar snap peas
- 1 pound medium asparagus spears, trimmed
- 3 tablespoons raspberry vinegar
- 1 tablespoon honey mustard
- ¼ teaspoon freshly ground pepper
- Dash salt
- ¼ cup cooking oil
- ¼ cup olive oil
- Shredded red cabbage (optional)
- Fresh raspberries (optional)

Why relegate tender asparagus to the side? Here, it stars as a fresh and light starter with a tangy dipping sauce. If you like, prepare the sauce ahead and refrigerate it for up to 4 hours before serving.

Start to finish: 25 minutes

DIRECTIONS

1. If desired, remove the strings and tips from snap peas. In a large deep skillet bring 1 inch of salted water to boiling. Add asparagus; reduce heat. Simmer, uncovered, about 4 minutes or until crisp-tender. Using tongs, transfer asparagus to a large bowl of ice water to cool quickly. Add snap peas to simmering water and cook about 2 minutes or until crisp-tender. Drain and transfer to bowl of ice water.

2. Meanwhile, for dipping sauce, in a blender container or food processor bowl combine the vinegar, honey mustard, pepper, and salt. Cover and blend or process until combined. With the blender or processor running, slowly add the oils in a thin, steady stream. Continue blending or processing until mixture is thickened.

3. If desired, line a serving platter with the shredded red cabbage. Arrange asparagus and sugar snap peas on top of the cabbage. Serve with the dipping sauce. If desired, garnish with raspberries. Makes 12 servings.

NUTRITION FACTS PER SERVING:

96 calories
9 g total fat
1 g saturated fat
0 mg cholesterol
14 mg sodium
3 g carbohydrate
1 g fiber
1 g protein

INGREDIENTS

- ¼ cup soft bread crumbs
- 2 tablespoons dry white wine or water
- 1 15- to 19-ounce can white kidney (cannellini) beans or Great Northern beans, rinsed and drained
- ¼ cup slivered almonds, toasted (see tip, page 63)
- 2 tablespoons lemon juice
- 2 tablespoons olive oil
- 3 cloves garlic, minced
- ¼ teaspoon salt
- ⅛ teaspoon ground red pepper
- 2 teaspoons snipped fresh oregano or basil
- 1 recipe Toasted Pita Chips
- 1 red and/or yellow sweet pepper, cut into 1-inch-wide strips (optional)

white bean dip with toasted pita chips

Almost everybody loves Mediterranean—and this creamy, aromatic dip is the essence of it. Inspired by hummus and skordalia, a Greek puree of potatoes, garlic, and almonds, it spices up predictable breads and crudités.

Prep time: 20 minutes
Baking time: 12 minutes

DIRECTIONS

1. In a small bowl combine bread crumbs and wine; set aside. In a food processor bowl or blender container combine beans, almonds, lemon juice, olive oil, garlic, salt, and ground red pepper. Cover and process or blend until almost smooth. Add bread-crumb mixture. Cover and process or blend until smooth. Stir in oregano. If desired, cover and refrigerate the dip for 3 to 24 hours to blend flavors.

2. Serve dip with Toasted Pita Chips and, if desired, sweet pepper strips. Makes 30 servings.

Toasted Pita Chips: Split 5 large pita bread rounds in half horizontally; cut each circle into 6 wedges (kitchen scissors work well for this task). Place the wedges in a single layer on large baking sheets. Brush wedges with 2 tablespoons olive oil or melted butter. If desired, sprinkle with paprika. Bake in a 350° oven for 12 to 15 minutes or until crisp and golden brown.

NUTRITION FACTS PER SERVING:

59 calories
2 g total fat
0 g saturated fat
0 mg cholesterol
96 mg sodium
8 g carbohydrate
1 g fiber
2 g protein

Even for the most casual

get-togethers, it's nice to have an assortment of nibbles for your guests to enjoy as a prelude to the main event. But if you're planning a no-fuss evening, just make one simple starter from scratch. Then fill in with purchased crudités, bagel chips, tortilla chips with salsa, purchased hummus with warm wedges of pita bread, or marinated olives. Stylish but easy!

fruited cheese spirals

Finger food gets a fresh new look! Dried fruit adds jewel tones to these clever spirals filled with prosciutto, cream cheese, and the cinnamon-pepper flavor of fresh basil.

INGREDIENTS

- ½ cup orange juice or apple juice
- 1 cup dried fruit (such as cranberries, snipped tart or sweet cherries, and/or snipped apricots)
- 1 8-ounce tub cream cheese
- ½ cup dairy sour cream or plain yogurt
- ¼ cup fresh basil leaves, finely snipped
- 2 14- to 15-inch soft cracker bread rounds or four 7- to 8-inch flour tortillas
- 4 very thin slices prosciutto (Italian ham) or cooked ham
- Fresh basil leaves (optional)
- Orange slices (optional)

Prep time: 25 minutes
Chilling time: 4 hours

DIRECTIONS

1. In a small saucepan bring orange juice to boiling. Stir in dried fruit; remove from heat. Let stand, covered, about 15 minutes or until fruit is softened. Drain. Meanwhile, in a medium bowl stir together cream cheese, sour cream, and the snipped basil.

2. Spread cream cheese mixture evenly over one side of each cracker bread. Sprinkle each with softened fruit. Place some of the prosciutto near an edge of each round. Starting from edge closest to meat, tightly roll up into a spiral. Wrap each roll in plastic wrap and refrigerate for 4 to 24 hours.

3. To serve, cut each roll into 1-inch slices. If desired, garnish with basil leaves and orange slices. Makes about 24 servings.

NUTRITION FACTS PER SERVING:

115 calories
6 g total fat
2 g saturated fat
12 mg cholesterol
142 mg sodium
14 g carbohydrate
0 g fiber
3 g protein

INGREDIENTS

- ⅓ cup balsamic vinegar
- 1 6-ounce jar marinated artichoke hearts
- 1 medium red sweet pepper, cut into 1-inch pieces
- 1 medium yellow sweet pepper, cut into 1-inch pieces
- 8 small whole or 4 halved medium cipollini or 8 pearl onions
- 8 large whole fresh cremini or button mushrooms, stems removed
- 2 ounces provolone cheese, cut into thin bite-size strips
- ¼ cup snipped fresh basil

grilled antipasto skewers

Not really onions at all—but sometimes called wild onions—cipollini are actually the bittersweet bulbs of the grape hyacinth. Fresh cipollini are available mostly in late summer and fall. If you can't find them at your supermarket, check at Italian markets.

Prep time: 25 minutes
Grilling time: 8 minutes

DIRECTIONS

1. In a small saucepan bring the vinegar to boiling; reduce heat. Simmer, uncovered, about 5 minutes or until vinegar is reduced to 3 tablespoons. Set vinegar aside to cool.

2. Drain artichoke hearts, reserving 2 tablespoons of the marinade; set aside. On 4 long skewers alternately thread peppers, cipollini, and mushrooms. In a small bowl combine the reduced vinegar and the reserved artichoke marinade. Brush half of the vinegar mixture over the vegetables.

3. Grill kabobs on the rack of an uncovered grill directly over medium heat for 8 to 10 minutes or until the vegetables are tender, turning once and brushing frequently with the remaining vinegar mixture. Remove vegetables from skewers and transfer to a large bowl. Add the drained artichokes, provolone cheese, and basil; toss gently to combine. Season to taste with salt and black pepper. Makes 6 servings.

NUTRITION FACTS PER SERVING:

106 calories
4 g total fat
2 g saturated fat
7 mg cholesterol
220 mg sodium
14 g carbohydrate
1 g fiber
4 g protein

257

antipasto on a stick

Salami, vegetables, and cheesy tortellini can marinate overnight, making this a cinch to fix today for travel tomorrow. Serve slices of crusty bread to catch the drips as you eat your antipasto off of skewers (no serving utensils required).

INGREDIENTS

8 ounces thinly sliced salami or other desired meat

½ of a 9-ounce package refrigerated cheese-filled tortellini, cooked and drained (about 40)

1 14-ounce can artichoke hearts, drained and halved

8 large pitted ripe olives

8 pepperoncini salad peppers

8 red or yellow cherry tomatoes

½ cup bottled reduced-calorie or fat-free Italian salad dressing

1 large clove garlic, minced

16 thin slices baguette-style French bread

Bottled reduced-calorie or fat-free Italian salad dressing

To vary this Italian-style

appetizer, substitute 1 cup cubed provolone or mozzarella cheese (4 ounces) for the cheese-filled tortellini.

Prep time: 25 minutes
Chilling time: 2 hours

DIRECTIONS

1. Fold the salami slices in quarters. On 16 short or 8 long wooden skewers alternately thread salami, tortellini, artichoke halves, olives, pepperoncini, and tomatoes. Place kabobs in a plastic food storage container.

2. Stir together the ½ cup salad dressing and garlic; drizzle over the kabobs. Cover and refrigerate for 2 to 24 hours.

3. Brush bread slices with additional salad dressing. Broil bread slices on the unheated rack of a broiler pan 4 to 5 inches from the heat about 1 minute or until slices are golden brown. Cool. Serve kabobs with toasted bread. Makes 8 servings.

NUTRITION FACTS PER SERVING:

233 calories
13 g total fat
4 g saturated fat
31 mg cholesterol
1,020 mg sodium
19 g carbohydrate
2 g fiber
11 g protein

258

baked kasseri cheese spread

When chilly winds blow, cozy up to the fire and linger over a glass of red wine, a loaf of crusty bread, and this creamy spread of kasseri cheese, piquant olives, and oregano.

INGREDIENTS

12 ounces kasseri or Scamorza cheese

⅔ cup kalamata olives, pitted and quartered

2 tablespoons snipped fresh oregano

1 clove garlic, minced

¼ teaspoon crushed red pepper French bread, apples, or crackers

Prep time: 20 minutes
Baking time: 8 minutes

DIRECTIONS

1. Cut cheese into ½-inch slices. Layer cheese in the bottom of a 1-quart quiche dish or a 9-inch pie plate, overlapping if necessary. Toss together the olives, oregano, garlic, and red pepper. Sprinkle over the cheese.

2. Bake in a 450° oven for 8 to 10 minutes or just until cheese begins to melt. Serve immediately on bread, apples, or crackers. Rewarm cheese as needed. Makes 12 servings.

Traditionally Greek, kasseri

cheese is made with either sheep's or goat's milk. Its sharp, salty flavor and meltability make it a natural for this dish.

NUTRITION FACTS PER SERVING (SPREAD ONLY):

141 calories
12 g total fat
7 g saturated fat
30 mg cholesterol
350 mg sodium
1 g carbohydrate
0 g fiber
7 g protein

mexicali stuffed zucchini

These savory stuffed zucchini "wheels" can be made a day ahead: Prepare them up to the baking step; then cover the dish with plastic wrap and refrigerate. About 25 minutes before serving, simply remove the wrap and bake.

INGREDIENTS

3 medium zucchini, ends trimmed (about 1¾ pounds total)

2 cloves garlic, minced

2 teaspoons cooking oil

1 medium red sweet pepper, chopped

3 green onions, thinly sliced

2 tablespoons snipped fresh cilantro

1 fresh or canned jalapeño pepper, seeded and finely chopped (see tip, page 158)

½ cup shredded Monterey Jack cheese (2 ounces)

1 recipe Cucumber Raita

Prep time: 25 minutes
Baking time: 21 minutes

DIRECTIONS

1. Cut the zucchini into 1½-inch rounds. Scoop out pulp, leaving ¼- to ½-inch-thick shells. Chop enough of the pulp to make ⅓ cup. In a medium skillet cook garlic in hot oil over medium-high heat for 1 minute. Add the reserved zucchini pulp, the sweet red pepper, green onions, 1 tablespoon of the cilantro, and the jalapeño pepper. Cook and stir about 2 minutes or until vegetables are crisp-tender.

2. Place zucchini shells in a lightly greased 2-quart rectangular baking dish. Fill each shell with pepper mixture. Bake, uncovered, in a 350° oven for 20 to 25 minutes or until zucchini is tender. Sprinkle with cheese and bake for 1 to 2 minutes more or until cheese is melted.

3. Sprinkle zucchini with the remaining 1 tablespoon cilantro. Serve with the Cucumber Raita. Makes 5 or 6 servings.

Cucumber Raita: In a small bowl combine ½ cup plain low-fat yogurt, ¼ cup peeled and finely chopped cucumber, 1 tablespoon snipped fresh cilantro, and ⅛ teaspoon salt.

NUTRITION FACTS PER SERVING:

101 calories
6 g total fat
3 g saturated fat
11 mg cholesterol
135 mg sodium
9 g carbohydrate
2 g fiber
5 g protein

roasted vegetables with balsamic vinegar

Roasting brings out the natural sweetness of vegetables. These earthy and elegant roasted green beans and summer squash balance just about any entrée—steaks, chicken, pork chops, or salmon.

INGREDIENTS

8 ounces green beans
1 small onion, cut into thin wedges
1 clove garlic, minced
1 tablespoon olive oil
Dash salt
Dash pepper
2 medium yellow summer squash, halved lengthwise and sliced ¼ inch thick
⅓ cup balsamic vinegar

Start to finish: 25 minutes

DIRECTIONS

1. If desired, remove the tips from green beans. In a shallow roasting pan combine beans, onion, and garlic. Drizzle with olive oil and sprinkle with salt and pepper. Toss mixture until beans are evenly coated. Spread into a single layer.

2. Roast in a 450° oven for 8 minutes. Stir in squash and roast for 5 to 7 minutes more or until vegetables are tender and slightly browned.

3. Meanwhile, in a small saucepan bring the balsamic vinegar to boiling over medium-high heat; reduce heat. Boil gently, uncovered, about 5 minutes or until reduced by half (vinegar will thicken slightly).

4. Drizzle the vinegar over roasted vegetables; toss to coat. Makes 4 to 6 servings.

Balsamic vinegar develops its intense, sweet-tart flavor through years of pampered rest in casks of differing woods. The most prized elixirs are concocted in the Italian city of Modena following ancient secret formulas. More a condiment than a cooking liquid, the best quality balsamic vinegar should be savored in small amounts.

NUTRITION FACTS PER SERVING:

81 calories
4 g total fat
1 g saturated fat
0 mg cholesterol
45 mg sodium
12 g carbohydrate
1 g fiber
1 g protein

261

eggplant with gorgonzola

The mild, sweet taste and meaty texture of eggplant lends itself especially well to grilling. This lovely combination of glossy purple eggplant, yellow summer squash, and red onion is the perfect accompaniment to grilled chicken.

INGREDIENTS

1 small eggplant (about 12 ounces)
1 medium yellow summer squash, halved lengthwise and sliced 1 inch thick
1 small red onion, cut into thin wedges
2 tablespoons pesto
¼ cup crumbled Gorgonzola or other blue cheese, goat cheese (chèvre), or feta cheese (1 ounce)

Prep time: 10 minutes
Grilling time: 20 minutes

DIRECTIONS

1. If desired, peel eggplant. Cut into 1-inch cubes. In a large bowl combine eggplant, squash, onion, and pesto; toss gently to coat.

2. Fold a 36×18-inch piece of heavy foil in half to make an 18-inch square. Place the vegetables in center of foil. Bring up 2 opposite edges of foil; seal with a double fold. Fold remaining ends to completely enclose the vegetables, leaving space for steam to build.*

3. Grill vegetables on the rack of an uncovered grill directly over medium heat for 20 to 25 minutes or until vegetables are crisp-tender, turning occasionally.

4. To serve, transfer the vegetables to a serving bowl and sprinkle with cheese. Makes 4 servings.

*Note: If desired, you may assemble the foil packet ahead of time and refrigerate until ready to grill. Add a few minutes to the grilling time.

NUTRITION FACTS PER SERVING:

116 calories
8 g total fat
2 g saturated fat
7 mg cholesterol
179 mg sodium
9 g carbohydrate
3 g fiber
4 g protein

INGREDIENTS

- 3½ cups broccoli flowerets
- ½ cup pitted ripe olives
- ½ of a 2-ounce can anchovy fillets, drained and finely chopped (optional)
- 2 tablespoons snipped fresh oregano or Italian flat-leaf parsley
- 2 tablespoons red wine vinegar
- 2 tablespoons olive oil
- 5 cloves garlic, minced
- ½ teaspoon crushed red pepper
- Dash salt

piquant grilled broccoli & olives

Broccoli on the grill? You bet! The grilled flowerets take on a pleasing smokiness and still stay crisp-tender. This intensely flavored side dish goes great with any grilled meat or poultry— or toss it with hot cooked pasta for a vegetarian entrée.

Prep time: 15 minutes
Marinating time: 10 minutes
Grilling time: 6 minutes

DIRECTIONS

1. In a covered large saucepan cook broccoli in a small amount of boiling water for 2 minutes. Drain well. In a medium bowl combine broccoli and olives. For marinade, in a small bowl whisk together anchovies (if desired), oregano, vinegar, oil, garlic, red pepper, and salt. Pour the marinade over the broccoli and olives. Marinate at room temperature for 10 minutes, stirring occasionally. Drain broccoli and olives, discarding marinade.

2. On long skewers alternately thread broccoli flowerets and olives. Grill on the rack of an uncovered grill directly over medium heat for 6 to 8 minutes or until broccoli is lightly browned and crisp-tender, turning occasionally. Remove the broccoli and olives from skewers. Makes 4 servings.

NUTRITION FACTS PER SERVING:

91 calories
8 g total fat
1 g saturated fat
0 mg cholesterol
125 mg sodium
6 g carbohydrate
3 g fiber
3 g protein

vegetable kabobs

These crisp-tender vegetable kabobs are the essence of simplicity—a swath of rosemary-scented oil-and-vinegar dressing is their only embellishment. Threaded onto rosemary stalks, the colorful components look like jewels on a string (to use fresh rosemary skewers, see tip, page 50).

INGREDIENTS

- 8 tiny new potatoes, quartered
- 2 tablespoons water
- 8 baby sunburst squash
- 4 miniature sweet peppers and/or 1 medium red sweet pepper, cut into 1-inch pieces
- 2 small red onions, each cut into 8 wedges, or 8 tiny red onions, halved
- 8 baby zucchini or 1 small zucchini, halved lengthwise and sliced
- ¼ cup bottled oil and vinegar salad dressing
- 2 teaspoons snipped fresh rosemary or ½ teaspoon dried rosemary, crushed

Prep time: 20 minutes
Grilling time: 10 minutes

DIRECTIONS

1. In a 2-quart microwave-safe casserole combine the potatoes and water. Microwave, covered, on 100% power (high) for 5 minutes. Gently stir in the sunburst squash, sweet peppers, and onions. Microwave, covered, on high for 4 to 6 minutes or until almost tender. Drain and cool slightly.

2. On eight 10-inch skewers alternately thread the potatoes, sunburst squash, sweet peppers, onions, and zucchini. In a small bowl combine salad dressing and rosemary; brush over the vegetables.

3. Grill kabobs on the rack of an uncovered grill directly over medium heat for 10 to 12 minutes or until the vegetables are crisp-tender and browned, turning and brushing occasionally with dressing mixture. Makes 4 servings.

NUTRITION FACTS PER SERVING:

161 calories
8 g total fat
1 g saturated fat
0 mg cholesterol
217 mg sodium
22 g carbohydrate
2 g fiber
3 g protein

264

grilled tomatoes with pesto

They say there are two things money can't buy: love and homegrown tomatoes. If you don't have the latter, search out a farmers' market for the makings of this summer dish. It will garner you love from all who are lucky enough to taste it.

INGREDIENTS

- 3 to 5 small to medium red, orange, and/or yellow tomatoes, cored and halved crosswise
- 2 tablespoons pesto
- 6 very thin onion slices
- ½ cup shredded Monterey Jack cheese (2 ounces)
- ⅓ cup smoky-flavored whole almonds, chopped
- 2 tablespoons snipped fresh parsley

Prep time: 15 minutes
Grilling time: 15 minutes

DIRECTIONS

1. Using a spoon, hollow out the top ¼ inch of tomato halves. Top with pesto, then onion slices. Place tomatoes in a disposable foil pie plate.

2. In a charcoal grill with a cover arrange medium-hot coals around edge of grill. Test for medium heat in center of the grill. Place the tomatoes in center of grill rack. Cover and grill for 10 to 15 minutes or until tomatoes are heated through. (For a gas grill, adjust for indirect cooking; grill as directed.)

3. Meanwhile, in a small bowl stir together cheese, almonds, and parsley. Sprinkle over the tomatoes. Cover and grill about 5 minutes more or until cheese is melted. Season to taste with salt and pepper. Makes 6 servings.

NUTRITION FACTS PER SERVING:

132 calories
10 g total fat
2 g saturated fat
9 mg cholesterol
119 mg sodium
6 g carbohydrate
2 g fiber
5 g protein

orange & new potato salad

What will you do with that jar of jalapeño jelly recently bestowed by your best friend? Quit wondering. Use the sweet-and-fiery condiment as the secret zing in this new potato salad that's great with grilled foods.

INGREDIENTS

- 2 oranges
- 1 pound tiny new potatoes, sliced
- 1 shallot, finely chopped
- 2 tablespoons cooking oil
- 2 tablespoons jalapeño jelly
- 2 tablespoons white wine vinegar
- ½ of a small red onion, thinly sliced and separated into rings
- Leaf lettuce (optional)
- 2 tablespoons snipped fresh chives (optional)

Prep time: 15 minutes
Cooking time: 10 minutes
Chilling time: 1 hour

DIRECTIONS

1. Finely shred 1 teaspoon orange peel; set aside. Peel the oranges, then halve lengthwise and slice. Set aside. In a covered large saucepan cook the potatoes in boiling, lightly salted water about 10 minutes or just until tender. Drain in colander. Rinse with cold water; drain again.

2. Meanwhile, in a small saucepan cook shallot in hot oil for 3 minutes. Stir in jelly and vinegar. Cook and stir until jelly is melted. Stir in reserved orange peel. In a medium bowl combine cooked potatoes, orange slices, and onion. Pour jelly mixture over potato mixture; toss gently to coat. Cover and refrigerate for 1 to 24 hours.

3. To serve, if desired, spoon potato mixture onto a lettuce-lined platter and sprinkle with chives. Makes 4 to 6 servings.

NUTRITION FACTS PER SERVING:

222 calories
7 g total fat
1 g saturated fat
0 mg cholesterol
13 mg sodium
38 g carbohydrate
2 g fiber
3 g protein

INGREDIENTS

- ¼ cup salad oil
- ¼ cup vinegar
- 1 tablespoon sugar (optional)
- 1 teaspoon snipped fresh tarragon or dill or ¼ teaspoon dried tarragon, crushed, or dried dillweed
- ½ teaspoon Dijon-style mustard
- 1 pound tiny new potatoes and/or small yellow potatoes, cut into bite-size pieces

- 2 teaspoons salad oil
- 1 cup chopped bok choy
- ½ cup chopped red radishes
- ½ cup thinly sliced green onions
- 2 thin slices Canadian-style bacon, chopped (1 ounce)
- ⅛ teaspoon freshly ground pepper
- 4 artichokes, cooked, halved lengthwise, and chokes removed (optional)

warm tarragon potato salad

A picnic favorite has been lightened and brightened up with a tangy fresh-herb and Dijon vinaigrette dressing, crunchy bok choy, and peppery radishes. Tarragon, with its aniselike flavor, makes a fine complement to mild foods such as potatoes.

Prep time: 10 minutes
Grilling time: 25 minutes

DIRECTIONS

1. For dressing, in a small bowl whisk together the ¼ cup oil, the vinegar, sugar (if desired), tarragon, and mustard. Set aside.

2. In a lightly greased 8×8×2-inch disposable foil baking pan combine potatoes and the 2 teaspoons oil; toss to coat.

3. In a charcoal grill with a cover arrange hot coals around edge of grill. Test for medium-hot heat in center of the grill. Place the potatoes in center of grill rack. Cover and grill about 25 minutes or just until potatoes are tender. (For a gas grill, adjust for indirect cooking; grill as directed.) Cool slightly.

4. In a large bowl combine potatoes, bok choy, radishes, green onions, Canadian bacon, and pepper. Add the dressing; toss gently to coat. If desired, spoon the salad into artichoke halves. Makes 8 servings.

NUTRITION FACTS PER SERVING:

135 calories
8 g total fat
1 g saturated fat
2 mg cholesterol
68 mg sodium
14 g carbohydrate
1 g fiber
2 g protein

fried green tomatoes on a bed of greens

This classic Southern side gets greener and tastier with the addition of mesclun, a mixture of tiny salad greens. Buy unripened green tomatoes at your market or harvest them from your garden.

INGREDIENTS

- ¼ cup yellow cornmeal
- ¼ teaspoon salt
- ⅛ teaspoon freshly ground pepper
- 2 large green tomatoes, sliced about ⅜ inch thick (8 center-cut slices)
- 3 tablespoons cooking oil or olive oil
- 4 cups mesclun
- 4 teaspoons olive oil
- 2 teaspoons balsamic vinegar

Mesclun has hit the mainstream!

This French mixture of tiny greens that may include peppery arugula, chervil, chickweed, dandelion, and oak leaf lettuce was once considered to be solely the domain of the gourmet, but now is often available at large supermarkets. Its greatest boon is flavor; unlike the mildly flavored iceberg, these spicy herblike greens together have a distinct taste, which is nicely accented by a drizzle of vinaigrette.

Prep time: 20 minutes
Cooking time: 8 minutes

DIRECTIONS

1. In a pie plate or shallow dish combine cornmeal, salt, and pepper. Coat both sides of tomato slices with the cornmeal mixture. In a large skillet heat the 3 tablespoons oil over medium heat. Add tomato slices, half at a time, and cook about 4 minutes or until golden brown, turning once halfway through cooking and adding more oil if necessary. Drain tomatoes on paper towels. Repeat with the remaining tomato slices.

2. In a medium bowl drizzle the mesclun with the 4 teaspoons olive oil and the vinegar; toss gently to coat. Season to taste with salt and pepper.

3. Divide mesclun mixture among 4 salad plates. Top with the tomatoes. Makes 4 servings.

NUTRITION FACTS PER SERVING:

188 calories
15 g total fat
2 g saturated fat
0 mg cholesterol
180 mg sodium
12 g carbohydrate
2 g fiber
2 g protein

INGREDIENTS

- 1 medium fennel bulb (about 1 pound)
- 2 tablespoons water
- 2 tablespoons olive oil
- ¼ teaspoon finely shredded lemon peel
- 4 teaspoons lemon juice
- ¼ teaspoon salt
- ⅛ teaspoon pepper
- 8 ounces asparagus spears, trimmed
- 4 cups spinach leaves
- ¼ cup shredded Parmesan cheese (1 ounce)
- 1 tablespoon thinly sliced fresh basil

warm asparagus, fennel, & spinach salad

This beautiful and sophisticated green-on-green salad may be monochromatic to the eye, but its components distinguish themselves on the palate: mild, licoricelike fennel; slightly bitter spinach; and tender, smoky-sweet asparagus.

Prep time: 15 minutes
Grilling time: 12 minutes

DIRECTIONS

1. Trim off the stem end of fennel; quarter the fennel lengthwise but do not remove core. Place fennel in a small microwave-safe dish or pie plate. Add the water. Cover with vented plastic wrap. Microwave on 100% power (high) about 4 minutes or until almost tender; drain.

2. Meanwhile, for dressing, in a small bowl combine oil, lemon peel, lemon juice, salt, and pepper; whisk until smooth. Brush the fennel and asparagus with 1 tablespoon of the dressing; set remaining dressing aside.

3. Grill fennel on the rack of an uncovered grill directly over medium heat for 5 minutes, turning fennel occasionally. Add asparagus to grill rack; grill vegetables for 7 to 8 minutes more or until crisp-tender, turning occasionally.

4. Transfer the fennel to a cutting board; cool slightly and cut into ¼- to ½-inch slices, discarding core. Divide fennel and asparagus among 4 dinner plates. Arrange the spinach on top. Drizzle with the remaining dressing. Top with Parmesan cheese and basil. Makes 4 servings.

NUTRITION FACTS PER SERVING:

111 calories
9 g total fat
1 g saturated fat
5 mg cholesterol
231 mg sodium
5 g carbohydrate
7 g fiber
4 g protein

269

pear & endive salad with honey vinaigrette

Made with pears and embellished with crunchy walnuts, this endive salad is ideal with Tuscan Lamb Chop Skillet (page 118). Assemble the salads while the chops are cooking, add some bakery bread, then settle in for an earthy but elegant dinner.

INGREDIENTS

- 2 ripe red Bartlett pears, Bosc pears, and/or apples, cored and thinly sliced
- 2 tablespoons lemon juice
- 8 ounces Belgian endive, leaves separated (2 medium heads)
- ¼ cup coarsely chopped walnuts
  Dash salt
  Dash pepper
- 3 tablespoons olive oil or salad oil
- 2 tablespoons sherry vinegar or white wine vinegar
- 1 shallot, finely chopped, or 1 tablespoon finely chopped onion
- 1 tablespoon honey
- ½ teaspoon ground cinnamon
  Pomegranate seeds (optional)

Start to finish: 20 minutes

DIRECTIONS

1. In a small bowl gently toss pear slices with lemon juice to prevent darkening. Place the endive leaves in 4 salad bowls or salad plates; top with the sliced pears. Sprinkle with walnuts, salt, and pepper.

2. For vinaigrette, in a small bowl combine olive oil, sherry vinegar, shallot, honey, and cinnamon; whisk until thoroughly blended.

3. Drizzle the vinaigrette over the salads. If desired, sprinkle with pomegranate seeds. Makes 4 servings.

NUTRITION FACTS PER SERVING:

216 calories
15 g total fat
2 g saturated fat
0 mg cholesterol
39 mg sodium
22 g carbohydrate
3 g fiber
2 g protein

INGREDIENTS

- 3 large baking potatoes (about 1¼ pounds total)
- 2 leeks, very thinly sliced (white and light green parts only)
- 2 slightly beaten eggs
- ¼ cup grated Parmesan cheese
- 3 tablespoons all-purpose flour
- 2 tablespoons snipped fresh parsley
- 2 tablespoons dairy sour cream
- ⅛ teaspoon salt
- ⅛ teaspoon pepper
- 1 tablespoon cooking oil

potato-leek pancakes

Potato pancakes with applesauce used to be a stand-alone Sunday night supper. Leeks, sour cream, parsley, and Parmesan cheese flavor these crisp coins of shredded potatoes. Try them with roasted chicken, grilled sausages, or a salad.

Prep time: 15 minutes
Cooking time: 16 minutes

DIRECTIONS

1. In a food processor coarsely shred the unpeeled potatoes. Pat dry with paper towels. In a large bowl combine potatoes, leeks, eggs, Parmesan cheese, flour, parsley, sour cream, salt, and pepper.

2. In a large skillet heat the oil over medium heat. For each pancake, drop about ¼ cup potato mixture into the hot oil and press each pancake with a spatula to flatten it to uniform thickness (cook 6 pancakes at a time).

3. Cook for 8 to 10 minutes or until crisp and brown, turning once when the edges brown. Remove from skillet. Repeat with remaining potato mixture. Makes 6 servings.

NUTRITION FACTS PER SERVING:

219 calories
9 g total fat
4 g saturated fat
82 mg cholesterol
164 mg sodium
28 g carbohydrate
2 g fiber
7 g protein

Leeks add a delicate onion-like flavor to these potato pancakes. To clean the leeks, loosen the leaves gently (or cut the leeks almost in half down the middle if they are very gritty) and rinse with cold water to remove the dirt. Or, first slice or chop the leeks; then rinse thoroughly in a colander.

corn cakes with fresh corn & chives

Everything old is new again! That most traditional of American foods, the corn cake, has been updated with fresh corn and just-snipped herbs. Try them with Tenderloin Steaks with Arugula-Cornichon Relish (page 92).

INGREDIENTS

- 1 fresh ear of corn, husked and cleaned, or ½ cup frozen whole kernel corn
- 2 tablespoons all-purpose flour
- 1½ teaspoons baking powder
- 1 teaspoon sugar
- ½ teaspoon salt
- 1 cup boiling water
- 1 cup yellow cornmeal
- ¼ cup milk
- 1 slightly beaten egg
- 1 tablespoon snipped fresh chives
- 3 tablespoons cooking oil
- 1 teaspoon snipped fresh chives or cilantro (optional)
- ⅓ cup dairy sour cream
  Fresh chives (optional)

Prep time: 20 minutes
Cooking time: 6 minutes

DIRECTIONS

1. Cut the corn kernels from cob and measure ½ cup. In a small bowl combine flour, baking powder, sugar, and salt. Set aside.

2. In a medium bowl stir boiling water into cornmeal to make a stiff mush. Stir in milk until smooth; then stir in fresh or frozen corn, egg, and the 1 tablespoon snipped chives. Add flour mixture and stir just until combined.

3. In a large skillet heat 2 tablespoons of the oil over medium heat. Drop batter by rounded tablespoons into hot oil. Cook for 3 to 4 minutes or until golden brown, turning once halfway through cooking. Transfer to a serving platter; cover and keep warm. Repeat with remaining batter, adding the remaining 1 tablespoon oil.

4. Meanwhile, if desired, stir the 1 teaspoon snipped chives into sour cream. Serve with corn cakes. If desired, garnish with additional chives. Makes 6 servings.

NUTRITION FACTS PER SERVING:

215 calories
11 g total fat
3 g saturated fat
42 mg cholesterol
295 mg sodium
25 g carbohydrate
2 g fiber
4 g protein

sweet & spicy pepper-pineapple salsa

INGREDIENTS

- 12 ounces peeled and cored fresh pineapple, sliced ½ inch thick
- 2 large red and/or green sweet peppers, quartered
- 1 ½-inch-thick slice sweet onion (such as Vidalia or Walla Walla)
- ¼ cup apricot jam
- 2 tablespoons rice vinegar
- ¼ teaspoon salt
- ¼ teaspoon ground cinnamon
- ¼ teaspoon ground allspice
- ¼ teaspoon bottled hot pepper sauce

To make this colorful salsa quickly, buy the peeled fresh pineapple that's available now in most grocery stores. The zippy condiment perks up grilled beef and pork (try it with Grilled Mustard-Glazed Pork, page 104) particularly well.

Prep time: 15 minutes
Grilling time: 13 minutes

DIRECTIONS

1. Grill the pineapple, sweet peppers, and onion on the rack of an uncovered grill directly over medium heat for 10 to 12 minutes or until sweet peppers are slightly charred, turning once halfway through cooking. Transfer pineapple and vegetables to a cutting board; cool slightly and coarsely chop.

2. Meanwhile, in a heavy medium saucepan* combine jam, vinegar, salt, cinnamon, allspice, and hot pepper sauce. Place saucepan on grill rack near edge of grill. Cook and stir for 3 to 5 minutes or until jam is melted. Stir the chopped pineapple, sweet peppers, and onion into the mixture in saucepan. Serve salsa warm or at room temperature over grilled meats or poultry. Makes 6 servings.

*Note: The heat from the grill will blacken the outside of the saucepan, so use an old one or a small cast-iron skillet.

NUTRITION FACTS PER SERVING:

76 calories
0 g total fat
0 g saturated fat
0 mg cholesterol
93 mg sodium
20 g carbohydrate
1 g fiber
1 g protein

273

grilled corn relish

Terrific as a side dish for grilled chicken or pork, this colorful corn relish also makes a light meal stirred with some cooked black beans, rolled up with some shredded Monterey Jack cheese in a flour tortilla, then warmed on the grill.

INGREDIENTS

- 3 tablespoons lime juice
- 1 tablespoon cooking oil
- 2 cloves garlic, minced
- 2 fresh ears of corn, husked and cleaned
- 1 teaspoon chili powder
- 1 small avocado, seeded, peeled, and cut up
- ½ cup chopped red sweet pepper
- ¼ cup snipped fresh cilantro
- ¼ teaspoon salt

Before buying avocados, think about how you'll be using them. Firm-ripe avocados are ideal for slicing and chopping; very ripe fruit is perfect for guacamole and mashing in recipes. Avocados peel most easily when they're firm-ripe. Simply cut them in half (moving the knife around the seed), remove the seed, then peel the halves. For a very ripe avocado being used for mashing, just halve the avocado and scoop the pulp away from the skin.

Prep time: 15 minutes
Grilling time: 25 minutes

DIRECTIONS

1. In a medium bowl combine lime juice, oil, and garlic. Brush corn lightly with juice mixture. Sprinkle with chili powder. Grill corn on the rack of an uncovered grill directly over medium heat for 25 to 30 minutes or until tender, turning corn occasionally.

2. Meanwhile, add the avocado, sweet pepper, cilantro, and salt to remaining lime juice mixture; toss gently to coat. Cut the corn kernels from cobs; stir into avocado mixture. Makes 4 servings.

NUTRITION FACTS PER SERVING:

159 calories
12 g total fat
2 g saturated fat
0 mg cholesterol
152 mg sodium
15 g carbohydrate
3 g fiber
3 g protein

INGREDIENTS

- 1 recipe Gingered Shortcake
- 1 cup whipping cream
- 2 tablespoons granulated sugar
- ½ teaspoon vanilla
- 3 tablespoons butter

- 3 medium cooking apples, Fuyu persimmons, and/or pears, cored (if necessary) and thinly sliced
- 3 tablespoons brown sugar
- ¼ teaspoon ground nutmeg
- 1 cup blueberries

gingered shortcake with spiced fruit

Shortcake isn't just for summer berries anymore! Enjoy this warming dessert with fall fruits such as apples, persimmons, or pears. The shortcake can be made ahead and refrigerated, then warmed—wrapped in foil—in a 350° oven about 25 minutes.

Prep time: 25 minutes
Baking time: 18 minutes
Cooling time: 40 minutes

DIRECTIONS

1. Prepare Gingered Shortcake. In a chilled bowl combine cream, granulated sugar, and vanilla. Beat with chilled beaters of an electric mixer until soft peaks form. Cover and refrigerate. In a large skillet melt butter over medium heat. Add apples; cook for 2 to 5 minutes or until almost tender. Stir in brown sugar and nutmeg. Cook for 1 to 3 minutes more or until apples are tender. Stir in blueberries.

2. Place bottom cake layer on serving plate. Spoon about two-thirds of the fruit mixture and half of the whipped cream over cake. Top with second cake layer and remaining fruit mixture. Pass remaining whipped cream. Makes 8 servings.

Gingered Shortcake:
Combine 2 cups all-purpose flour, ¼ cup granulated sugar, and 2 teaspoons baking powder. Cut in ½ cup butter until mixture resembles coarse crumbs. Combine 1 beaten egg, ⅔ cup milk, and 1 tablespoon grated fresh ginger; add to dry mixture. Stir just until moistened. Spread batter in a greased 8×1½-inch round baking pan. Bake in a 450° oven for 18 to 20 minutes or until a wooden toothpick inserted near center comes out clean. Cool in pan for 10 minutes. Remove from pan; cool on a wire rack for 30 minutes. Split into 2 layers.

NUTRITION FACTS PER SERVING:

457 calories
28 g total fat
17 g saturated fat
111 mg cholesterol
280 mg sodium
47 g carbohydrate
2 g fiber
5 g protein

275

espresso-orange sauce

Italians may drink their espresso in an express fashion at coffee bars and train stations, but you can savor this ice-cream sauce featuring the famed Italian coffee. If your market carries them, use sweet, juicy, cabernet-colored blood oranges.

INGREDIENTS

- 2 oranges
- ⅓ cup packed brown sugar
- 4 teaspoons cornstarch
- 1 cup water
- 1 tablespoon instant espresso coffee powder
- 2 inches stick cinnamon
- 1 tablespoon coffee liqueur (optional)
- Vanilla ice cream
- Sliced almonds, toasted (see tip, page 63), or honey-roasted almonds

Start to finish: 20 minutes

DIRECTIONS

1. Using a vegetable peeler, cut a few strips of peel from 1 of the oranges. Cut the strips into very thin strips and place in a small bowl of water. Cover and refrigerate. Peel the oranges; then halve oranges lengthwise and slice. Set aside.

2. In a medium saucepan combine the brown sugar and cornstarch. Stir in water, espresso powder, and stick cinnamon. Cook and stir over medium heat until thickened and bubbly. Cook and stir for 2 minutes more. Remove from heat. Remove stick cinnamon. Stir in orange slices and, if desired, liqueur.

3. Drain the orange strips. Serve the sauce warm or cool over ice cream. Sprinkle with the orange strips and almonds. Makes 16 servings.

NUTRITION FACTS PER SERVING (WITH ICE CREAM):

106 calories
5 g total fat
2 g saturated fat
15 mg cholesterol
28 mg sodium
14 g carbohydrate
1 g fiber
2 g protein

INGREDIENTS

- 2 medium ripe, yet firm, bananas
- 3 tablespoons sugar
- 2 tablespoons orange liqueur
- 2 tablespoons orange juice
- 1 tablespoon butter
- ⅛ teaspoon ground nutmeg
- ½ of a 10¾-ounce package frozen pound cake, thawed and cut into 4 slices
- Shredded orange peel (optional)
- Ground nutmeg (optional)

bananas suzette over grilled pound cake

Here is all the drama of crepes suzette without laboring over the crepes—and no chafing dish required! This elegant dessert is made easily in a skillet right on your grill. For company, garnish each slice with a few delicate strands of orange peel.

Prep time: 10 minutes
Grilling time: 6 minutes

DIRECTIONS

1. Peel bananas; bias-slice each banana into 8 pieces. Preheat a heavy 8-inch skillet* on the rack of an uncovered grill directly over medium heat for 2 minutes. Add sugar, liqueur, juice, and butter. Cook about 1 minute or until butter is melted and sugar begins to dissolve. Add the bananas and cook about 4 minutes more or just until bananas are tender, stirring once. Stir in the ⅛ teaspoon nutmeg. Set skillet to the side of the grill rack. Add pound cake slices to grill rack; grill cake about 1 minute or until golden brown, turning once halfway through cooking.

2. To serve, spoon bananas and sauce over pound cake slices. If desired, garnish with shredded orange peel and additional nutmeg. Makes 4 servings.

*Note: The heat from the grill will blacken the outside of the skillet, so use a cast-iron or old skillet.

NUTRITION FACTS PER SERVING:

292 calories
12 g total fat
7 g saturated fat
67 mg cholesterol
139 mg sodium
42 g carbohydrate
1 g fiber
3 g protein

red wine-marinated peaches

Carpe diem, meaning "seize the day" in Latin, must refer to that much-anticipated though fleeting time in late summer when juicy peaches are at their peak. Embellish this golden fruit with red wine, cinnamon, and cloves.

INGREDIENTS

- 6 ripe medium peaches, peeled, pitted, and sliced, or pears, cored and sliced
- 1½ cups fruity red wine (such as Beaujolais) or dry white wine
- ¾ cup sugar
- ½ teaspoon ground cinnamon
- ⅛ teaspoon ground cloves

If you're short on time, dessert doesn't have to be a lost prospect. Try one of these super-simple ideas:

- Fresh fruit sliced and tossed with a little honey and sprinkled with toasted almonds.
- A tea bar set up with several kinds of teabags, lemon, milk, honey, and sugar—and purchased tea biscuits.
- A cheese course featuring a selection of cheeses and fresh fruit. Ripe pears with blue cheese, berries and apples with brie, and oranges with thin wedges of Parmesan are great choices.

Prep time: 15 minutes
Marinating time: 30 minutes

DIRECTIONS

1. Place peaches in a large bowl. For marinade, in a medium saucepan combine the wine, sugar, cinnamon, and cloves. Cook and stir over medium heat until sugar is dissolved.

2. Pour the marinade over peaches; toss gently to coat. Marinate at room temperature for 30 to 60 minutes, stirring occasionally. To serve, spoon the peaches and marinade into 6 dessert dishes. Makes 6 servings.

NUTRITION FACTS PER SERVING:

262 calories
0 g total fat
0 g saturated fat
0 mg cholesterol
6 mg sodium
51 g carbohydrate
3 g fiber
1 g protein

almond cookie cups with sorbet

Like pastel eggs in an Easter basket, scoops of sorbet are nestled prettily in crisp, almond-flavored cups. In addition to raspberry and lemon sorbet, try other flavors, such as lime, grapefruit, peach, and pear.

INGREDIENTS

- 1 cup all-purpose flour
- 1 cup sliced almonds, finely chopped
- ¾ cup packed dark brown sugar
- ½ cup light-colored corn syrup
- ½ cup butter
- 1 teaspoon vanilla
- 3 cups raspberry and/or lemon sorbet
- Fresh raspberries

Prep time: 15 minutes
Baking time: 10 minutes per batch

DIRECTIONS

1. In a small bowl combine the flour and almonds; set aside. In a medium saucepan bring the brown sugar, corn syrup, and butter to a full boil over medium heat. Remove from heat. Stir in the flour mixture and vanilla.

2. Line a large cookie sheet with parchment paper. For each cookie cup, drop about 3 tablespoonfuls of batter about 5 inches apart onto prepared cookie sheet (bake 3 or 4 at a time). Bake in a 350° oven for 10 to 12 minutes or until bubbly and deep golden brown (cookies will form irregular shapes). Let stand on cookie sheet about 2 minutes. When firm but still pliable, place on top of inverted custard cups to form small bowls. Cool to room temperature.

3. To serve, fill 6 of the cups with scoops of sorbet. Garnish with raspberries. Serve immediately. Store the remaining cups in an airtight container in the freezer for up to 3 months. Makes 6 servings.

NUTRITION FACTS PER SERVING:

380 calories
15 g total fat
6 g saturated fat
25 mg cholesterol
121 mg sodium
60 g carbohydrate
1 g fiber
4 g protein

chocolate ricotta-filled pears

Discover all the wonderful flavors of the classic Sicilian ricotta-chocolate-fruit-filled cake called cassata—without turning on your oven or chopping a thing. Be sure the pears are ripe. Serve them with an Italian dessert wine, such as Vin Santo.

INGREDIENTS

- 1 cup ricotta cheese
- ⅓ cup sifted powdered sugar
- 1 tablespoon unsweetened cocoa powder
- ¼ teaspoon vanilla
- 2 tablespoons miniature semisweet chocolate pieces
- 1 teaspoon finely shredded orange peel
- 3 large ripe Bosc, Anjou, or Bartlett pears
- 2 tablespoons orange juice
- 2 tablespoons slivered or sliced almonds, toasted (see tip, page 63)
- Fresh mint leaves (optional)
- Orange peel curls (optional)

Start to finish: 20 minutes

DIRECTIONS

1. In a medium bowl beat the ricotta cheese, powdered sugar, cocoa powder, and vanilla with an electric mixer on medium speed until combined. Stir in chocolate pieces and the 1 teaspoon orange peel. Set aside.

2. Peel the pears; cut in half lengthwise and remove the cores. Remove a thin slice from the rounded sides so the pear halves will sit flat. Brush the pears all over with orange juice. Place the pears on 6 dessert plates. Spoon the ricotta mixture on top of the pears and sprinkle with almonds. If desired, garnish with mint leaves and orange curls. Makes 6 servings.

NUTRITION FACTS PER SERVING:

166 calories
6 g total fat
2 g saturated fat
13 mg cholesterol
52 mg sodium
24 g carbohydrate
3 g fiber
6 g protein

INGREDIENTS

- ⅓ cup granulated sugar
- 5 tablespoons all-purpose flour
- 1 tablespoon lemon juice
- 1¼ teaspoons apple pie spice or ground nutmeg
- 6 medium nectarines (about 2 pounds total), pitted and cut into 1-inch chunks
- 1 cup fresh raspberries
- ¼ cup packed brown sugar
- ¼ cup rolled oats
- ¼ cup cold butter
- ⅓ cup pecans, coarsely chopped
- Vanilla ice cream (optional)

nectarine-raspberry crisp

Chock-full of juicy nectarines and jewel-toned raspberries, this juicy crisp takes full advantage of the best of summer's sweet fruits. If you're pressed for time, assemble it up to 6 hours ahead; then refrigerate until it's time to put it on the grill.

Prep time: 15 minutes
Grilling time: 20 minutes

DIRECTIONS

1. In a large bowl combine the granulated sugar, 2 tablespoons of the flour, the lemon juice, and ¼ teaspoon of the apple pie spice. Gently stir in the nectarines and raspberries. Transfer the fruit mixture to an 8×8×2-inch or 8½×1½-inch round disposable foil baking pan.

2. For topping, combine the brown sugar, rolled oats, the remaining flour, and the remaining apple pie spice. Using a pastry blender, cut in butter until mixture resembles coarse crumbs. Stir in nuts. Sprinkle topping evenly over fruit mixture.

3. In a charcoal grill with a cover arrange medium coals in a donut-shape, leaving a 9-inch circle in the center without coals. Test for medium-low heat in center of the grill. Place the crisp in center of grill rack. Cover and grill for 20 to 25 minutes or until fruit mixture is bubbly in center. (For a gas grill, adjust for indirect cooking; grill as directed.) Serve the crisp warm. If desired, serve with ice cream. Makes 6 servings.

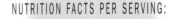

NUTRITION FACTS PER SERVING:

291 calories
13 g total fat
5 g saturated fat
20 mg cholesterol
80 mg sodium
45 g carbohydrate
4 g fiber
3 g protein

281

A-B

Allspice Meatball Stew, 140
Almond Cookie Cups with Sorbet, 279
Antipasto on a Stick, 258
Appetizers *(see also Dips)*
    Antipasto on a Stick, 258
    Baked Kasseri Cheese Spread, 259
    Fruited Cheese Spirals, 256
    Grilled Antipasto Skewers, 257
Apple-Glazed Lamb Chops, 119
Asian Beef & Noodle Bowl, 139
Asian Chicken Noodle Soup, 83
Asian Dressing, 168
Asian Grilled Salmon Salad, 168
Asparagus & Cheese Potato Soup, 238
Asparagus with Raspberry-Dijon Dipping
    Sauce, 254
Baked Kasseri Cheese Spread, 259
Balsamic-Glazed Springtime Lamb Salad, 137
Bananas Suzette over Grilled Pound Cake, 277
Barbecued Turkey Tenderloins, 59
Basil Dressing, 220
Bayou Shrimp Soup, 180
Beans
    Allspice Meatball Stew, 140
    Black & White Bean Chili, 244
    Caribbean-Style Pork Stew, 142
    Chicken, Long Beans, & Tomato Stir-Fry, 53
    Chicken Chili with Rice, 87
    Christmas Limas with Pesto Bulgur, 191
    Chunky Chicken Chili, 86
    Chunky Ratatouille Stew, 232
    Corn Waffles with Tomato Salsa, 190
    Fennel-Asparagus Soup, 146
    Garbanzo Bean Stew, 246
    Greek Lamb Salad with Yogurt Dressing, 136
    Greek Minestrone, 245
    Grilled Gazpacho Medley Open-Faced
        Sandwich, 202
    Italian Mozzarella Salad, 220
    Mexican Fiesta Salad, 222
    Middle Eastern Bulgur-Spinach Salad, 230
    Mixed Bean & Portobello Ragout, 247
    Mostaccioli with Green Beans &
        Tomatoes, 32
    Pasta Coleslaw, 224
    Penne Salad with Italian Beans &
        Gorgonzola, 226
    Peppery Artichoke Pitas, 204
    Red Beans & Grains, 134
    Roasted Vegetables Parmesan, 208
    Roasted Vegetables with Balsamic
        Vinegar, 261

Rosemary-Orange Shrimp Kabobs, 167
    Southwestern Black Bean Cakes with
        Guacamole, 194
    Southwestern Chicken & Black Bean
        Salad, 71
    Spaghetti Squash with Balsamic Beans, 193
    Summer Pasta with Pork, 109
    Tangy Bean Salad Wraps, 192
    Thai Pork & Vegetable Curry, 110
    Tuscan Lamb Chop Skillet, 118
    Warm Beet Salad with Roasted Garlic
        Dressing, 221
    White Bean & Sausage Rigatoni, 9
    White Bean Dip with Toasted Pita Chips, 255
    White Bean Soup with Sausage & Kale, 145
    Wide Noodles with Chicken & Lima Beans, 7
Beef
    Allspice Meatball Stew, 140
    Asian Beef & Noodle Bowl, 139
    Beef & Apple Salad, 125
    Beef & Avocado Tacos, 100
    Beef & Curry Pinwheels on Spinach, 124
    Beef & Fruit Salad, 126
    Beef & Vegetable Ragout, 138
    Beef with Cucumber Raita, 96
    Bistro Beef & Mushrooms, 94
    Flank Steak with Pineapple Salsa, 127
    Garlic Steaks with Nectarine-Onion
        Relish, 95
    Gingered Beef & Pasta Salad, 128
    Grilled Beef, Red Onion, & Blue Cheese
        Salad, 129
    Lemony Flank Steak, 93
    Linguine with Steak & Spicy Garlic
        Sauce, 14
    Roasted Vegetable & Pastrami Panini, 101
    Sesame Beef, 97
    Spanish Meat Loaves, 98
    Spicy Steak & Ranch Salad, 123
    Sun-Dried Tomato Burgers, 99
    Tenderloin Steaks with Arugula-Cornichon
        Relish, 92
    Thai Cobb Salad, 132
Bistro Beef & Mushrooms, 94
Black & White Bean Chili, 244
Blackened Catfish with Roasted Potatoes, 160
BLT Salad with Crostini, 78
Border Grilled Turkey Salad, 74
Bow Ties with Sausage & Sweet
    Peppers, 11
Braised Chicken Thighs with Peppers &
    Olives, 49
Broccoli Rabe over Polenta, 217
Broiled Turkey Salad with Pineapple
    Wedges, 76
Bulgur
    Christmas Limas with Pesto Bulgur, 191
    Middle Eastern Bulgur-Spinach Salad, 230
    Peppers Stuffed with Cinnamon Bulgur, 210

C-D

Canadian Bacon
    Canadian Bacon Pizza, 114
    Sweet Potato Frittata with Fresh Cranberry
        Salsa, 115
Capellini with Shrimp in Pesto Sauce, 20
Caribbean Clam Chowder, 187
Caribbean-Style Pork Stew, 142
Cavatelli with Arugula & Dried Cranberries, 29
Cheese
    Asparagus & Cheese Potato Soup, 238
    Baked Kasseri Cheese Spread, 259
    Cheese Frittata with Mushrooms & Dill, 196
    Chicken & Pears with Pecan Goat
        Cheese, 63
    Chocolate Ricotta-Filled Pears, 280
    Corn & Tomato Bread Pudding, 197
    Fontina & Melon Salad, 227
    Fruited Cheese Spirals, 256
    Grilled Eggplant & Sweet Pepper
        Sandwiches, 203
    Grilled Gazpacho Medley Open-Faced
        Sandwich, 202
    Grilled Sicilian-Style Pizza, 207
    Hawaiian-Style Barbecue Pizza, 54
    Italian Mozzarella Salad, 220
    Muffuletta Salad, 135
    Pasta with Chèvre, 28
    Sautéed Onion & Tomato Sandwiches, 206
    Smoky Chicken Wraps, 51
    Three-Cheese Orzo Salad, 225
    Tomato, Mozzarella, & Polenta Platter, 229
    Vegetable Cheese Chowder, 240
    Wild Rice Quesadillas, 212
Chicken
    Asian Chicken Noodle Soup, 83
    Braised Chicken Thighs with Peppers &
        Olives, 49
    Chicken, Long Beans, & Tomato Stir-Fry, 53
    Chicken, Pear, & Blue Cheese Salad, 61
    Chicken & Banana Curry, 47
    Chicken & Pasta Primavera, 6
    Chicken & Pears with Pecan Goat
        Cheese, 63
    Chicken & Prosciutto Roll-Ups, 36
    Chicken & Shrimp Tortilla Soup, 182
    Chicken Chili with Rice, 87
    Chicken Souvlaki, 50
    Chicken Stew with Tortellini, 81
    Chicken with Mango Chutney, 40
    Chicken with Roquefort Sauce, 44
    Chipotle Chile Pepper Soup, 79
    Chunky Chicken Chili, 86
    Chutney-Chicken Salad, 65
    Citrusy Chicken Salad, 68
    Cool-as-a-Cucumber Chicken Salad, 64
    Crab & Pasta Gazpacho, 186
    Curried Chicken Salad, 69
    Fabulous Focaccia Sandwiches, 55

Grilled Vietnamese Chicken Breasts, 41
Hawaiian-Style Barbecue Pizza, 54
Herb-Rubbed Grilled Chicken, 46
Keys-Style Citrus Chicken, 42
Mexican Chicken Posole, 84
Mushroom Medley Soup, 80
Pesto Chicken Breasts with Summer
 Squash, 45
Poached Chicken & Pasta with Pesto
 Dressing, 66
Raspberry Chicken with Plantains, 43
Sautéed Chicken Breasts with Tomatillo
 Salsa, 38
Sautéed Chicken with Brandied Fruit &
 Almonds, 39
Scarlet Salad, 70
Sesame Chicken Kabob Salad, 62
Sesame-Ginger Barbecued Chicken, 48
Smoky Chicken Wraps, 51
Soba Noodles with Spring Vegetables, 8
Soup with Mixed Pastas, 85
Southwest Chicken Salad, 60
Southwestern Chicken & Black Bean
 Salad, 71
Spicy Chicken & Star Fruit, 37
Spring Vegetable Stew, 82
Strawberry Vinaigrette with Turkey, 72
Teriyaki Chicken Noodle Salad, 67
Thai Chicken Wraps, 52
Thai Cobb Salad, 132
Wide Noodles with Chicken & Lima
 Beans, 7
Chipotle Chile Pepper Soup, 79
Chocolate Ricotta-Filled Pears, 280
Christmas Limas with Pesto Bulgur, 191
Chunky Chicken Chili, 86
Chunky Ratatouille Stew, 232
Chutney-Chicken Salad, 65
Citrusy Chicken Salad, 68
Clam Chowder, Caribbean, 187
Cool-as-a-Cucumber Chicken Salad, 64
Corn
 Corn & Tomato Bread Pudding, 197
 Corn Cakes with Fresh Corn & Chives, 272
 Corn Waffles with Tomato Salsa, 190
 Grilled Corn Relish, 274
 Jalapeño Corn Chowder, 239
 Oyster & Corn Chowder, 184
Couscous Burritos, 215
Crab
 Crab & Pasta Gazpacho, 186
 Crab Chowder, 185
 Curried Crab Salad, 175
Creamy Carrot & Pasta Soup, 241
Crisp Tortilla Shreds, 182
Cucumber Raita, 260
Curried Chicken Salad, 69
Curried Crab Salad, 175
Curried Lentil Soup, 248
Curry Catsup, 57

Desserts
 Almond Cookie Cups with Sorbet, 279
 Bananas Suzette over Grilled Pound
  Cake, 277
 Chocolate Ricotta-Filled Pears, 280
 Espresso-Orange Sauce, 276
 Gingered Shortcake with Spiced Fruit, 275
 Nectarine-Raspberry Crisp, 281
 Red Wine-Marinated Peaches, 278
Dilled Spinach Soup, 88
Dilly Salmon Fillets, 153
Dipping Sauce, 201
Dips
 Asparagus with Raspberry-Dijon Dipping
  Sauce, 254
 White Bean Dip with Toasted Pita
  Chips, 255

E-J

Eggplant with Gorgonzola, 262
Eggs
 Cheese Frittata with Mushrooms & Dill, 196
 Corn & Tomato Bread Pudding, 197
 Egg & Apple Bruschetta, 198
 Egg Ragout, 200
 Moo Shu Vegetable & Egg Crepes, 195
 Southwest Skillet, 199
 Sweet Potato Frittata with Fresh Cranberry
  Salsa, 115
Espresso-Orange Sauce, 276
Fabulous Focaccia Sandwiches, 55
Fennel-Asparagus Soup, 146
Fire-&-Ice Rice Salad, 170
Fish
 Asian Grilled Salmon Salad, 168
 Blackened Catfish with Roasted
  Potatoes, 160
 Dilly Salmon Fillets, 153
 Fish Provençale, 177
 Grilled Rosemary Trout with Lemon
  Butter, 161
 Grilled Swordfish with Spicy Tomato
  Sauce, 158
 Grilled Tuna with Wilted Spinach, 156
 Honey-Glazed Tuna & Greens, 169
 Pan-Seared Salmon with Stir-Fried
  Vegetables, 151
 Pasta with Smoked Salmon & Lemon
  Cream, 18
 Poached Orange Roughy with Lemon
  Sauce, 159
 Quick Cioppino, 176
 Salmon with Cucumber Kabobs, 152
 Salmon with Fresh Pineapple Salsa, 154
 Seared Tuna with Grapefruit-Orange
  Relish, 157
 Shark with Nectarine Salsa, 150

Strawberries, Salmon, & Fettuccine, 19
Wasabi-Glazed Whitefish with Vegetable
 Slaw, 155
Flank Steak with Pineapple Salsa, 127
Fontina & Melon Salad, 227
Fresh Tomato Fusilli, 15
Fried Green Tomatoes on a Bed of Greens, 268
Fruited Cheese Spirals, 256
Garbanzo Bean Stew, 246
Garlic Asparagus & Pasta with Lemon
 Cream, 33
Garlic Pilaf with Cajun Eggplant, 216
Garlic Steaks with Nectarine-Onion Relish, 95
Gingered Beef & Pasta Salad, 128
Gingered Pork & Cabbage Soup, 143
Gingered Shortcake with Spiced Fruit, 275
Greek-Inspired Lamb Pockets, 121
Greek Lamb Salad with Yogurt Dressing, 136
Greek Minestrone, 245
Grilled Recipes
 Apple-Glazed Lamb Chops, 119
 Asian Grilled Salmon Salad, 168
 Bananas Suzette over Grilled Pound
  Cake, 277
 Barbecued Turkey Tenderloins, 59
 Beef & Avocado Tacos, 100
 Beef & Fruit Salad, 126
 Beef with Cucumber Raita, 96
 Blackened Catfish with Roasted
  Potatoes, 160
 Border Grilled Turkey Salad, 74
 Canadian Bacon Pizza, 114
 Chicken & Prosciutto Roll-Ups, 36
 Chicken with Mango Chutney, 40
 Chicken with Roquefort Sauce, 44
 Dilly Salmon Fillets, 153
 Eggplant with Gorgonzola, 262
 Garlic Steaks with Nectarine-Onion
  Relish, 95
 Greek-Inspired Lamb Pockets, 121
 Grilled Antipasto Skewers, 257
 Grilled Beef, Red Onion, & Blue Cheese
  Salad, 129
 Grilled Corn Relish, 274
 Grilled Eggplant & Sweet Pepper
  Sandwiches, 203
 Grilled Gazpacho Medley Open-Faced
  Sandwich, 202
 Grilled Italian Sausage with Sweet & Sour
  Peppers, 116
 Grilled Lambburger Roll-Ups, 122
 Grilled Mustard-Glazed Pork, 104
 Grilled Rosemary Trout with Lemon
  Butter, 161
 Grilled Sicilian-Style Pizza, 207

Grilled Swordfish with Spicy Tomato Sauce, 158
Grilled Tomatoes with Pesto, 265
Grilled Tuna with Wilted Spinach, 156
Grilled Vegetable Salad with Garlic Dressing, 223
Grilled Vietnamese Chicken Breasts, 41
Herb-Rubbed Grilled Chicken, 46
Honey-Glazed Tuna & Greens, 169
Jamaican Pork Chops with Melon Salsa, 106
Jamaican Pork Kabobs, 112
Lemony Flank Steak, 93
Nectarine-Raspberry Crisp, 281
Peach-Mustard Glazed Ham, 113
Pepper Shrimp in Peanut Sauce, 166
Pineapple-Rum Turkey Kabobs, 58
Piquant Grilled Broccoli & Olives, 263
Pork Chops with Savory Mushroom Stuffing, 108
Raspberry Chicken with Plantains, 43
Rosemary-Orange Shrimp Kabobs, 167
Saffron Pilaf with Grilled Vegetables, 213
Salmon with Cucumber Kabobs, 152
Salmon with Fresh Pineapple Salsa, 154
Sesame-Ginger Barbecued Chicken, 48
Shark with Nectarine Salsa, 150
Shrimp & Tropical Fruit, 172
Smoky Chicken Wraps, 51
Southwest Chicken Salad, 60
Southwestern Black Bean Cakes with Guacamole, 194
Southwest Pork Chops with Corn Salsa, 107
Spanish Meat Loaves, 98
Spicy Chicken & Star Fruit, 37
Stuffed Turkey Tenderloins, 56
Sun-Dried Tomato Burgers, 99
Sweet & Spicy Pepper-Pineapple Salsa, 273
Tandoori-Style Lamb Chops, 120
Thai-Spiced Scallops, 163
Tomato Ravioli with Grilled Portobellos & Spinach, 24
Turkey Burgers with Fresh Curry Catsup, 57
Turkey-Peach Salad, 75
Veal Chops with Pesto-Stuffed Mushrooms, 102
Vegetable Kabobs, 264
Warm Asparagus, Fennel, & Spinach Salad, 269
Warm Tarragon Potato Salad, 267
Wasabi-Glazed Whitefish with Vegetable Slaw, 155

Ham
Dilled Spinach Soup, 88
Fresh Tomato Fusilli, 15
Muffuletta Salad, 135
Peach-Mustard Glazed Ham, 113

Red Beans & Grains, 134
Southern Ham Chowder, 144
Spaetzle with Caramelized Onions, 12
Spinach, Ham, & Melon Salad, 133
Hawaiian-Style Barbecue Pizza, 54
Herb-Rubbed Grilled Chicken, 46
Honey-Glazed Tuna & Greens, 169
Indian-Spiced Squash, 209
Italian Greens & Cheese Tortellini, 242
Italian Mozzarella Salad, 220
Jalapeño Corn Chowder, 239
Jamaican Pork & Sweet Potato Stir-Fry, 111
Jamaican Pork Chops with Melon Salsa, 106
Jamaican Pork Kabobs, 112

K-O

Keys-Style Citrus Chicken, 42
Lamb
Apple-Glazed Lamb Chops, 119
Balsamic-Glazed Springtime Lamb Salad, 137
Greek-Inspired Lamb Pockets, 121
Greek Lamb Salad with Yogurt Dressing, 136
Grilled Lambburger Roll-Ups, 122
Lamb Chops with Sweet Potato Chutney, 117
Moroccan Lamb Tagine, 147
Tandoori-Style Lamb Chops, 120
Tuscan Lamb Chop Skillet, 118
Lemon & Scallop Soup, 178
Lemon-Oregano Vinaigrette, 228
Lemony Flank Steak, 93
Lentils
Curried Lentil Soup, 248
Lentil & Veggie Tostadas, 214
Shells Stuffed with Turkey & Lentils, 10
Linguine with Fennel & Shrimp in Orange Sauce, 22
Linguine with Steak & Spicy Garlic Sauce, 14
Meatless Recipes *(see also Chapter 5, Vegetarian Dinners)*
Cavatelli with Arugula & Dried Cranberries, 29
Garlic Asparagus & Pasta with Lemon Cream, 33
Mostaccioli with Green Beans & Tomatoes, 32
Pasta Rosa-Verde, 31
Pasta with Chèvre, 28
Penne with Broccoli & Dried Tomatoes, 27
Rotini & Sweet Pepper Primavera, 30
Teriyaki Penne, 26
Tomato Ravioli with Grilled Portobellos & Spinach, 24
Trattoria-Style Spinach Fettuccine, 23
Wild Mushroom Ravioli with Sage Butter, 25
Meats *(see specific meat and pages 90–91)*
Mediterranean Couscous Salad, 228
Mexicali Stuffed Zucchini, 260

Mexican Chicken Posole, 84
Mexican Fiesta Salad, 222
Middle Eastern Bulgur-Spinach Salad, 230
Mixed Bean & Portobello Ragout, 247
Moo Shu Vegetable & Egg Crepes, 195
Moroccan Lamb Tagine, 147
Mostaccioli with Green Beans & Tomatoes, 32
Muffuletta Salad, 135
Mushroom Medley Soup, 80
Mushroom, Noodle, & Tofu Soup, 236
Mushroom Tortelloni in Curry Cream, 243
Nectarine-Raspberry Crisp, 281
Open-Face Portobello Sandwiches, 205
Orange & New Potato Salad, 266
Orange-Poppy Seed Dressing, 133
Oyster & Corn Chowder, 184

P-R

Paella Soup, 179
Paella-Style Shrimp & Couscous, 164
Pancakes
Corn Cakes with Fresh Corn & Chives, 272
Potato-Leek Pancakes, 271
Pan-Seared Salmon with Stir-Fried Vegetables, 151
Pan-Seared Scallops, 162
Papaya & Olives with Brown Rice, 231
Party Pancit, 21
Pasta *(see also pages 4–5)*
Pasta Coleslaw, 224
Peach-Mustard Glazed Ham, 113
Peanut Sauce, 52
Pear & Endive Salad with Honey Vinaigrette, 270
Penne Salad with Italian Beans & Gorgonzola, 226
Penne with Broccoli & Dried Tomatoes, 27
Peppered Pork & Apricot Salad, 131
Peppered Vinaigrette, 134
Pepper Shrimp in Peanut Sauce, 166
Peppers Stuffed with Cinnamon Bulgur, 210
Peppery Artichoke Pitas, 204
Pesto Chicken Breasts with Summer Squash, 45
Pesto-Vegetable Soup, 249
Pineapple-Rum Turkey Kabobs, 58
Piquant Grilled Broccoli & Olives, 263
Pita Chips, 228
Pizzas
Canadian Bacon Pizza, 114
Grilled Sicilian-Style Pizza, 207
Hawaiian-Style Barbecue Pizza, 54
Poached Chicken & Pasta with Pesto Dressing, 66
Poached Orange Roughy with Lemon Sauce, 159
Polenta
Broccoli Rabe over Polenta, 217
Polenta with Fresh Tomato Sauce, 219

Polenta with Mushrooms & Asparagus, 218
Tomato, Mozzarella, & Polenta Platter, 229
Pork
Caribbean-Style Pork Stew, 142
Gingered Pork & Cabbage Soup, 143
Grilled Mustard-Glazed Pork, 104
Jamaican Pork & Sweet Potato Stir-Fry, 111
Jamaican Pork Chops with Melon Salsa, 106
Jamaican Pork Kabobs, 112
Paella Soup, 179
Peppered Pork & Apricot Salad, 131
Pork Chops with Savory Mushroom
Stuffing, 108
Pork, Corn, & Three-Pepper Soup, 141
Pork Medallions with Cherry Sauce, 105
Pork Medallions with Fennel &
Pancetta, 103
Pork Salad with Cabbage Slaw, 130
Shanghai Pork Lo Mein, 13
Southwest Pork Chops with Corn Salsa, 107
Spaetzle with Caramelized Onions, 12
Summer Pasta with Pork, 109
Thai Cobb Salad, 132
Thai Pork & Vegetable Curry, 110
Potatoes
Asparagus & Cheese Potato Soup, 238
Blackened Catfish with Roasted
Potatoes, 160
Caribbean Clam Chowder, 187
Creamy Carrot & Pasta Soup, 241
Jamaican Pork & Sweet Potato Stir-Fry, 111
Lamb Chops with Sweet Potato Chutney, 117
Orange & New Potato Salad, 266
Oyster & Corn Chowder, 184
Potato-Leek Pancakes, 271
Scarlet Salad, 70
Southern Ham Chowder, 144
Sweet Potato Frittata with Fresh Cranberry
Salsa, 115
Vegetable Kabobs, 264
Warm Sweet Potato, Apple, & Sausage
Salad, 77
Warm Tarragon Potato Salad, 267
**Poultry (see Chicken, Turkey, and
pages 34–35)**
Prosciutto
Chicken & Prosciutto Roll-Ups, 36
Fresh Tomato Fusilli, 15
Quick Cioppino, 176
Raspberry Chicken with Plantains, 43
Red Beans & Grains, 134
Red Wine-Marinated Peaches, 278
Relish, Grilled Corn, 274
Rice
Papaya & Olives with Brown Rice, 231
Saffron Pilaf with Grilled Vegetables, 213
Spinach Risotto with Acorn Squash, 211
Wild Rice Quesadillas, 212
Roasted Garlic Dressing, 223
Roasted Red Pepper Sauce over Tortellini, 16

Roasted Vegetable & Pastrami Panini, 101
Roasted Vegetables Parmesan, 208
Roasted Vegetables with Balsamic Vinegar, 261
Rosemary-Orange Shrimp Kabobs, 167
Rotini & Sweet Pepper Primavera, 30

S

Saffron Pilaf with Grilled Vegetables, 213
Salad Dressings
Asian Dressing, 168
Basil Dressing, 220
Lemon-Oregano Vinaigrette, 228
Orange-Poppy Seed Dressing, 133
Peppered Vinaigrette, 134
Roasted Garlic Dressing, 223
Sesame Dressing, 62
Strawberry-Peppercorn Vinaigrette, 72
Salads, Main Dish
Asian Grilled Salmon Salad, 168
Balsamic-Glazed Springtime Lamb
Salad, 137
Beef & Apple Salad, 125
Beef & Curry Pinwheels on Spinach, 124
Beef & Fruit Salad, 126
BLT Salad with Crostini, 78
Border Grilled Turkey Salad, 74
Broiled Turkey Salad with Pineapple
Wedges, 76
Chicken & Pears with Pecan Goat Cheese, 63
Chicken, Pear, & Blue Cheese Salad, 61
Chutney-Chicken Salad, 65
Citrusy Chicken Salad, 68
Cool-as-a-Cucumber Chicken Salad, 64
Curried Chicken Salad, 69
Curried Crab Salad, 175
Fire-&-Ice Rice Salad, 170
Flank Steak with Pineapple Salsa, 127
Fontina & Melon Salad, 227
Gingered Beef & Pasta Salad, 128
Greek Lamb Salad with Yogurt Dressing, 136
Grilled Beef, Red Onion, & Blue Cheese
Salad, 129
Grilled Vegetable Salad with Garlic
Dressing, 223
Honey-Glazed Tuna & Greens, 169
Italian Mozzarella Salad, 220
Mediterranean Couscous Salad, 228
Mexican Fiesta Salad, 222
Middle Eastern Bulgur-Spinach Salad, 230
Muffuletta Salad, 135
Papaya & Olives with Brown Rice, 231
Pasta Coleslaw, 224
Penne Salad with Italian Beans &
Gorgonzola, 226
Peppered Pork & Apricot Salad, 131
Poached Chicken & Pasta with Pesto
Dressing, 66
Pork Salad with Cabbage Slaw, 130

Red Beans & Grains, 134
Scandinavian Shrimp Salad, 171
Scarlet Salad, 70
Seared Scallop & Spinach Salad, 174
Sesame Chicken Kabob Salad, 62
Shrimp & Tropical Fruit, 172
Southwest Chicken Salad, 60
Southwestern Chicken & Black Bean
Salad, 71
Spicy Steak & Ranch Salad, 123
Spinach, Ham, & Melon Salad, 133
Strawberry Vinaigrette with Turkey, 72
Teriyaki Chicken Noodle Salad, 67
Thai Cobb Salad, 132
Three-Cheese Orzo Salad, 225
Tomato, Mozzarella, & Polenta Platter, 229
Turkey & Pasta Salad, 73
Turkey-Peach Salad, 75
Warm Beet Salad with Roasted Garlic
Dressing, 221
Warm Scallop Salad with Toasted Sesame
Dressing, 173
Warm Sweet Potato, Apple, & Sausage
Salad, 77
Salads, Side Dish
Fried Green Tomatoes on a Bed of
Greens, 268
Orange & New Potato Salad, 266
Pear & Endive Salad with Honey
Vinaigrette, 270
Warm Asparagus, Fennel, & Spinach
Salad, 269
Warm Tarragon Potato Salad, 267
Salmon with Cucumber Kabobs, 152
Salmon with Fresh Pineapple Salsa, 154
Salsa, Sweet & Spicy Pepper-Pineapple, 273
Sausage
Bayou Shrimp Soup, 180
Bow Ties with Sausage & Sweet Peppers, 11
Grilled Italian Sausage with Sweet & Sour
Peppers, 116
Muffuletta Salad, 135
White Bean Soup with Sausage & Kale, 145
Sautéed Chicken Breasts with Tomatillo
Salsa, 38
Sautéed Chicken with Brandied Fruit &
Almonds, 39
Sautéed Onion & Tomato Sandwiches, 206
Scallops
Lemon & Scallop Soup, 178
Pan-Seared Scallops, 162
Seared Scallop & Spinach Salad, 174
Thai-Spiced Scallops, 163
Warm Scallop Salad with Toasted Sesame
Dressing, 173

Scandinavian Shrimp Salad, 171
Scarlet Salad, 70
Seared Scallop & Spinach Salad, 174
Seared Tuna with Grapefruit-Orange
    Relish, 157
Sesame Beef, 97
Sesame Chicken Kabob Salad, 62
Sesame Dressing, 62
Sesame-Ginger Barbecued Chicken, 48
Shanghai Pork Lo Mein, 13
Shark with Nectarine Salsa, 150
Shells Stuffed with Turkey & Lentils, 10
Shrimp
    Bayou Shrimp Soup, 180
    Capellini with Shrimp in Pesto Sauce, 20
    Chicken & Shrimp Tortilla Soup, 182
    Dilled Spinach Soup, 88
    Fire-&-Ice Rice Salad, 170
    Linguine with Fennel & Shrimp in Orange
       Sauce, 22
    Paella Soup, 179
    Paella-Style Shrimp & Couscous, 164
    Party Pancit, 21
    Pepper Shrimp in Peanut Sauce, 166
    Quick Cioppino, 176
    Rosemary-Orange Shrimp Kabobs, 167
    Scandinavian Shrimp Salad, 171
    Shrimp & Greens Soup, 181
    Shrimp & Tropical Fruit, 172
    Spicy Pumpkin & Shrimp Soup, 183
    Thai Shrimp & Fresh Vegetable Rice, 165
    Warm Scallop Salad with Toasted Sesame
       Dressing, 173
Sides (*see Salads, Side Dish; Vegetables;*
    and pages 252–253)
Smoky Chicken Wraps, 51
Soba Noodles with Spring Vegetables, 8
Soups and Stews
    Allspice Meatball Stew, 140
    Asian Beef & Noodle Bowl, 139
    Asian Chicken Noodle Soup, 83
    Asparagus & Cheese Potato Soup, 238
    Bayou Shrimp Soup, 180
    Beef & Vegetable Ragout, 138
    Black & White Bean Chili, 244
    Caribbean Clam Chowder, 187
    Caribbean-Style Pork Stew, 142
    Chicken & Shrimp Tortilla Soup, 182
    Chicken Chili with Rice, 87
    Chicken Stew with Tortellini, 81
    Chipotle Chile Pepper Soup, 79
    Chunky Chicken Chili, 86
    Chunky Ratatouille Stew, 232
    Crab & Pasta Gazpacho, 186
    Crab Chowder, 185
    Creamy Carrot & Pasta Soup, 241

Curried Lentil Soup, 248
Dilled Spinach Soup, 88
Fennel-Asparagus Soup, 146
Fish Provençale, 177
Garbanzo Bean Stew, 246
Gingered Pork & Cabbage Soup, 143
Greek Minestrone, 245
Italian Greens & Cheese Tortellini, 242
Jalapeño Corn Chowder, 239
Lemon & Scallop Soup, 178
Mexican Chicken Posole, 84
Mixed Bean & Portobello Ragout, 247
Moroccan Lamb Tagine, 147
Mushroom Medley Soup, 80
Mushroom, Noodle, & Tofu Soup, 236
Mushroom Tortelloni in Curry Cream, 243
Oyster & Corn Chowder, 184
Paella Soup, 179
Pesto-Vegetable Soup, 249
Pork, Corn, & Three-Pepper Soup, 141
Quick Cioppino, 176
Shrimp & Greens Soup, 181
Soba Noodles with Spring Vegetables, 8
Soup with Mixed Pastas, 85
Southern Ham Chowder, 144
Spicy Pumpkin & Shrimp Soup, 183
Spring Green Pasta Soup, 237
Spring Vegetable Soup, 233
Spring Vegetable Stew, 82
Squash & Papaya Soup, 251
Tomato & Wild Mushroon Soup, 234
Tomato-Basil Soup, 235
Turkey & Wild Rice Chowder, 89
Vegetable Cheese Chowder, 240
White Bean Soup with Sausage & Kale, 145
Wild Rice, Barley, & Mushroom Soup, 250
Southern Ham Chowder, 144
Southwest Chicken Salad, 60
Southwestern Black Bean Cakes with
    Guacamole, 194
Southwestern Chicken & Black Bean Salad, 71
Southwest Pork Chops with Corn Salsa, 107
Southwest Skillet, 199
Spaetzle with Caramelized Onions, 12
Spaghetti Squash with Balsamic Beans, 193
Spanish Meat Loaves, 98
Spicy Chicken & Star Fruit, 37
Spicy Pumpkin & Shrimp Soup, 183
Spicy Steak & Ranch Salad, 123
Spinach, Ham, & Melon Salad, 133
Spinach Risotto with Acorn Squash, 211
Spring Green Pasta Soup, 237
Spring Vegetable Soup, 233
Spring Vegetable Stew, 82
Squash & Papaya Soup, 251
Stir-Fries
    Chicken, Long Beans, & Tomato Stir-Fry, 53
    Jamaican Pork & Sweet Potato Stir-Fry, 111
    Sesame Beef, 97
    Shanghai Pork Lo Mein, 13

Thai Pork & Vegetable Curry, 110
Thai Shrimp & Fresh Vegetable Rice, 165
Strawberries
    Strawberries, Salmon, & Fettuccine, 19
    Strawberry-Peppercorn Vinaigrette, 72
    Strawberry Vinaigrette with Turkey, 72
Stuffed Turkey Tenderloins, 56
Summer Pasta with Pork, 109
Sun-Dried Tomato Burgers, 99
Sweet & Spicy Pepper-Pineapple Salsa, 273
Sweet & Spicy Spring Rolls, 201
Sweet Potato Frittata with Fresh Cranberry
    Salsa, 115

T-Z

Tandoori-Style Lamb Chops, 120
Tangy Bean Salad Wraps, 192
Tenderloin Steaks with Arugula-Cornichon
    Relish, 92
Teriyaki Chicken Noodle Salad, 67
Teriyaki Penne, 26
Thai Chicken Wraps, 52
Thai Cobb Salad, 132
Thai Pork & Vegetable Curry, 110
Thai Shrimp & Fresh Vegetable Rice, 165
Thai-Spiced Scallops, 163
Three-Cheese Orzo Salad, 225
Toasted Pita Chips, 255
Tofu
    Mushroom, Noodle, & Tofu Soup, 236
    Sweet & Spicy Spring Rolls, 201
Tomatoes
    Antipasto on a Stick, 258
    Asian Grilled Salmon Salad, 168
    Asparagus & Cheese Potato Soup, 238
    Bayou Shrimp Soup, 180
    Beef & Vegetable Ragout, 138
    BLT Salad with Crostini, 78
    Border Grilled Turkey Salad, 74
    Canadian Bacon Pizza, 114
    Capellini with Shrimp in Pesto Sauce, 20
    Caribbean-Style Pork Stew, 142
    Chicken, Long Beans, & Tomato Stir-Fry, 53
    Chipotle Chile Pepper Soup, 79
    Corn Waffles with Tomato Salsa, 190
    Couscous Burritos, 215
    Crab & Pasta Gazpacho, 186
    Fish Provençale, 177
    Fresh Tomato Fusilli, 15
    Fried Green Tomatoes on a Bed of
       Greens, 268
    Garbanzo Bean Stew, 246
    Gingered Beef & Pasta Salad, 128
    Gingered Pork & Cabbage Soup, 143
    Greek Minestrone, 245
    Greek-Inspired Lamb Pockets, 121
    Grilled Beef, Red Onion, & Blue Cheese
       Salad, 129

Grilled Gazpacho Medley Open-Faced Sandwich, 202
Grilled Rosemary Trout with Lemon Butter, 161
Grilled Sicilian-Style Pizza, 207
Grilled Swordfish with Spicy Tomato Sauce, 158
Grilled Tomatoes with Pesto, 265
Grilled Tuna with Wilted Spinach, 156
Honey-Glazed Tuna & Greens, 169
Italian Mozzarella Salad, 220
Mexican Fiesta Salad, 222
Mostaccioli with Green Beans & Tomatoes, 32
Muffuletta Salad, 135
Mushroom Tortelloni in Curry Cream, 243
Open-Face Portobello Sandwiches, 205
Paella-Style Shrimp & Couscous, 164
Pasta Rosa-Verde, 31
Pasta with Chèvre, 28
Poached Chicken & Pasta with Pesto Dressing, 66
Polenta with Fresh Tomato Sauce, 219
Red Beans & Grains, 134
Salmon with Cucumber Kabobs, 152
Sautéed Onion & Tomato Sandwiches, 206
Shells Stuffed with Turkey & Lentils, 10
Southwestern Chicken & Black Bean Salad, 71
Southwest Pork Chops with Corn Salsa, 107
Southwest Skillet, 199
Spanish Meat Loaves, 98
Strawberry Vinaigrette with Turkey, 72
Three-Cheese Orzo Salad, 225
Tomato, Mozzarella, & Polenta Platter, 229
Tomato & Wild Mushroon Soup, 234
Tomato-Basil Soup, 235
Tomatoes & Ravioli with Escarole, 17
Tomato Ravioli with Grilled Portobellos & Spinach, 24
Trattoria-Style Spinach Fettuccine, 23
White Bean Soup with Sausage & Kale, 145
Trattoria-Style Spinach Fettuccine, 23

Turkey
Asian Chicken Noodle Soup, 83
Barbecued Turkey Tenderloins, 59
BLT Salad with Crostini, 78
Border Grilled Turkey Salad, 74
Broiled Turkey Salad with Pineapple Wedges, 76
Chicken Chili with Rice, 87
Chutney-Chicken Salad, 65
Citrusy Chicken Salad, 68
Curried Chicken Salad, 69
Dilled Spinach Soup, 88
Pineapple-Rum Turkey Kabobs, 58
Scarlet Salad, 70
Shells Stuffed with Turkey & Lentils, 10
Soba Noodles with Spring Vegetables, 8

Southern Ham Chowder, 144
Southwestern Chicken & Black Bean Salad, 71
Strawberry Vinaigrette with Turkey, 72
Stuffed Turkey Tenderloins, 56
Turkey & Pasta Salad, 73
Turkey & Wild Rice Chowder, 89
Turkey Burgers with Fresh Curry Catsup, 57
Turkey-Peach Salad, 75
Warm Sweet Potato, Apple, & Sausage Salad, 77
White Bean & Sausage Rigatoni, 9
Tuscan Lamb Chop Skillet, 118
Veal Chops with Pesto-Stuffed Mushrooms, 102

Vegetables (*see also specific vegetable*)
Eggplant with Gorgonzola, 262
Mexicali Stuffed Zucchini, 260
Piquant Grilled Broccoli & Olives, 263
Roasted Vegetables with Balsamic Vinegar, 261
Vegetable Cheese Chowder, 240
Vegetable Kabobs, 264

Vegetarian Dinners (*see Meatless Recipes and pages 188–189*)
Warm Asparagus, Fennel, & Spinach Salad, 269
Warm Beet Salad with Roasted Garlic Dressing, 221
Warm Scallop Salad with Toasted Sesame Dressing, 173
Warm Sweet Potato, Apple, & Sausage Salad, 77
Warm Tarragon Potato Salad, 267
Wasabi-Glazed Whitefish with Vegetable Slaw, 155
White Bean & Sausage Rigatoni, 9
White Bean Dip with Toasted Pita Chips, 255
White Bean Soup with Sausage & Kale, 145
Wide Noodles with Chicken & Lima Beans, 7
Wild Mushroom Ravioli with Sage Butter, 25
Wild Rice, Barley, & Mushroom Soup, 250
Wild Rice Quesadillas, 212

TIPS

Appetizers, assorted, 255
Arugula, 204
Asparagus, trimming, 165
Avocados, buying, 274
Beans, dried, cooking, 191
Beans, dried, using, 192
Beverages, 99
Broth, options, 240
Broth, vegetable, options, 143
Cheese, kasseri, 259
Cheese, mozzarella, fresh, 207
Cheese, Scamorza, 220
Chicken, cooked, 64
Chili toppings, 86
Chutney, defined, 124

Desserts, simple ideas, 278
Eggs, hard-cooking, 198
Escarole, defined, 17
Fennel, selecting, 22
Fish, buying, 157
Fish, grilling, 150
Garam masala, 120
Garlic, cooking, 42
Ginger, fresh, storing, 117
Grilling, testing temperature of coals, 48
Herbs, fresh, buying and storing, 187
Herbs, fresh, cooking, 219
Jamaican jerk seasoning, 106
Jicama, defined, 244
Leeks, cleaning, 271
Lox, defined, 18
Mango and papaya, in jars, 40
Marinating meats, 104
Mesclun, defined, 268
Mushrooms, exotic, 234
Mushrooms, fresh, storing, 236
Mushrooms, portobello, 24
Nectarines, substituting, 39
Nuts, toasting, 63
Olives, buying, 28
One-pot meals, 138
Oranges, blood, defined, 167
Orzo, defined, 80
Pasta serving dishes, warming, 14
Peppers, chili, handling, 158
Pesto, 45
Pizza party ideas, 54
Pork, cooking, 112
Rice, brown, cooking, 231
Rice, cooking extra, 89
Rice, wild, cooking, 212
Saffron, defined, 147
Salad greens, selecting, 70
Scallops, 173
Sesame oil, toasted, 169
Shrimp, fresh, buying, 20
Shrimp, frozen, buying, 180
Skewers, rosemary, 50
Soup garnishes, 79
Soups, bread bowls for, 233
Soups, chowder versus bisque, 144
Tahini, defined, 59
Thai ingredients, 110
Thawing fish, seafood, or meats, 183
Tomatoes, plum, seeding, 32
Vinegar, balsamic, defined, 261
Vinegar, rice, defined, 128
Wheat berries, cooking, 251
Wine, adding to soup, 177

Metric Cooking Hints

By making a few conversions, cooks in Australia, Canada, and the United Kingdom can use the recipes in this book with confidence. The charts on this page provide a guide for converting measurements from the U.S. customary system, which is used throughout this book, to the imperial and metric systems. There also is a conversion table for oven temperatures to accommodate the differences in oven calibrations.

Product Differences: Most of the ingredients called for in the recipes in this book are available in English-speaking countries. However, some are known by different names. Here are some common U.S. American ingredients and their possible counterparts:

• Sugar is granulated or castor sugar.
• Powdered sugar is icing sugar.
• All-purpose flour is plain household flour or white four. When self-rising flour is used in place of all-purpose flour in a recipe that calls for leavening, omit the leavening agent (baking soda or baking powder) and salt.
• Light-colored corn syrup is golden syrup.
• Cornstarch is cornflour.
• Baking soda is bicarbonate of soda.
• Vanilla is vanilla essence.
• Green, red, or yellow sweet peppers are capsicums.
• Golden raisins are sultanas.

Volume and Weight: U.S. Americans traditionally use cup measures for liquid and solid ingredients. The following chart shows the approximate imperial and metric equivalents. If you are accustomed to weighing solid ingredients, the following approximate equivalents will help.

• 1 cup butter, castor sugar, or rice = 8 ounces = about 230 grams
• 1 cup flour = 4 ounces = about 115 grams
• 1 cup icing sugar = 5 ounces = about 140 grams

Spoon measures are used for smaller amounts of ingredients. Although the size of the tablespoon varies slightly in different countries, for practical purposes and for recipes in this book, a straight substitution is all that's necessary.

Measurements made using cups or spoons always should be level unless stated otherwise.

EQUIVALENTS: U.S. = AUSTRALIA/U.K.

⅛ teaspoon = 1 ml	½ cup = 120 ml
¼ teaspoon = 1.25 ml	⅔ cup = 160 ml
½ teaspoon = 2.5 ml	¾ cup = 180 ml
1 teaspoon = 5 ml	1 cup = 240 ml
1 tablespoon = 15 ml	2 cups = 475 ml
1 fluid ounce = 30 ml	1 quart = 1 liter
¼ cup = 60 ml	½ inch = 1.25 cm
⅓ cup = 80 ml	1 inch = 2.5 cm

BAKING PAN SIZES

U.S. American	Metric
8×1½-inch round baking pan	20×4-cm cake tin
9×1½-inch round baking pan	23×4-cm cake tin
11×7×1½-inch baking pan	28×18×4-cm baking tin
13×9×2-inch baking pan	32×23×5-cm baking tin
2-quart rectangular baking dish	28×18×4-cm baking tin
15×10×1-inch baking pan	38×25.5×2.5-cm baking tin (Swiss roll tin)
9-inch pie plate	22×4- or 23×4-cm pie plate
7- or 8-inch springform pan	18- or 20-cm springform or loose-bottom cake tin
9×5×3-inch loaf pan	23×13×8-cm or 2-pound narrow loaf tin or pâté tin
1½-quart casserole	1.5-liter casserole
2-quart casserole	2-liter casserole

OVEN TEMPERATURE EQUIVALENTS

Fahrenheit Setting	Celsius Setting*	Gas Setting
300°F	150°C	Gas Mark 2 (very low)
325°F	170°C	Gas Mark 3 (low)
350°F	180°C	Gas Mark 4 (moderate)
375°F	190°C	Gas Mark 5 (moderately hot)
400°F	200°C	Gas Mark 6 (hot)
425°F	220°C	Gas Mark 7 (hot)
450°F	230°C	Gas Mark 8 (very hot)
475°F	240°C	Gas Mark 9 (very hot)
Broil		Grill

*Electric and gas ovens may be calibrated using Celsius. However, for an electric oven, increase the Celsius setting 10 to 20 degrees when cooking above 160°C. For convection or forced-air ovens (gas or electric), lower the temperature setting 10°C when cooking at all heat levels.

exclusive offer!

claim your
free
year

of America's favorite idea-packed, recipe-filled magazines ...

mail today!

hurry...
limited-time offer!

rush!
free-year request

BUSINESS REPLY MAIL
FIRST-CLASS MAIL PERMIT NO. 120 BOONE, IA

POSTAGE WILL BE PAID BY ADDRESSEE

Better Homes and Gardens®
Hometown Cooking™
MAGAZINE
PO BOX 37456
BOONE IA 50037-2456

rush!
free-year request

BUSINESS REPLY MAIL
FIRST-CLASS MAIL PERMIT NO. 120 BOONE, IA

POSTAGE WILL BE PAID BY ADDRESSEE

Better Homes and Gardens
MAGAZINE
PO BOX 37428
BOONE IA 50037-2428